"Who would have thought that the financial in
cave in to civil society groups? In her David-
Kastner does not downplay the lobbying power c
establishes that finance has moved from a back-room expertise to normal
politics. A must-read for anybody interested in the politics of financial
regulation."
— *Cornelia Woll, Professor of Political Sciences, Sciences Po, France*

Civil Society and Financial Regulation

Coalitions of consumer groups, NGOs, and trade unions have traditionally been considered politically weak compared to well-organized and resourceful financial sector groups which dominate or "capture" financial regulatory decisions. However, following the 2008 financial crisis, civil society groups have been seen to exert much more influence, with politicians successfully implementing financial reform in spite of industry opposition.

Drawing on literature from social movement research and regulatory politics, this book shows how diffuse interests were represented in financial regulatory overhauls in both the United States (US) and the European Union (EU). Four cases of reform in the post-crisis regulatory context are analyzed: the creation of a new Consumer Financial Protection Bureau in the US; the introduction of new consumer protection regulations through EU directives; the failure of attempts to introduce a financial transaction tax in the US; and the agreement of 11 EU member states to introduce such a tax. It shows how building coalitions with important elite allies outside and inside government helped traditionally weak interest groups transcend a lack of material resources to influence and shape regulatory policy.

By engaging with a less well-known side of the debate, it explains how business power was curbed and diverse interests translated into financial regulatory policy.

Lisa Kastner is a policy advisor at the Foundation for European Progressive Studies in Brussels and associated research fellow at Sciences Po Paris. Her research on the politics of financial markets in the US and the EU was awarded the Research Award by the Erasmus academic network on Parliamentary Democracy in Europe (PADEMIA) and the Otto Hahn Medal of the Max Planck Society.

RIPE Series in Global Political Economy

Series Editors: James Brassett *(University of Warwick, UK)*,
Eleni Tsingou *(Copenhagen Business School, Denmark)* and
Susanne Soederberg *(Queen's University, Canada)*

The RIPE Series published by Routledge is an essential forum for cutting-edge
scholarship in International Political Economy. The series brings together new
and established scholars working in critical, cultural and constructivist political
economy. Books in the RIPE Series typically combine an innovative contribution
to theoretical debates with rigorous empirical analysis.

The RIPE Series seeks to cultivate:

- Field-defining theoretical advances in International Political Economy
- Novel treatments of key issue areas, both historical and contemporary, such
  as global finance, trade, and production
- Analyses that explore the political economic dimensions of relatively
  neglected topics, such as the environment, gender relations, and migration
- Accessible work that will inspire advanced undergraduates and graduate students
  in International Political Economy.

The *RIPE Series in Global Political Economy* aims to address the needs of students
and teachers.

For a full list of titles in this series, please visit www.routledge.com/RIPE-
Series-in-Global-Political-Economy/book-series/RIPE

**Critical Methods in Political and
Cultural Economy**
Johnna Montgomerie

**Neoliberalism and
Climate Policy in
the United States**
From Market Fetishism to the
Developmental State
Robert MacNeil

Beyond Defeat and Austerity
Disrupting (the Critical Political
Economy of) Neoliberal Europe
*David Bailey, Monica Clua-Losada,
Nikolai Huke and Olatz Ribera-Almandoz*

Civil Society and Financial Regulation
Consumer Finance Protection and
Taxation after the Financial Crisis
Lisa Kastner

Civil Society and Financial Regulation

Consumer Finance Protection and Taxation after the Financial Crisis

Lisa Kastner

LONDON AND NEW YORK

First published 2018 by Routledge

2 Park Square, Milton Park, Abingdon, Oxfordshire OX14 4RN
52 Vanderbilt Avenue, New York, NY 10017

Routledge is an imprint of the Taylor & Francis Group, an informa business

First issued in paperback 2019

British Library Cataloguing-in-Publication Data
A catalogue record for this book is available from the British Library

Library of Congress Cataloging-in-Publication Data
Names: Kastner, Lisa, author.
Title: Civil society and financial regulation consumer finance protection
    and taxation after the financial crisis / Lisa Kastner.
Description: Abingdon, Oxon ; New York, NY : Routledge, 2018. |
    Series: RIPE series in global political economy | Includes bibliographical
    references and index.
Identifiers: LCCN 2017007043| ISBN 9781138634428 (hardback) |
    ISBN 9781315206806 (e-book)
Subjects: LCSH: Financial institutions—State supervision. |
    Financial institutions—Law and legislation. | Financial services
    industry—Law and legislation. | Global Financial Crisis, 2008–2009. |
    Consumer protection. | Civil society.
Classification: LCC HG173 .K357 2018 | DDC 332.1—dc23
LC record available at https://lccn.loc.gov/2017007043

ISBN: 978-1-138-63442-8 (hbk)
ISBN: 978-0-367-88720-9 (pbk)

Typeset in Times New Roman
by Book Now Ltd, London

To my parents

Contents

x *Contents*

Illustrations

Figures

Tables

Acknowledgments

This book would not have been possible without the encouragement and support of Cornelia Woll during the years she invited me to spend as a doctoral and post-doctoral fellow at the Max Planck Sciences Po Center on Instability in Market Societies (MaxPo). Special thanks go to Christine Trampusch at the Max Planck Institute for the Study of Societies who gave clear directions to this project.

This research was made possible by the financial support of the Max Planck Sciences Po Center on Instability in Market Societies (MaxPo), the DAAD fellowship for a two-month stay at the American Institute for Contemporary German Studies (AICGS) of Johns Hopkins University and the logistical support of the Max Planck Institute in Cologne, the Centre d'études européennes at Sciences Po as well as the Elliott School of George Washington University during a short stay in Washington, D.C.

Faculty and colleagues at Sciences Po, the Max Planck Institute, and elsewhere commented generously on my work in a series of conferences, workshops, and seminars. I would like to thank Jens Beckert, Sigrid Quack, Martin Höpner, André Kaiser, Marion Fourcade, Olivier Rozenberg, Emiliano Grossman, Nicolas Sauger, and Bruno Palier who have all read parts of the manuscript. For advice and stimulating discussions during different stages of the research project, I would also like to thank Olivier Godechot, Jeanne Lazarus, Peter Gourevitch, Cathie Jo Martin, Josh Whitford, Neil Fligstein, Kevin Young, Pepper Culpepper, and Nick Ziegler. Many thanks as well to a number of people for never growing tired of discussing my research topic with me: Mirjam Dageförde, Camille Allé, Rahul Prabhakar, Tom Chevalier, Inga Rademacher, Betsy Carter, Adel Daoud, Charlotte Haberstroh, Alexander Spielau, and Agnes Orban. At Routledge, I thank Eleni Tsingou for seeing me through the publication process so pleasantly and three anonymous reviewers for a number of excellent suggestions. I am especially grateful to all the individuals who agreed to be interviewed for this project.

I would like to express a very special thanks to Helge and to my parents. Without their encouragement and patience this book would not have been possible.

Parts of chapter 3 and the introduction have first appeared in "Much ado about nothing? Transnational civil society, consumer protection and financial regulatory reform", *Review of International Political Economy*, 21 (6), 2014, 1313–1345.

Parts of chapter 4 have appeared in "From Outsiders to Insiders: A Civil Society Perspective on EU Financial Reforms", *Journal of Common Market Studies*, forthcoming 2017 (Online, DOI: 10.1111/jcms.12644) and parts of chapter 6 in "Business Lobbying under Salience – Financial Industry Mobilization against the European Financial Transaction Tax", *Journal of European Public Policy*, 2017 (Online, DOI: 10.1080/13501763.2017.1330357). I thank the publishers for allowing me to use these materials.

Acronyms

AARP	American Association of Retired Persons
ABA	American Bankers' Association
ABI	Association of British Insurers
ADICAE	Asociación de Usuarios de Bancos Cajas y Seguros
AFL-CIO	American Federation of Labor and Congress of Industrial Organizations
AFR	Americans for Financial Reform
AILO	Association of International Life Offices
ALDE	Alliance of Liberals and Democrats for Europe
ALTER-EU	Alliance for Lobbying Transparency and Ethics Regulation
ATTAC	Association for the Taxation of Financial Transactions for the Aid of Citizens
BBA	British Bankers' Association
BEUC	European Consumers' Organisation
CDU	Christian-Democratic Union of Germany
CFA	Consumer Federation of America
CEED	Center for the Environmental Economic Development
CFPA	Consumer Financial Protection Agency
CFPB	Consumer Financial Protection Bureau
C20	Civil 20
CI	Consumers International
COP	Congressional Oversight Panel
CPSC	Consumer Product Safety Commission
CRA	Community Reinvestment Act
CRIS	Special Committee on the Financial, Economic and Social Crisis
CSO	Civil Society Organization
CU	Consumers Union
CRL	Center for Responsible Lending
DG	Directorate General
DGB	Confederation of German Trade Unions
DG TAXUD	Directorate General for Taxation and Customs Union
DG MARKT	Directorate General for Internal Market and Services

EACB	Federation European Association of Cooperative Banks
EAPB	European Association of Public Banks
EBA	European Banking Authority
EBF	European Banking Federation
EBIC	European Banking Industry Committee
ECON	Committee on Economic and Financial Affairs
ECP	Enhanced Co-operation Procedure
ECR	European Conservatives and Reformists
ECRC	European Coalition for Responsible Credit
EFAMA	European Fund and Asset Management Association
EFFR	Europeans for Financial Reform
EFIN	European Financial Inclusion Network
EFRA	European Financial Regulatory Authority
EIOPA	European Insurance and Occupational Pensions Authority
EMF	European Mortgage Federation
EP	European Parliament
EPP	Group of the European People's Party
ESA	European Supervisory Authority
ESBG	European Savings Bank Group
ESMA	European Securities and Markets Authority
ETUC	European Trade Union Confederation
EU	European Union
FFB CFE-CGC	Fédération nationale de la finance et de la banque
FinForum	Financial Forum Ljubljana
FIN-USE	Forum of financial services users
FSCG	Financial Services Consumers Group
FSUG	Financial Services Users Group
FAT	Financial Activities Tax
FTT	Financial Transaction Tax
GFMA	Global Financial Market Association
GPF	Global Progressive Forum
IFI	International Financial Institution
IMF	International Monetary Fund
ICBA	Independent Community Bankers Association
ITUC	International Trade Union Confederation
KID	Key Information Document
L20	Labour 20
MBA	Mortgage Bankers' Association
MCD	Mortgage Credit Directive
MEP	Member of the European Parliament
MiFID	Markets in Financial Instruments Directive
NACA	National Associations of Consumer Advocates
NAACP	National Association for the Advancement of Colored People
NCL	National Consumers League
NCRC	National Community Reinvestment Coalition

NGO	Non-governmental organization
NNU	National Nurses United
PC	Public Citizen
PRIP	Packaged Retail Investment Products
PSI	Public Services International
S&D	Progressive Alliance of Socialists and Democrats
SME	Small and medium-sized enterprise
SPD	Social Democratic Party of Germany
SEIU	Service Employees International Union
SIFMA	Securities Industry and Financial Markets Association
TACD	Transatlantic Consumer Dialogue
TUC	British Trades Union Congress
UNDP	United Nations Development Programme
US PIRG	Federation of State Public Interest Research Groups
VERDI	Vereinte Dienstleistungsgewerkschaft
VÖB	Association of German Public Sector Banks
VZBV	German national consumer organization (Verbraucherzentrale)
WEED	World Economy, Ecology and Development
ÖGB	Austrian Trade Union Federation

1 Introduction

Non-financial groups and financial reforms

In this book we analyze the role of non-financial groups in political conflicts about financial regulation. The principal aim of this research is to ascertain the particular social mechanisms by which groups outside finance, such as consumer organizations and labor unions, can successfully promote their advocacy aims with regard to financial regulation despite having fewer resources at their disposal than dominant financial industry groups. What is the role of organized civil society in influencing and redirecting regulatory reforms?

The involvement of alternative societal actors or "outsider" groups—such as NGOs and consumer groups—in the financial reform debate was arguably one of the most striking aspects of the 2007/2008 credit crisis. A number of scholars have identified the mobilization of groups beyond the financial industry in response to the crisis as a new research agenda for political scientists looking for sources of change (Helleiner and Pagliari 2011, 179). By paying greater attention to the role of non-financial advocacy groups in shaping financial regulatory policies, as suggested by scholars of international political economy (IPE), this book aims to fill a gap in the burgeoning literature on financial reform-making. By taking the questions of "why" and "how" seriously, and developing a theoretical model with scope, as well as necessary and sufficient conditions the book seeks to make an important contribution to opening up the black box of interest politics in domains that are typically considered to be dominated by narrow industry interests and the technical expertise of small elite groups.

Contrary to the conventional wisdom about the relative weakness of post-crisis financial regulation and the image of financial reforms as being manipulated and watered down by financial sector lobbyists (see for example, Wolf 2014; Admati and Hellwig 2013; Johnson and Kwak 2011), we will show that policy-makers have introduced a number of reforms against the expressed preferences of the financial services industry. These actions have set new regulations and imposed costs on the industry. A theoretical position that claims massive and ongoing impact of business power appears difficult to reconcile with this empirical evidence. This book looks beyond the impact of material resources on policy decisions. To understand post-crisis regulatory dynamics, we need a framework that goes beyond concentrated interest group pressure and takes a closer look at interest group dynamics in terms of a wider range of actors.

By empirically studying the question of how actors usually classified as weak mobilized successfully against resourceful and dominant actors after the 2007/2008 financial crisis, this study aims to contribute to broader debates in international political economy. In recent years, a large amount of social science literature has emerged analyzing US or EU financial regulatory reforms (Woolley and Ziegler 2016; 2014; Kirsch and Mayer 2013; Pagliari 2013; Pagliari and Young 2013a/b; Woll 2013; Clapp and Helleiner 2012; Mayer 2012; Engelen et al. 2011; Johnson and Kwak 2011; Morgan 2010; Helleiner, Pagliari, and Zimmermann 2010; Quaglia 2010). Only rarely do these studies pay any real attention to comparative material from both sides of the Atlantic as a source of insight. Both the US and the EU cases are addressed here.

This analysis is also a contribution to the recent findings in political economy on how business power can be curbed by diffuse interests (Trumbull 2012; Bell and Hindmoor 2014; Culpepper 2011). Elected officials might be especially inclined to step up to represent diffuse interests when political salience is high (Culpepper 2011; Smith 2000; Woll 2013). In the theoretical framework adopted in the book, I follow the lead of these studies in focusing on factors that enable civil society groups to restrain business power. The account here will thereby deal with a side that is less known to researchers. The model presented here offers a close empirical analysis of a causal mechanism at work that allows civil society groups to leave their imprint on financial regulatory reforms, but it should also be stressed what it does not cover: it is not a comprehensive explanation of how the power of the financial industry is checked or constrained, but rather one route to that end. Likewise, the analysis is not a general guide to understanding the state of post-crisis financial regulation, but focuses on specific reforms.

This research also has practical policy relevance. Not only have financial reform issues become a topic of broad public interest but the reform debates remain important on the policy agenda. Bills proposing to strip the new US consumer regulator of its powers have been repeatedly introduced into Congress since the passage of the reform law. Likewise, in the EU, lobbying of industry groups aimed at watering down the proposed tax on the financial sector continues since an EU directive was proposed. By examining reform issues of greater public interest, this research tries to inform and contribute to public discussions. Also, focusing on cases in which the financial industry did not win—even if they are few and far between—is crucial because it is the first step to understanding how regulatory capture can be prevented in the future.

The puzzle: why did regulatory change occur?

The history of the deregulation of financial markets dominated by industry interests raises the highly interesting theoretical puzzle of how special and well-organized interests could successfully be subordinated to diffuse and less-well-organized interests in recent financial reform cases. Diffuse interests are generally understood as "collective interests held by large numbers of individuals," such as consumer protection policies (Pollack 1997, 572). Accordingly, interest groups can be classified as diffuse or specific, depending on the underlying interests of the constituencies they represent. While diffuse interest groups represent a broad, collective interest (such as consumers), specific interest groups represent a narrow self-interest (such as industry groups) (Beyers 2004, 216). As material resources are usually considered a major determinant of political influence, reform outcomes diametrically opposed to the interests of the dominant industry groups are puzzling.

In order to better understand the underlying dynamics of when and how such diffuse interests can gain influence on the policy process we analyze four cases of reform in the post-crisis regulatory context:

(i)   the creation of a new Consumer Financial Protection Bureau (CFPB) in the United States (US);
(ii) the introduction of new consumer protection regulations through EU directives;
(iii) the failure of attempts to introduce a financial transaction tax (FTT) in the US; and
(iv) the agreement of 11 EU member states to introduce such a tax, albeit without much progress in implementation up to date.

The positive cases that we have picked to analyze in depth are not the only recent examples of regulatory reforms running counter to concentrated financial industry interests. Other studies include the regulation of hedge funds (Woll 2013; Pagliari 2013), agricultural derivatives (Clapp and Helleiner 2012), over-the-counter (OTC) derivatives (Woolley and Ziegler 2011), and capital requirement rules (Young 2014). The cases I chose pitted concentrated industry interests even more clearly against diffuse interests. In all cases, policymakers either proposed or enacted legislation that industry groups had opposed.

In the first case studied here, the creation of a new consumer bureau in the US, Congress agreed to a new regulatory agency, which had been fiercely opposed by dominant financial sector groups, including the American Bankers Association (ABA) and the Mortgage Bankers Association (MBA). The Dodd-Frank Act contained major consumer protection provisions, which fundamentally changed the regulatory landscape for financial services. Under title X, the reform law established the CFPB, a new federal regulator with the sole responsibility of protecting consumers from unfair, deceptive, or abusive practices. As title XIV, Dodd-Frank also passed the Mortgage Reform and Anti-Predatory Lending Act which contains new regulations of the residential mortgage market, including new duties on mortgage originators and enhanced consumer protections with a requirement that all lenders must base their loan decisions on the consumers' ability to repay the loan. A third overhaul, the Credit Card Act was passed in 2009, just prior to the Dodd-Frank Act, and included major improvements on consumer protections in relation to credit cards such as limits on rate increases and improved disclosures. Both laws, along with most of the existing consumer protection regulations, fall within the jurisdiction of the new consumer regulator.

Some critics might object that the new regulator for consumer products was merely a fig leaf covering the influence of concentrated interests in the financial overhaul. A reason to think that this was not the case is, as the case study will demonstrate, the amount of resources the industry invested to defeat the new bureau. Industry groups had clearly preferred the status quo and the regulation passed in spite of an enormous industry campaign to block it. Private sector actors were concerned about conflicts that might arise among banking regulators and the new consumer watchdog.[1] When he testified before the Senate Finance Committee in July 2009, the then-president of the ABA complained that the new regulator would "simply complicate our existing financial regulatory structure by adding another extensive layer of regulation" (Yingling 2009). Interviews with leading banking lobbyists confirmed that the defeat of the consumer bureau was among the industry's top advocacy goals.[2] Those industry pressures failed to dissuade the administration from its course of action. Second, there is wide agreement among regulators, legal scholars, activists, and industry representatives that the consumer protection reforms introduced in response to the crisis go beyond "gesture politics" (Buckley and Howarth 2010). Most importantly, from a legal perspective, the array of new measures introduces an alternative regulatory paradigm or "paradigm shift" (Pridgen 2013; Caggiano et al. 2011), based on "a renewed recognition that when the competitive market place suffers from a lack of transparency and fairness, it will not fulfill its proper function" (Pridgen 2013, 30).

New consumer protection regulations at the EU level, the second case study under analysis here, were more moderate and compromised, aimed at the harmonization of consumer protection policies, but they still introduced new binding mortgage rules and improved protection for retail investors through enhanced information and transparency, as well as stricter disclosure rules. Industry attempts to block regulatory change remained largely unsuccessful. As a cross-sectional issue, consumer protection was a relevant dimension in several legislative proposals that were brought forward by the European Commission in response to the crisis. Drawing on Hall's (1993) distinction between three different levels of policy change (changes in settings of regulations, the institutional structure, or—most transformative—the normative nature of regulation or policy), Moloney (2012, 118) concludes that "the financial crisis has reshaped the context in which reform is taking place and is driving innovation in the form of change to the nature and policy goals of market and consumer protection regulation." This paradigm shift is accompanied by first- and second-order change "in the form of the emergence of product intervention as a retail market regulatory mechanism, at Member State and at EU levels" (Moloney 2012, 168). The in-depth analyses of four Directives dealing with consumer finance protection regulation will demonstrate that final reform legislations were a compromise, with both lobbying sides—industry groups and consumer associations—achieving some of their goals. Overall, however, the reform advances fall short of structural changes.

The financial transaction tax, with its redistributive effects, appears to be a hard case to demonstrate the policy influence of diffuse interest groups. Dominant industry groups in the EU and the US overwhelmingly opposed reform proposals. The US Congress subsequently failed to enact legislation and several bills introduced into Congress proposing a financial transaction tax stalled. Attempts by newly mobilized civil society coalitions pushing for regulatory change remained unheard by policymakers. While this outcome seems scarcely surprising in light of the potentially disruptive effects of a transaction tax on a sector that is considered structurally important in capitalist systems, the question arises, why 11 European countries nevertheless decided to introduce a financial transaction tax in 2013. In February 2013 the Commission adopted a directive proposing a broad-based financial transaction tax, in line with preferences of a mobilized civil society network and despite a unified industry that was violently opposed to it. Although the proposed EU financial transaction tax has been watered down since it was initially proposed, capture theories cannot explain why it made it onto the EU's reform agenda although the financial sector was bitterly opposed to it.

The findings of our case studies are at odds with prevailing capture theories of financial regulatory reforms. The purpose of this book is to solve the puzzle that these cases present. It poses a simple question: how can interest groups, usually considered weak and peripheral in the context of finance, such as consumer associations, successfully have their preferences met in financial reforms despite the opposition of the financial industry that sought to preserve the status quo?

The overall argument in brief

This book provides a more "pluralistic" view of financial reform-making. Situating this study in the larger context of interest group research, we argue that the image of politics as exclusively dominated by resourceful business lobbies moves us in the wrong direction. As Haunss and Kohlmorgen (2010, 243) rightly observe, interest group research with its emphasis on strong actors "is not well-suited to explain the occasional success of actors it regards as weak." The challenge is thus to explain the successful lobbying efforts of diffuse interests, traditionally considered as weak, in the context of post-crisis financial reforms. To explain the power of weak interests, the book will refocus our attention on non-material political resources, such as the capacity to organize, to provide expertise and to forge coalitions with like-minded policymakers.

We argue that the outcome of regulatory reforms can be fully understood only with reference to diffuse interests and their translation into policy. Drawing on insights of existing political and sociological literature into how presumably weak consumer interests can win over concentrated industry interests in the policy process, the main argument of the book is that an alliance of "weak" or "diffuse" interests—including small consumer groups, labor unions, and community groups as a "countervailing force"—has increased actor plurality around financial reform issues and thereby prevented industry groups from dominating the legislative process of financial reform to the degree that the regulatory capture literature predicts. The mobilization of countervailing interest groups is considered one necessary element in a larger causal chain to explain policy change in response to the financial crisis. While the financial crisis can be interpreted as the catalyst for institutional change, the explanation for policy change has to be much more agent-centered, as Baumgartner et al. (2009, 122) suggest: "crises do offer opportunities for the advocates of change, and if they are ready to seize on them, then major change becomes far more likely."

The theoretical contributions developed in Chapter 2 outline an alternative political account, integrating the demand and supply side factors of regulatory change, representing diffuse interests in one causal mechanism. Specifically, I examine coalition-building efforts among outsider groups, as well as between these and policymakers and the influence of these relationships on policy reforms. The causal mechanism is set in the post-crisis context which enhanced the capacity of actor groups usually classified as weak to capitalize on the moral outrage caused by the credit crisis and to take advantage of the (temporary) disempowerment of concentrated interests. I will show that the ability of concentrated industry interests to affect either the policy agenda or the specific content of regulatory rules has been weakened in the context of the financial crisis, thereby changing interest group dynamics and giving political leverage to groups traditionally considered "outsider groups" to finance.

Four necessary conditions that come from the political science literature on institutional change and the sociology literature on social movements provide a framework for the possible influence of these outsider groups. The various forces are viewed as interrelated: first, it is hypothesized that politicians due to public salience and electoral constraints become more receptive and grant new access points to diffuse interest groups. In other words, in the wake of the crisis a policy window opens up for diffuse interest groups, in terms of access to the reform process and political responsiveness to their reform demands.

The second hypothesis is that perceived political opportunities incentivized the formation of collective action among pro-reform groups and strengthened their collective action capacity. I argue that small advocacy organizations have contributed to policymakers' quest for more substantial reforms by acting as transmitters of public opinion, deploying expertise during legislative debates and exploiting the (temporary) weakness of the opposition. A third hypothesis is that the policy impact of newly mobilized groups is leveraged, if a well-positioned policy entrepreneur as a source of innovation, expertise, institutional resources, and political connections helps in exploiting the new political opportunities. A fourth hypothesis is that this intense pro-reform mobilization leads to a bandwagon effect that strengthens the reform side of the debate and encourages policymakers to actively defend diffuse interest groups on the political stage. The outcome is regulatory change that is not captured by industry interests.

Capture theories of financial regulatory reforms

The sizable literature on interest groups reminds us that interests of the consumers often remain unorganized, inactive, and subordinate to the power and influence of business lobbies. More resourceful actors have a much better chance of getting their voice heard than less well-resourced groups (Eising 2007, 356). This is even more so in the field of finance, where financial industry groups enjoy a structurally privileged position due to the rise of finance capitalism (Streeck 2014). According to Olson's (1965) *Logic of Collective Action*, this fact is hardly surprising, because large groups in particular are faced with a collective action dilemma when they try to influence policy. The barrier to efficient coordination is higher for large or diffuse groups of individuals than it is for smaller, concentrated groups. Large groups of individuals have difficulties organizing themselves because they lack incentives and face higher organizational costs than smaller groups who share a specialized or particular interest, which allows them to organize into active lobbies. Diffuse interests have therefore traditionally been considered politically weak. Olson's view was echoed in the Chicago School "capture" theories of regulation and applied to regulatory behavior by Stigler (1971), Posner (1974), and Peltzman (1989), who argued that interests of small groups (producer groups) consistently prevail over the interests of large groups (consumers as voters) with more diffuse interests.

When we look at past developments in financial regulation, Olson's reasoning has held true: concentrated costs and more political leverage for the tightly organized financial industry have generally led to more industry-friendly than consumer-friendly policies. Following the Olsonian interest group approach to public policy, most research on financial reform-making sees diffuse interest groups at a disadvantage relative to the financial industry lobby. Echoing Olson's presumptions, Hacker and Pierson (2010), for instance, explain striking income inequalities among Americans in terms of the organizational capacity of resourceful private interests to bring public policy in line with their interests. This pattern has been most pronounced in the field of finance, they argue, where the massive political leverage of financial industry lobbyists accounts for overly industry-friendly regulatory politics. From this perspective, American politics needs to be understood as "organized combat" of groups that only the most resourceful ones can win. According to their view, general elections make little difference to politics; they are just "spectacle" (Hacker and Pierson 2010, 154).

While effective financial industry lobbying on the international level is only part of the story to explain why the expected backlash against market-friendly standards failed to appear (Helleiner and Pagliari 2010; Moschella and Tsingou 2013), domestic financial elites are the most prominent explanatory factor in the literature for a lack of national-level financial reforms. Most scholars evaluating specific aspects of post-crisis financial regulation have linked modest reform efforts—despite the magnitude of the crisis—to continued private sector influence. Tsingou (2010), for instance, testifies to the persistence of the influence of a transnational policy network of financial experts. Emphasizing "close financial, personal and ideological ties" between policymakers and the banking industry, Johnson and Kwak (2011, 12) argue that Wall Street returned to "business as usual" after the crisis, with its political influence in Washington as powerful as ever. Similarly, political scientists studying post-crisis reforms in the EU recorded incremental change, often due to successful lobbying of domestic financial industries aimed at preventing regulation (Quaglia 2010; Buckley and Howarth 2010; Moschella and Tsingou 2013; Moschella 2014).

This study contests the conventional wisdom. Due to the assumption of regulatory capture scholars have neglected to systematically examine reform cases in which industry groups did not succeed. As Carpenter and Moss (2014, 3) observe: "All too often, observers are quick to see regulatory capture as the explanation for almost any regulatory problem, making large-scale inference [...] without a careful look at the evidence." This bias is particularly true for scholarship unfolding in response to the financial crisis. Given the actor constellation involved in the financial reform debate, capture theories focused on the ability of actors to have their interests heard based on their resourcefulness would predict clear outcomes. From this perspective, where regulatory change depends upon the means and power of the financial industry lobby to (re-)shape regulatory reform, we would expect the outcome to reflect domestic financial sector preferences. In the case of the US consumer protection agency, where all "strong" actors representing the financial services industry opposed a new regulator and only "weak" actors, including consumer associations, labor groups and other public interest groups supported the provision, we would expect an easy defeat of the reform proposal. Despite massive protest and considerable investment of lobbying resources by business groups, organized by the US Chamber of Commerce, the new consumer regulator became law and there were only minor modifications to the original proposal. With reference to the consumer protection regulations in the EU case, the situation is less clear-cut. In the case of the Mortgage Credit Directive, for instance, industry groups were generally opposed to new regulations, while consumer groups pushed for reforms. After legislative debate, a new Directive was adopted, harmonizing European mortgage regulations by setting the minimum regulatory requirements in a consistent way across member states, reflecting a compromise solution among the various interests involved. These results suggest that factors other than material resourcefulness may have actually been decisive in these conflicts.

Restraining capture: salience and actor plurality

Accounts of recent reform efforts based on capture theory have not gone entirely uncontested. New research evaluating industry influence on post-crisis regulatory reforms in more detail is indeed more sophisticated than the narrative of pure capture that preceded it. Recent studies on financial regulation in response to the crisis have found counter-evidence to traditional capture analyses. Literature on post-crisis regulatory change has shown that the lobbying strategies of the financial industry were affected by two factors: political pressures in times of increased salience and increased actor plurality.

Highlighting the role of public salience, scholars increasingly emphasize that electoral contingencies and public opinion are causal factors that influence decision-makers. Some scholars emphasize populist pressures on policymakers, together with an increased awareness of the distributional consequences of regulatory failures due to the crisis as driving factors for more stringent regulation of the financial sector (Baker 2010; Pagliari 2013). A small but growing number of studies testify that the crisis was a catalyst in changing interest group dynamics with regard to financial regulation. Woll (2012) argues that regulatory reform had become subject to public outrage which forced financial industry lobbyists—in this case the hedge fund industry—to adapt their strategies to governments' preferences in order to be successful. Recent research has also shown that altered social relations within the financial policy network considerably weakened the industry's capacity to veto or block reform proposals. Drawing on empirical material gathered from interviews with private sector associations in the US and the EU during the reform debates in 2011 and 2012, Young (2013) finds that increased issue salience was accompanied by a qualitative shift in policymaking, with decision-makers becoming more reluctant to exchange information with industry groups and overall communication levels dropping significantly. Adjusting to these shifts, the financial industry changed its advocacy strategy, putting more emphasis on self-regulatory moves and delaying implementation instead of vetoing policy proposals.

Increased actor plurality, closely linked to and motivated by heightened issue salience, is a second factor that can account for decreasing industry influence. Quantitative analyses confirm that the mobilization of interest groups beyond financial groups in the regulatory debate following the crisis increased in the EU (Eising, Rasch, and Rozbicka 2013), as well as in the US (Pagliari and Young 2013b). In general, the circle of actors involved in financial regulatory policymaking has become less restricted (Quaglia 2010). So far there is little evaluation of how this increased plurality has affected financial reform outcomes. Indeed, the role of newly mobilizing non-financial groups in redirecting regulatory reform in response to the crisis has not attracted much attention to date among political scientists who study financial markets. Those few scholars who have explored the subject, however, have offered some important insights into how groups beyond financial industry groups matter. This brings us to the small but growing number of studies that analyze the growing mobilization of non-financial groups surrounding financial regulation and the effects of this mobilization on regulatory policies in more detail. What is the precise role of those newly mobilized groups beyond finance that occurred in the aftermath of the financial crisis in redirecting regulatory reforms?

The literature identifies two differing effects of increased actor plurality in financial reform debates: increased actor plurality might either allow industry groups to form coalitions with supportive non-industry groups to leverage their influence (Pagliari and Young 2013b, 6) or it might have the opposite effect and reduce industry impact on regulatory politics when outsider groups successfully oppose industry preferences as a "countervailing force" (Clapp and Helleiner 2012). Scholars analyzing the US Dodd-Frank Act have found that a new network of small advocacy groups successfully opposed industry lobby campaigns against stricter regulations. At the same time, they disagree on the mechanism by which capture of financial regulation can be tempered. Kastner (2014), for example, argues that "a polymorphous network of civil society organizations was able to gain momentum after the financial crisis and to influence the financial reform process." Examining the greater strength of regulatory reform efforts in the US in comparison with Europe, Griffith-Jones, Silvers, and Thiemann (2010, 6) conclude that the key explanatory factors for regulatory change are political leadership combined with "a particularly strong coordinated lobbying effort [...] by trade unions, consumer and civil rights advocates, and a wide range of civil society organizations" which could capitalize on the public outrage in response to the crisis. Highlighting two variables—institutional context and interest group coalitions—Clapp and Helleiner (2012, 200) argue that the financial industry's power in preventing agricultural derivatives regulation was curbed by "the presence of an alternative coalition of agricultural interests, energy sector groups and NGOs who favored tougher regulation as well as by the broader political environment that favored financial regulatory reform after the 2008 financial crisis."

Existing case studies of Dodd-Frank suggest that new pro-reform actors, including smaller advocacy groups under the umbrella of AFR, played an important role during the reform-making process. Mayer and Kirsch (2013), for example, offer a detailed journalistic account of mobilizing efforts on the part of civil society coalitions in favor of a new consumer agency. Although it provides a rich factual account of lobbying efforts and Congressional actions during the passage of Dodd-Frank, the book lacks the theoretical and analytical depth of an academic work and presents only one side of lobbying, namely civil society activities. In contrast, the present analysis draws on a wide range of empirical material, including all sides of the debate.

Stressing the role of electoral incentives and interest groups dynamics, Woolley and Ziegler suggest that the new consumer protection framework in the US was "a settlement between concentrated industry interests and consumer-oriented advocacy groups" (Woolley and Ziegler 2011, 1). While the authors provide a compelling narrative, the analyses fall short of a systematic discussion of the role of advocacy groups. The story actually moves away from these groups to explain regulatory change with reference to strong policy entrepreneurs (such as Elizabeth Warren and Timothy Geithner) and key legislators (such as Congressmen Barney Frank and Chris Dodd), as well as new ideas held by those actors. In a recent article, Woolley and Ziegler show how a new network of advocacy organizations, the so-called "stability alliance," led by AFR, was able to prevent capture of the rule-making process by the industry-supported "self-regulation" alliance. In the battle over the shape of post-crisis regulation, the pro-reform groups formed a political alliance based on public philosophies that underpin financial market practices ("knowledge regimes"), and provided the necessary expertise to policymakers.

This book complements the existing approach by offering a clearly circumscribed causal mechanism. To explain the power of weak interests, we will focus on non-material political resources. Intellectual resources and specific expertise are considered here as only one element in a larger causal chain that can account for the increased policy influence of newly mobilized non-financial groups in financial reforms following the crisis. This study also differs in an important way from existing case studies, because it approaches the question of diffuse interest representation in financial regulatory reforms, employing comparative case analysis.

Taken together, then, where does existing scholarship on recent financial reform leave us? Given the public outcry and emerging popular pressures in response to the financial crisis, recent efforts on the part of scholars to explain regulatory change pay surprisingly little attention to newly mobilizing societal groups as change agents. While the above accounts—which represent the state of the art on the international political economy literature on Dodd-Frank—have acknowledged that traditional capture dynamics surrounding financial regulatory policymaking were significantly altered by the shock of the credit crisis, the precise role of newly mobilized interest groups beyond the traditional financial groups remains theoretically implicit or at best underdeveloped. Given this weakness of the existing analyses, the contribution of the book is to open up the black box of interest group politics in domains that are typically considered to be dominated by narrow industry interests and technical expertise of small elite groups. We need a precise account of how diffuse interest groups were able to confront the powerful financial lobby to have their preferences met in regulatory reforms in a more systematic manner. The next section will discuss some explanatory factors for the power of diffuse interests, as suggested by the existing literature.

The power of diffuse interests

The puzzle of how diffuse interests can become powerful in public policymaking has been addressed by a substantial body of political science and sociological literature. Numerous studies, focused mainly on the American political system, testify to the recurring success of weak interests such as workers, consumer or public interest groups in spite of a conflict with more powerful business groups (Grossmann 2012; Berry 1999; Vogel 1997; Trumbull 2012; Smith 2000). Grossman (2012) finds, for instance, that advocacy groups, including public interest groups, are more often associated with policy change than business groups. These conclusions are consistent with Berry's (1999) findings, in his book *The New Liberalism*, about the successful advocacy of citizen groups in American politics when it comes to agenda setting. For the EU, a recent study found that business groups are less influential than citizen groups during the decision-making stage and in particular when policy issues are highly conflictual (Dür, Bernhagen, and Marshall 2013, 33).

Diffuse interest groups might be able to compensate for their structurally weak position through different mechanisms, by mobilizing and employing framing strategies (Dobusch and Quack 2013), by coalescing with resourceful groups, or by the intervention of elected officials who take up their cause (Baumgartner et al. 2009). Scholars have also sought to use network analysis to understand how relationships might lead to policy influence on the part of weak interests (Haunss and Kohlmorgen 2010; Grossmann 2012).

To begin with, weak interests, such as consumer associations, can successfully be translated into public policy by means of coalition-building with industry groups. The idea that meaningful legislation is enacted only when a consumer interest coincides with a powerful producer interest is a common assumption about consumer protection politics (Nadel 1971, 145). In *Trading Up*, Vogel (1997) argues that a strengthening of consumer protection standards can generally be driven by domestic producers keen to secure a competitive advantage due to stricter product standards vis-à-vis other jurisdictions. Consumer organizations and producers—which Vogel dubbed "Baptist-bootlegger" coalitions—might act together to promote stricter environmental regulations to raise entry barriers to foreign competitors (Vogel 1997, 20). In their study of a random sample of policy issues, based on more than 300 interviews, Baumgartner et al. (2009) find that money is not a good predictor of groups' policy influence, precisely because poor interest groups ally with rich groups in the legislative process. Although material resources matter, these kinds of mixed alliances even out material advantages one group might have vis-à-vis another group and therefore compensate for the weaker stance of public interest groups vis-à-vis business.

A second approach to explaining the successful representation of diffuse interests has relied on favorable institutional structures. Transferring this framework to the EU, Pollack (1997) argues that weak actors—such as interest groups for women's rights, environmental protection or consumer protection—can prevail over concentrated business groups by taking advantage of political opportunity structures providing access points and receptivity to demands from diffuse interests.

As another set of actors to promote diffuse interests, the literature on the politics of regulation introduces "entrepreneurs": public officials such as bureaucrats, experts, legislators, or judges. Entrepreneurs in this sense "know how to mobilize public sentiment by capitalizing on a crisis or failure" and how to involve themselves "in the process of change, offering counsel, logistics, financial and technical expertise, or otherwise empowering poorly resourced societal groups adversely affected by the regulatory status quo" (Mattli and Woods 2009, 28).

Finally, elected officials might be especially inclined to step up for the representation of diffuse interests when political salience is high. As we have learned from Culpepper (2011) and Smith (2000), public salience can severely constrain business power. In particular in situations of high public salience, electoral considerations motivate politicians to listen less to business lobbies and more to the electorate (Culpepper 2011, 7). Salience is therefore a strong predictor of interest group influence, as Danielian and Page (1994, 1076) point out: "when the spotlight is on and the public gets involved, political equality tends to prevail and special interests lose." Hence, for highly salient policy decisions, organized diffuse interests are a force to be reckoned with.

In his book *Strength in Numbers* Trumbull (2012) recently drew our attention to processes through which Olson's logic of collective action can be inverted by consumer groups' ability to increase policy legitimacy in the public eye. Trumbull offers a compelling explanation for why diffuse interests, such as consumer interests, can win over business interests. Including the role of elected officials under public scrutiny, he argues that diffuse interests have a clear advantage in their ability to seemingly legitimize policy decisions, whereas concentrated interests are viewed with suspicion. From this perspective, the ability of diffuse groups to make policy appear legitimate accounts for their increased policy influence, especially when decision-makers are under public scrutiny. In their extensive study on lobbying success or failure, Baumgartner et al. (2009, 241) also confirmed the importance of heightened public attention on issues to explain policy change.

However, while this book builds on this prior work, it goes beyond it in carefully specifying the causal mechanism that allows diffuse interests to confront industry power. With such a perspective, the causes of diffuse interests' policy impact are found partly on the supply side of regulatory change and partly on the demand side.

Research methods and case selection

In order to explain the determinants of the reform shift set in motion by the financial and economic crisis, this study draws on qualitative case-oriented research. The book tries to explain how diffuse interests were translated into post-crisis financial regulatory policy by systematically applying process-tracing to test the presence or absence of a hypothesized causal mechanism. Process-tracing—arguably the only method that allows us to study causal mechanisms—is used here to open the black box of the preference attainment of interest groups. The analysis closely follows Beach and Pedersen (2013) who offered a detailed and comprehensive guide for researchers on how to use process-tracing methods in practice. I also follow the guidelines for good process-tracing as proposed by two recent contributions to the subject, an article by Trampusch and Palier (2016) and a book by Bennett and Checkel (2015).

The case selection follows the case selection strategy for theory-testing process-tracing. The ambition here is to select cases "where X and Y are present, along with the relevant scope conditions" in order to test whether a hypothesized causal mechanism linking X and Y is present (Beach and Pedersen 2013, 147). The case studies illuminate the ways weak interests can affect policy outcomes in finance through their engagement in the regulatory process, their capacity to organize, lobby, provide expertise, and forge coalitions with legislative allies and the institutional setting within which they participate. The cases range from instances in which diffuse interests have been successful (especially consumer finance protection regulations passed as part of financial overhauls) to other cases in which the success of diffuse interests was confined largely to the agenda-setting stage or where diffuse interests had to succumb entirely to concentrated industry interests. The latter cases, focused on regulation of speculation through a financial transaction tax, provide the strongest evidence for capture theories, albeit revealing important limits on industry influence. By asking why and how diffuse interests came to be represented in some policies, but not in others, we can start to single out the underlying mechanisms of diffuse interest representation in financial regulation.

The case logic follows a "least-likely" design (Levy 2008, 11; Gerring 2007, 116). Although diffuse consumer interests have "systematically dominated national policy processes" in the postwar period (Trumbull 2012, 10) and are more likely to succeed under conditions of high salience (Culpepper 2011, Woll 2013), the effect of civic non-state actors is expected to be low in a highly technical policy field such as financial regulation, which is dominated by savvy and resourceful financial industry groups. Indeed, in the cases of consumer protection as well as taxation, diffuse interests were pitched against intense industry opposition to new regulations. Since a theory that succeeds in explaining a case in which it is least likely to apply increases our confidence in its validity, the aim here is to show the policy influence of weak interests under difficult conditions.

Empirically, I will focus on the EU rather than on member states for a comparison with the US. Many of the crucial decisions regarding financial reforms in response to the crisis were taken in Brussels. Although comparing regulatory reforms in the US with those in the EU can be viewed critically from an analytical standpoint given that the former is a state and the latter is an international organization, one can argue that they are both federal systems and therefore comparable. More importantly, due to the sheer size of their capital markets, the US and the EU are relevant cases whose financial reforms are likely to have a large impact on financial regulation worldwide. Insights from these two cases can be considered quite relevant to the overall international financial architecture.

For the theory test, I have collected data from three different types of sources: this research uses elite interviews with different participants (as primary source), as well as newspaper articles and academic and professional publications about financial reforms (as publicly available secondary sources). Elite interviewing is the key data collection technique employed in this research project, as it is the research tool best suited to the method of process-tracing for reconstructing political events (George and Bennett 2005, 6; Tansey 2007; Beach and Pedersen 2013; Mosley 2013). Elites can be defined as "those with close proximity to power or policymaking," including elected representatives, executive officers of organizations, and senior state employees (Lilleker 2003, 207). Hence, first and foremost the case study analysis draws on empirical material gathered through 116 semi-structured interviews conducted between May 2011 and March 2014 with representatives from civil society, international organizations, policymakers, industry, and regulators mainly in Brussels, London, Paris, Washington, D.C., and New York. In addition to the interview transcripts,[3] publicly available secondary data—including memoirs of participants, newspapers, press releases, position papers, and industry reports in the aftermath of the crisis— offered a sizeable amount of data and therefore an excellent opportunity for social scientists to study the politics of financial regulatory reform. The financial press and other journalistic sources represented an important secondary source to reconstruct and assess the mobilization strategies and expressed preferences of different actors.

Plan of the book

This study analyzes how interest groups traditionally considered to be weak successfully had their preferences met in financial reforms in response to the 2007/2008 financial crisis, despite the opposition of powerful private sector groups. The narrative of the following chapters tells the story of how non-financial groups were able to tap into public sentiment in order to bring about policy change in the realm of financial regulation. The empirical part of the study will focus on the policy process itself, and the ways in which diffuse interests have been able to gain access to policymakers and influence policy outcomes after the crisis.

Chapter 2 develops the theoretical framework and derives testable hypotheses for a causal mechanism linking diffuse interests to regulatory change.

In order to interpret the policy process, the next three chapters, 3–5, use process-tracing to apply theoretically derived hypotheses to the empirical record of the case studies. A preliminary task in each chapter is to establish reforms of the financial regulatory system in the EU and the US as developments characterizing a more nuanced influence of private sector groups than commonly thought. The positive and mixed case studies attempt to trace social mechanisms linking weak interests to policy change in financial regulation, trying to identify analogous mechanisms in multiple cases that contribute to producing the same outcomes: the creation of a US consumer regulator; the harmonization of EU level consumer protection reforms; and the decision of 11 EU countries to introduce a transaction tax—all reforms proposed despite private sector resistance.

Chapter 6 takes the analysis further by extending the process-tracing analysis of the cases in which the outcome to be explained occurs to cases in which it does not occur. By analyzing the failed attempts of mobilized civil society to get the financial transaction tax on the legislative agenda of Congress, we will be able to identify which elements of the mechanism I consider to be systemic and transportable.

Our story spans the time period from 2008 to 2014. The starting point that sets the causal mechanism in motion is the beginning of the financial crisis and the preliminary policy responses to it in 2008, while the end point is roughly the end of the reform negotiations and the signing into law of reforms. Political reform dynamics addressed as long-term re-regulation proximately started in spring 2009, after a first phase of measures addressed at fire-fighting the ramifications of the bankruptcy of the investment bank Lehman Brothers in September 2008 had been implemented. Subsequent research will have to unpack the full implementation process of the financial reforms enacted in response to the crisis.

Making inferences from the commonalities among the positive cases and the contrasts with the mixed and negative cases, I attempt in a cross-case analysis in Chapter 7 to explain what made regulatory change corresponding to preferences of diffuse interests possible even though the odds against them seemed high. The conclusion reflects on the implications for our understanding of regulatory capture.

Notes

1 Interview 113 with a financial industry lobbyist, Washington, D.C., February 25, 2015.
2 Interview with a banking lobbyist, Washington, D.C., September 16, 2013.
3 A complete list of anonymized transcripts of the conducted interviews can be found in the appendix.

References

Admati, A. and Hellwig, M. (2013) *The Bankers' New Clothes: What's Wrong with Banking and What to Do about It*, Princeton, Oxford: Princeton University Press.

Baker, A. (2010) 'Restraining Regulatory Capture? Anglo-America, Crisis Politics and Trajectories of Change in Global Financial Governance', *International Affairs* 86 (3): 647–63.

Baumgartner, F. R. et al. (2009) *Lobbying and Policy Change: Who Wins, Who Loses, and Why*, Chicago, London: University of Chicago Press.

Beach, D. and Pedersen, R. B. (2013) *Process-Tracing Methods: Foundations and Guidelines*, Ann Arbor: University of Michigan Press.

Bell, S. and Hindmoor, A. (2014) 'The Structural Power of Business and the Power of Ideas: The Strange Case of the Australian Mining Tax', *New Political Economy* 19 (3): 470–86.

Bennett, A. and Checkel, J. T. (2015) *Process Tracing: From Metaphor to Analytic Tool*, Cambridge: Cambridge University Press.

Berry, J. M. (1999) *The New Liberalism: The Rising Power of Citizen Groups*, Brookings Institution Press, 1 March, available at www.brookings.edu/book/the-new-liberalism (accessed September 2016).

Beyers, J. (2004) 'Voice and Access. Political Practices of European Interest Associations', *European Union Politics* 5 (2): 211–40.

Buckley, J. and Howarth, D. (2010) 'Internal Market: Gesture Politics? Explaining the EU's Response to the Financial Crisis', *Journal of Common Market Studies* 48 (September): 119–41.

Caggiano, J. R. et al. (2011) 'Mortgage Lending Developments: A New Federal Regulator and Mortgage Reform under the Dodd–Frank Act', *Business Lawyer* 66 (2): 457–72.

Carpenter, D. P. and Moss, D. A. (eds) (2014) *Preventing Regulatory Capture: Special Interest Influence and How to Limit It*, New York: Cambridge University Press.

Clapp, J. and Helleiner, E. (2012) 'Troubled Futures? The Global Food Crisis and the Politics of Agricultural Derivatives Regulation', *Review of International Political Economy* 19 (2): 181–207.

Culpepper, P. D. (2011) *Quiet Politics and Business Power: Corporate Control in Europe and Japan*, Cambridge: Cambridge University Press.

Danielian, L. H. and Page, B. I. (1994) 'The Heavenly Chorus: Interest Group Voices on TV News', *American Journal of Political Science* 38 (4): 1056–78.

Dobusch, L. and Quack, S. (2013) 'Framing Standards, Mobilizing Users: Copyright versus Fair Use in Transnational Regulation', *Review of International Political Economy* 20 (1): 52–88.

Dür, A., Bernhagen, P. and Marshall, D. J. (2013) 'Interest Group Success in the European Union: When (and Why) Does Business Lose?', Paper presented at the annual conference of the European Political Science Association, Barcelona, 20–22 June, available at papers.ssrn.com/abstract=2225099 (accessed September 2016).

Eising, R. (2007) 'Institutional Context, Organizational Resources and Strategic Choices Explaining Interest Group Access in the European Union', *European Union Politics* 8 (3): 329–62.

Eising, R., Rasch, D. and Rozbicka, P. (2013) 'EU Financial Market Regulation and Stakeholder Consultations', Paper presented at the Institute for European Studies, Université Libre de Bruxelles, 18–19 April, available at www.intereuro.eu/public/downloads/publications/Eising_Rasch_Rozbicka_2013_EU_financial_market_regulation_and_stakeholder_consultations.pdf?phpMyAdmin=bc921356f086070c90aa893e9eb2bead (accessed September 2016).

Engelen, E. et al. (eds) (2011) *After the Great Complacence: Financial Crisis and the Politics of Reform*, Oxford, New York: Oxford University Press.

George, A. L. and Bennett, A. (2005) *Case Studies and Theory Development in the Social Sciences*, Cambridge, MA: MIT Press.

Gerring, J. (2007) *Case Study Research: Principles and Practices*, New York: Cambridge University Press.

Griffith-Jones, S., Silvers, D. and Thiemann, M. (2010) 'Turning the Financial Sector from a Bad Master to a Good Servant; the Role of Regulation and Taxation', Unpublished working paper, available at www.stephanygj.net/papers/Fin-Regulation-SGJ.pdf (accessed September 2016).

Grossmann, M. (2012) 'Interest Group Influence on US Policy Change: An Assessment Based on Policy History', *Interest Groups & Advocacy* 1 (2): 171–92.

Hacker, J. S. and Pierson, P. (2010) 'Winner-Take-All Politics: Public Policy, Political Organization, and the Precipitous Rise of Top Incomes in the United States', *Politics & Society* 38 (2): 152–204.

Hall, P. (1993) 'Policy Paradigms, Social Learning, and the State: The Case of Economic Policymaking in Britain', *Comparative Politics* 25 (3), 275–96.

Haunss, S. and Kohlmorgen, L. (2010) 'Conflicts about Intellectual Property Claims: The Role and Function of Collective Action Networks', *Journal of European Public Policy* 17 (2): 242–62.

Helleiner, E., Pagliari S., and Zimmermann, H. (2010) *Global Finance in Crisis: The Politics of International Regulatory Change*, London: Routledge.

Helleiner, E. and Pagliari, S. (2011) 'The End of an Era in International Financial Regulation? A Postcrisis Research Agenda', *International Organization* 65 (1): 169–200.

Johnson, S. and Kwak, J. (2011) *13 Bankers: The Wall Street Takeover and the Next Financial Meltdown*, New York: Vintage Books.

Kastner, L. (2014) 'Much Ado about Nothing? Transnational Civil Society, Consumer Protection and Financial Regulatory Reform', *Review of International Political Economy* 21 (6): 1313–45.

Kirsch, L. and Mayer, R. N. (2013) *Financial Justice: The People's Campaign to Stop Lender Abuse*, Santa Barbara: Praeger Frederick.

Levy, J. (2008) 'Case Studies: Types, Designs, and Logics of Inference', *Conflict Management and Peace Science* 25 (1): 1–18.

Lilleker, D. G. (2003) 'Interviewing the Political Elite: Navigating a Potential Minefield', *Politics* 23 (3): 207–14.

Mattli, W. and Woods, N. (2009) 'In Whose Benefit? Explaining Regulatory Change in Global Politics', in W. Mattli and N. Wood (eds), *The Politics of Global Regulation*, Princeton: Princeton University Press, pp. 1–43.

Mayer, R. N. (2012) 'The US Consumer Movement: A New Era Amid Old Challenges', *Journal of Consumer Affairs* 46 (2): 171–89.

Mayer, R. N. and Kirsch, L. (2013) *Financial Justice: The People's Campaign to Stop Lender Abuse*, Santa Barbara: Praeger Frederick.

Moloney, N. (2012) 'The Legacy Effects of the Financial Crisis on Regulatory Design in the EU', in E. Ferran et al. (eds), *The Regulatory Aftermath of the Global Financial Crisis*, Cambridge: Cambridge University Press, pp. 111–202.

Morgan, G. (2010) 'Legitimacy in Financial Markets: Credit Default Swaps in the Current Crisis', *Socio-Economic Review* 8 (1): 17–45.

Moschella, M. (2014) 'The Institutional Roots of Incremental Ideational Change: The IMF and Capital Controls after the Global Financial Crisis', *The British Journal of Politics & International Relations* 17 (3): 442–60.

Moschella, M. and Tsingou, E. (2013) *Great Expectations, Slow Transformation: Incremental Change in Post-Crisis Regulation*, Colchester: ECPR Press.

Mosley, L. (ed.) (2013) *Interview Research in Political Science*, Ithaca, NY: Cornell University Press.

Nadel, M. V. (1971) *The Politics of Consumer Protection*, Mishawaka, IN: Macmillan.

Olson, M. (1965) *The Logic of Collective Action: Public Goods and the Theory of Groups*, Cambridge, MA: Harvard University Press.

Pagliari, S. (2013) 'Public Salience and International Financial Regulation. Explaining the International Regulation of OTC Derivatives, Rating Agencies, and Hedge Funds', Ph.D. dissertation, University of Waterloo, available at www.stefanopagliari.net/ pagliari_-_phd_thesis_-.pdf (accessed September 2016).

Pagliari, S. and Young, K. L. (2013a) 'The Wall Street–Main Street Nexus in Financial Regulation: Business Coalitions Inside and Outside the Financial Sector in the Regulation of OTC Derivatives', in M. Moschella and E. Tsingou (eds), *Great Expectations, Slow Transformations: Incremental Change in Financial Governance*, Colchester: ECPR Press, pp. 125–48.

Pagliari, S. (2013) 'Public Salience and International Financial Regulation. Explaining the International Regulation of OTC Derivatives, Rating Agencies, and Hedge Funds,' PhD thesis, Canada: University of Waterloo.

Pagliari, S. and Young, K. L. (2013b) 'Leveraged Interests: Financial Industry Power and the Role of Private Sector Coalitions', *Review of International Political Economy* 21 (3): 575–610.

Peltzman, S. (1989) 'The Economic Theory of Regulation After a Decade of Deregulation', Brookings Papers on Economic Activity, Brookings Institution, Washington, DC, available at www.brookings.edu/bpea-articles/the-economic-theory-of-regulation-after-a-decade-of-deregulation/ (accessed September 2016).

Pollack, M. A. (1997) 'Representing Diffuse Interests in EC Policy-Making', *Journal of European Public Policy* 4 (4): 572–90.

Posner, R. A. (1974) 'Theories of Economic Regulation', *The Bell Journal of Economics and Management Science* 5 (2): 335–58.

Pridgen, D. (2013) 'Sea Changes in Consumer Financial Protection: Stronger Agency and Stronger Laws', *Wyoming Law Review* 13 (2): 1–36.

Quaglia, L. (2010) *Governing Financial Services in the European Union: Banking, Securities and Posttrading*, London: Routledge.

Smith, M. A. (2000) *American Business and Political Power*, Chicago, London: The University of Chicago Press.

Stigler, G. J. (1971) 'The Theory of Economic Regulation', *The Bell Journal of Economics and Management Science* 2 (1): 3–21.

Streeck, W. (2014) *Buying Time: The Delayed Crisis of Democratic Capitalism*, Brooklyn, NY: Verso.

Tansey, O. (2007) 'Process Tracing and Elite Interviewing: A Case for Non-Probability Sampling', *Political Science & Politics* 40 (4): 765–72.

Trampusch, C. and Palier, B. (2016), 'Between X and Y: How Process Tracing Contributes to Opening the Black Box of Causality', *New Political Economy* 21 (5): 437–54.

Trumbull, G. (2012) *Strength in Numbers: The Political Power of Weak Interests*, Cambridge, MA: Harvard University Press.

Tsingou, E. (2010) 'Regulatory Reaction to the Global Credit Crisis: Analyzing a Policy Community under Stress', in E. Helleiner, S. Pagliari and H. Zimmermann (eds), *Global Finance in Crisis: The Politics of International Regulatory Change*, London: Routledge, pp. 21–36.

Vogel, D. (1997) *Trading Up: Consumer and Environmental Regulation in a Global Economy*, Cambridge, MA: Harvard University Press.

Young, K. L. (2013) 'Financial Industry Groups' Adaptation to the Post-Crisis Regulatory Environment: Changing Approaches to the Policy Cycle', *Regulation & Governance* 7 (4): 460–80.

Wolf, M. (2014) *The Shifts and the Shocks: What We've Learned – and Have Still to Learn – from the Financial Crisis*, London: Allen Lane, Penguin Press.

Woll, C. (2012) 'The Brash and the Soft-Spoken: Lobbying Styles in a Transatlantic Comparison', *Interest Groups & Advocacy* 1 (2): 193–214.

Woll, C. (2013) 'Lobbying under Pressure: The Effect of Salience on European Union Hedge Fund Regulation', *Journal of Common Market Studies* 51 (3): 555–72.

Woolley, J. T. and Ziegler, J. N. (2011) 'The Two-Tiered Politics of Financial Reform in the United States', IRLE Working Paper 111-11. Berkeley: Institute for Research on Labor and Employment, University of California, available at irle.berkeley.edu/workingpapers/111-11.pdf (accessed September 2016).

Woolley, J. T. and Ziegler, J. N. (2014) 'Who Shapes Institutional Reform: A Process-Tracing Approach to the Politics of Financial Reform in the United States, 2008–2010', Paper presented at a workshop, Sciences Po, Paris, 22–23 May.

Woolley, J. T. and Ziegler, J. N. (2016) 'After Dodd-Frank: Ideas and the Post-Enactment Politics of Financial Reform in the United States', *Politics & Society* 44 (2): 249–80.

Yingling, E. (2009) *Testimony On Behalf of the American Bankers Association Before the Committee on Banking, Housing and Urban Affairs, United States Senate*. Washington, DC, available at www.aba.com/archive/Testimony_Archive/Testimony%20Document%20Archive/July14EdYinglingSenateBankingCommitteeConsume.pdf

Young, K. L. (2014) 'Losing Abroad but Winning at Home: European Financial Industry Groups in Global Financial Governance since the Crisis', *Journal of European Public Policy* 21 (3): 367–88.

Part I

A theory of financial regulatory change

2 Towards a causal mechanism of post-crisis regulatory reform dynamics

Contrary to the prevailing assumption that financial regulatory outcomes are always geared towards powerful industry preferences, detailed analysis of the cases of post-crisis consumer protection reforms in the United States (US) and the European Union (EU) and taxation reforms in the latter suggest that we should look elsewhere for the precise causal mechanism shaping regulatory reforms in the field of finance. The case studies presented here challenge "capture" explanations, suggesting that the proverbial "fire power" of the financial industry has been much more circumscribed in the post-crisis regulatory environment than is commonly assumed. This chapter will outline a plausible causal mechanism of relations between interest groups and government officials in a post-crisis context that can explain reform trajectories that represent diffuse interests.

Diffuse interests shall be understood as the initial condition. The outcome studied here is the degree of influence of diffuse interest groups on regulatory reforms in response to the crisis. For the sake of simplicity, this is conceptualized as a spectrum that goes from relatively low, to moderate and high influence. In order to find a plausible causal mechanism behind relations between interest groups and government officials, we have cast the net widely to find inspiration in the literature on the representation of diffuse interests in public policy, but also in the literature on social movements, regulation, and public policy studies. While this approach is predominantly deductive, recent studies by sociologists and political scientists on the financial reform process have also served as a source of ideas on how a theorized mechanism could work.

In order to explain how diffuse interests can become powerful in public policy-making, the analytical framework employed here combines perspectives of IPE research on financial regulation with insights of the social movement and lobbying literature. Following Mattli and Woods (2009), I suggest integrating demand- and supply-side factors into a causal theory in order to explore the institutional conditions under which diffuse interests can become change agents in times of crisis. we will turn to the scope conditions first, before I lay out the different steps of a hypothesized theoretical mechanism—institutional context, diffuse interest coalitions, and elite allies on the outside and inside of government—to explain the outcome. The parts of the causal mechanism are understood as individually necessary elements that are jointly sufficient to produce the outcome. Each part taken individually is understood to be insufficient to produce the outcome.

Scope conditions: crises and limits of capture

We need to pay close attention to how the crisis altered the contextual conditions for regulatory reforms in order to understand the increased political receptivity to pro-reform demands and sudden (at least partial) redistribution of power away from concentrated industry interests to more diffuse consumer interests. The outcome of the causal process, which begins with the critical juncture, was influenced by a variety of contextual factors, notably a legitimacy crisis of global finance, which subsequently allowed for the opening of a policy window for newly mobilizing actors. The structural power of finance might be considerably weakened by a crisis, as Capoccia and Keleman (2007, 343) point out: "Critical junctures are characterized by a situation in which the structural (that is, economic, cultural, ideological, organizational) influences on political action are significantly relaxed for a relatively short period."

According to the literature, the recipe for success of diffuse interests in public policy includes processes that neutralize the organizational advantages of clientele groups (Patashnik 2008, 21). The retreat of affected financial sector groups, mobilized in opposition to regulatory change, is also one of the main explanatory factors for the success of diffuse interests. Sectoral opposition may be weakened by several factors, but in particular, when political disorganization inhibits a sector from effectively putting its economic resources to political use (Derthick and Quirk 1985, 245). When faced with an opposed public opinion, groups defending the status quo have two incentives to back down: the first incentive is that lobbying in the face of public opinion opposition is not likely to be successful (Kollman 1998) and second, groups have an incentive not to have their name associated with a publicly unpopular stance, which can incur reputational costs (Dür and Mateo 2014, 1204). Negative publicity can therefore strongly affect traditional interest groups dynamics, as Birkland (1998, 57) argues: "The suddenness of an event means that politically disadvantaged groups gain a strategic advantage [...], while the members of the policy monopoly are placed in the position of managing negative publicity and defending the status quo in a highly charged, politically embarrassing environment." In those situations, groups on the defensive might decide to refrain from active counter-lobbying.

According to recent IPE research, the financial crisis had several important effects that at least temporarily neutralized the organizational advantage of financial sector groups. First and foremost, the post-crisis financial regulatory environment was generally marked by increased issue salience and negative publicity for the financial sector. Heightened media attention raised by the financial crisis certainly increased the perception of undue sectoral influence. Applying his theory of "quiet politics" to post-crisis politics, Culpepper (2011) predicts "a weakened bargaining position" for organized interests in a "radically changed political environment" and "under intense public scrutiny."

The global crisis delegitimized the financial industry and its practices, throwing the existing neoliberal order and financial community into a "legitimacy crisis" (Morgan 2010). Financial sector groups were thereby deprived of a valuable source of power. Several studies stressed how this delegitimization and increased public attention, in turn, led to a change in lobbying strategies, with industry groups refraining from vetoing policy proposals (Young 2014; Steinlin and Trampusch 2012), focusing their attention on different stages of the policy cycle or on the reversal of legislative decisions during the implementation stage (Young 2013). Baker (2010, 656) observed that the "lobbying capacity and voice of bank lobbies are not what they were prior to the crisis. Their oppositional attitudes to regulation are softening, while regulators are emboldened."

The crisis also led to a divide among financial sector groups, thereby diminishing their collective action capacity. In the aftermath of the crisis, the financial community was highly divided over the desirability of reform and policy-makers started to call into question the expertise of the existing financial epistemic community and their past consensus on light-touch regulation. Divisions emerged not only between parts of the financial sector but also among politicians, regulators, and industry representatives, thereby reducing the sector's post-crisis political influence (Helleiner and Pagliari 2011; Engelen et al. 2011). While the financial sector had largely enjoyed privileged access to the technocratic decision-making process before the crisis (Tsingou 2008; Baker 2010), recent works within IPE have illustrated that the regulatory reform context was characterized by increased issue salience, accompanied by qualitative shifts in policy-making, displaying increasing divisions among policy-makers and the private sector (Young 2013, 4). To sum up, the contextual conditions allowing the causal mechanism to operate are marked by a (temporal) delegitimization of the financial sector after the financial crisis, which somewhat neutralized its organizational advantage and led to increasing fractions with policy-makers, thereby changing interest group dynamics. We shall see in the next section how this crisis context affected the political opportunity structure for diffuse interest groups.

Political opportunities: access and receptivity

The financial crisis and the subsequent industry retreat provide the contextual conditions for the political opportunities that opened up for diffuse interest groups and spurred the formation of collective action in the post-crisis regulatory environment. This section will consider qualitative changes in the institutional and procedural context of decisions; the supply side of regulatory change in economic theories. Research on social movement and political contention provides particularly relevant insights for institutional factors that determine the roles of weak actors in politics. As Tarrow (1996, 54) writes: "Unlike money or power, this opens the possibility that even weak and disorganized challengers can take advantage of opportunities created by others to organize against powerful opponents." According to this strand of literature, institutional factors present risks and opportunities for diffuse interest groups (Tilly 1978; Tarrow 2011; McAdam et al. 2001; Kriesi 1989). Drawing on the existing social movement literature, McAdam (1996, 27) defines the formal legal and institutional structure of a political system as one dimension of "political opportunity" that constrains or facilitates the organization of collective action.

Political opportunities are understood to encompass the following two dimensions: "The first is a structural aspect, which relates to the openness of a political system and, hence, the ease of access for political actors. The second concerns the receptivity of the political system to the claims of those political actors" (Princen and Kerremans 2008, 1131). The successful representation of diffuse interests hinges on two factors, as Vogel (1993, 237) points out: access to the political process and officials' receptiveness to demands from diffuse interest groups. Although it remains unclear whether access will actually translate into influence, access increases the likelihood that influence will occur. According to McAdam's dimensions of political opportunities the "emergence of new [elite] allies within a previously unresponsive political system" (McAdam 1996, 30) is a key condition for collective action. From this perspective, political opportunity structures offer incentives to the formation of collective action among challenger groups. Indeed, advocacy groups are more likely to mobilize if a governing party is supportive of an advocacy group's position (Mahoney and Baumgartner 2008, 1268). Following this conceptualization of opportunity structures, I will argue that two institutional factors—access and receptivity—provided diffuse interest groups with a favorable political opportunity structure in the context of the financial crisis.

The analysis suggests that qualitative changes in the institutional context in which financial regulatory policies were developed after the crisis granted access to a variety of non-financial sector groups previously excluded from the decision-making process. Legislative bodies such as the US Congress and the European Parliament got involved in the debate and directly shaped regulatory reforms (Helleiner and Pagliari 2011, 178). This involvement, in turn, allowed for better access of interest groups. As Pagliari and Young (2013) observe,

> the deepening of the crisis moved the focal point away from the technocratic policy network and toward the agency of elected politicians. The greater involvement in the design of financial regulatory reform initiatives of bodies such as the US Congress and the European Parliament has opened up new access points [...] to a broader range of stakeholders.

With respect to the reform of agricultural derivatives after the crisis, Clapp and Helleiner (2012), for instance, observe the importance of the US Congressional Agricultural Committee as a locus of reform debate which provided access points to a variety of stakeholder groups. Similarly, Baker (2010, 656) writes that the "dominance of the terrain of the regulatory debate has clearly shifted away from the largest banks towards newly invigorated regulators and policy-makers." In this sense, the openness of the institutional context is considered here to be a necessary condition for the success of diffuse interests.

The receptivity of decision-makers to their concerns and demands depends on contingent factors, such as shifts in the political mood or public opinion due to focusing events, preferences of government officials, or divisions among political elites (Princen and Kerremans 2008, 1131). Public salience in particular affects diffuse groups' political opportunities. The financial crisis can be interpreted as "a shock that triggers a significant and long-lasting increase in the level of public attention towards a financial domain [...] likely to create strong electoral incentives for elected politicians to reform the regulatory framework, even when these reforms run against the preferences of the domestic financial industry groups" (Pagliari 2013). As a result of the crisis as focusing event, regulatory reform had become susceptible to public outrage, pushing financial regulatory reform out of the arena of what Culpepper (2011) termed "quiet politics," in which interest group politics are shielded from public debate, into the arena of "noisy politics," which force elected politicians to react to popular opinion or interest groups representing it. In particular under conditions of noisy politics, when the public pays attention, highly organized business groups often lose. In both cases, in the US and the EU, it should have been clear to decision-makers that there was very little appetite among voters for a soft line on the industry. In other words, by shifting the political mood, the crisis opened up a "policy window" (Kingdon 2010, 165) (at least temporarily) increasing political receptivity to alternative societal actors promoting reform. We expect the following conditions to be present in the case studies: *qualitative changes in the post-crisis institutional context in which financial regulatory policies were developed, combined with political receptivity allowed for increased access of diffuse interest groups.*

Mobilization of diffuse interests

A necessary condition for regulatory change is therefore the capacity of diffuse interest groups to successfully overcome their organizational disadvantage, because "[g]aining and using control over political authority requires organization" (Hacker and Pierson 2010, 172). Since Olsons insight that diffuse interests are notoriously difficult to organize, many political scientists have drawn our attention to the capacity of diffuse interests to affect policies despite problems of collective action. Wilson observed about American regulatory politics in the 1980s that "an important organizational change has occurred [...] – the emergence of watchdog or public interest associations that have devised ways of maintaining themselves without having to recruit and organize people who will be affected by a policy" (Wilson 1980, 369). Keck and Sikkink (1998, 117) ascribe a key role to the activities of advocacy networks, including NGOs and consumer organizations in changing human rights practices. Similarly, Trumbull (2012) found that consumer interests prevailed in French and UK credit regulations, as well as in other policy areas including retail, pharmaceutical, and agricultural sectors. Drawing on social movement scholarship, Dobusch and Quack (2013, 59) regard organizing capacities as "preconditions and catalysts of mobilizing processes." According to them, "establishing a formal organization or a mobilizing network of organizations not only strengthens stability and public visibility but also helps in mobilizing financial and human resources." Networking among groups considerably reduces transaction costs and facilitates advocacy work (Price 1998). Coalition-building among diffuse interest groups to enhance their collective action capacity can therefore be considered a necessary condition of regulatory change.

The organization as a coalition can provide sufficient resources to pro-reform groups to serve as a link between public opinion and decision-makers. Especially in situations of uncertainty generated, for instance, by a financial crisis that turns institutional arrangements or parts of it upside down, policy-makers turn to interest groups as new sources of advice (Haas 1992; Keck and Sikkink 1998). From the perspective of resource exchange theories, groups can provide necessary information about domestic electoral preferences for legislators pursuing re-election, as well as expert knowledge (Bowen 2004). For Kollman (1998) interest group mobilization serves as a powerful signal to decision-makers about the state of public opinion. Indeed, Dür and Mateo (2014) could show empirically that mobilized public interest groups can influence public policy, when they can transmit information to policy-makers about public opinion backing their cause. Especially in the EU, in the absence of a European public sphere, organized civil society can be proxy for public opinion for policy-makers.

Crises, in particular, are dramatic events that can facilitate collective action and spur interest group mobilization. The literature converges on the view that "a focusing event can trigger extensive interest group mobilization [...] where public interest is relatively high or easily mobilized" (Birkland 1998, 73). Crises entail also "demonstration effects," which reveal distributional consequences of regulations, thereby motivating the mobilization of a broader range of societal actors (Mattli and Woods 2009). Meins (2000) argues that by redistributing political leverage from producers to consumers, public outrage helps pressure groups such as consumer associations to overcome the collective action problem that is inherently linked to groups' efforts at providing a public good, consumer protection.

Public salience has another important effect, namely that it raises the diversity of groups involved in a political contestation. In turn, business groups' political influence might be severely restricted, in particular if groups mobilize against their preferences. Smith (2000) argues that even a united business lobby might lose because issues they jointly mobilize for are likely to be accompanied by increased public attention and by the counter-mobilization of public interest groups. This in turn amplifies electoral motives for decision-makers to act in the public interest rather than pander to business preference.

The explanation provided here regards the crisis as catalyst—not as a cause for policy change. In the words of Birkland (1998, 72), "[w]ithout any sort of policy community or advocacy coalition [...] there is no one to take advantage of an event." Kingdon (2010, 170) suggests that a "window of opportunity" exists in the perception of participants who have to perceive its presence to take advantage of it. As McAdam et al. (1996, 8; italic in orig.) write, "[n]o matter how momentous a change appears in retrospective, it only becomes an opportunity when defined as such by a *group* of actors sufficiently well organized to act on this shared definition of the situation."

Mobilized diffuse groups might also be influential due to another factor, namely fragmentation within the financial sector. A splitting of the industry's opposition can be helpful for diffuse interest groups because it diminishes the sector's overall political influence. The conventional wisdom predicts that consumer interests win when they coincide with a powerful producer interest and so-called "Baptist–bootlegger" coalitions emerge. A split can therefore be particularly helpful if consumer groups find themselves on the same lobbying side with financial sector groups against other financial sector groups. This gives rise to the following causal proposition: *the crisis-induced organization as an advocacy coalition spurred by the perception of a window of opportunity allows diffuse interest groups to effectively promote reform goals (A) by serving as link between public opinion and policy-makers and (B) by exploiting the (temporary) weakness of the opposition.*

Policy entrepreneurs

As with political opportunities and organizational resources, powerful allies remain just as important to the fate of diffuse interests in public policy. Diffuse interest groups are dependent on elite allies that act as entrepreneurs on their behalf to actively promote policy change. Policy entrepreneurs are important actors to help diffuse interests in their efforts to identify and exploit opportunities that arise with crises. In general, crises or scandals that evoke anti-business sentiments are presumed to make easier the work of policy entrepreneurs trying to defend diffuse interests. In Kingdon's (2010, 182) words, "any crisis is seized as an opportunity." When policy windows open, policy entrepreneurs are central actors to promote policy positions as "advocates who are willing to invest their resources – time, energy, reputation, money" (Kingdon 2010, 179). This requires that policy entrepreneurs have developed their ideas or policy proposals well in advance of a crisis that opens a policy window (ibid. 181). Levine (1976, 58) writes that "economic disruptions often change the distribution of political power and create opportunities for public policy entrepreneurs to rearrange things to their advantage." Entrepreneurs are also instrumental in building coalitions: "It is during times of crisis or uncertainty when political entrepreneurs can offer alternative or competing narratives that redefine political interests in a manner that open up new coalitional possibilities" (Sheingate 2003, 192).

The importance of policy entrepreneurs in remedying industry capture and facilitating the mobilization of diffuse interests had already occurred to critics of economic theories of regulation. Focusing on the distributional consequences of regulatory policy, James Q. Wilson offered an extension of capture theories of economic regulation, arguing that diffuse interests do not necessarily go unrepresented. Wilson ascribed the raise of social regulation in the 1960s and 1970s that conferred benefits on society as a whole at the expense of a narrow few to "entrepreneurial politics" in which an entrepreneur "serves as the vicarious representative of groups not directly part of the legislative process" (Wilson 1980, 370). Policy entrepreneurs "mobilize latent public sentiment (by revealing a scandal or capitalizing on a crisis), put the opponents of the plan publicly on the defensive (by accusing them of killing babies or deforming motorists) and associate the legislation with widely shared values (clean air, pure water, health, and safety)" (ibid.). This kind of "entrepreneurial politics"—which distributes benefits widely and concentrates costs more narrowly—is needed for the representation of diffuse interests in public policy. One example of how a skilled policy entrepreneur was instrumental in passing consumer protection legislation is provided by consumer advocate Ralph Nader in the passage of the Auto Safety Act of 1966.

According to Mattli and Woods, "the entrepreneur involves himself or herself to the best of his or her abilities in the process of change, offering counsel, logistics, financial and technical expertise, or otherwise empowering poorly resourced societal groups adversely affected by the regulatory status quo" (Mattli and Woods 2009, 28). In relation to Dodd-Frank, Woolley and Ziegler (2011; 2014) found Elizabeth Warren, a Harvard law professor, to be a crucial figure in their research on consumer finance protection reforms. A more precise understanding of political entrepreneur is, however, needed in order to specify entrepreneurial success in defending diffuse interests.

The notion of entrepreneurship or political entrepreneur has been attributed to Schumpeter (1934). While he was writing about capitalist entrepreneurs who introduce new products, create new markets, or invent new methods of production in a process he famously described as "creative destruction," his ideas bear some resemblance to the policy process. Policy entrepreneurs can also invest in the development of new ideas to bring about policy change and attack existing power monopolies (Patashnik 2008, 28). In an often-quoted essay on political entrepreneurship Sheingate (2003, 188) finds that political science literature converges on the view of entrepreneurs "as creative, resourceful, and opportunistic leaders whose skillful manipulation of politics somehow results in the creation of a new policy or a new bureaucratic agency [...]." Two attributes of entrepreneurs are considered relevant here: first, entrepreneurs shape political debates by defining problems and second, entrepreneurs are a source of innovation, putting forward ideas and building supportive coalitions to get new policies adopted. Entrepreneurial innovation is key to understanding institutional change, as Sheingate (2003, 203; italics in original) put it, "[c]rises *do* precipitate change, but not always." Instead, entrepreneurial innovation can be an important source of endogenous institutional change.

The specific placement of entrepreneurs will differ among case studies. Political entrepreneurs are here considered separate from the leaders of consumer, labor, civil rights, and other advocacy groups. From the perspective of Salisbury's "exchange theory of interest groups," entrepreneurs provide selective benefits to group members and negotiate deals on the political stage, thereby serving as central connectors among two different spheres. In other words, entrepreneurs can organize new forms of collective action and make them politically relevant. Following Wilson (1980) and Salisbury (1969), policy entrepreneurs are here conceptualized as not directly part of the legislative process. Entrepreneurs therefore also differ from government officials. Experts are one category often evoked as important advocates for diffuse interests as policy entrepreneurs (Mattli and Woods 2009, 32). Expertise alone will not bring about policy change, however. For entrepreneurs to be heard, they also must have an ability to speak for others (such as an interest group leader) or an authoritative position (such as the presidency or a chairmanship). Entrepreneurs are most influential when they are politically savvy (meaning they have the relevant political connections or negotiating skill). Moreover, entrepreneurs need to be willing to invest a considerable amount of resources (Kingdon 2010, 181). We will test the following claim: *activism of a well-positioned entrepreneur, as a source of innovation, expertise, institutional resources, and political connections can exploit perceived political opportunities and leverage diffuse groups' policy influence.*

Government allies

Elected officials, often considered key actors in promoting regulatory change in the public interest (Mattli and Woods 2009, 32), might not just become more receptive to consumer demands but they might actually turn into active "government allies" to promote the consumer cause in coalitions with interest groups. There are several incentives for elected officials to act on behalf of diffuse interests. Promoting one's personal interests and career goals can be a strong motivator. Politicians might promote diffuse interests when they expect electoral benefits (Levine 1976, 48), or they might want to promote their ideology or values and affect the shape of public policy accordingly (Wilson 1980, 123). In particular when officeholders are in a position of leadership, their actions are publicly visible and command a sense of responsibility. As Derthick and Quirk (1985, 239) argue: "If any officeholders have adequate incentives to prefer diffuse over special interests, leaders do." In the terminology of social movement scholars, elites (such as government officials or parties) become "influential allies" pushing for the same policy goals (Tarrow 1996, 55; McAdam 1996, 30). In the EU, the Commission and the Parliament have traditionally been allies for diffuse interest groups (Pollack 1997, 579). Although there are no electoral incentives for Commission officials, the Commission in trying to expand its competencies in areas such as consumer protection has found an important ally in civil society groups in pushing for pro-integrationist EU policies. In general, diffuse interests figure prominently on the political agenda when the leading role of high-standard countries and lobbying demands for harmonization by producers and consumers are reinforced by the "entrepreneurial role of the Commission eager to increase its substantive competencies" (ibid. 585). In this view, the Commission and the European Parliament, with their pro-integrationist agendas, are considered to be champions of diffuse interests, "providing a natural ally" (Ibid. 580). In particular, individual Commissioners can become forceful promoters of diffuse interests (Greenwood 2011, 37)

The advancement of public policy—for electoral or ideological reasons—can be a strong incentive for politicians to promote diffuse interests. Mahoney and Baumgartner (2015) highlight the centrality of active policy advocacy of government allies to explain policy change. They conceptualize "lobbying groups and government officials as parts of collective efforts to move policy in one direction or another" in so-called insider–outsider coalitions (Mahoney and Baumgartner 2015, 203). From this perspective, the road to success in Washington is gaining government allies. Successful legislative battles are usually fought by coalitions of insiders (government officials) and outsiders (lobbying groups) with shared policy goals, and not, as many interest group scholars have depicted it, by outsider groups trying to lobby largely inactive government officials. Government officials are likely to invest resources in the promotion of a particular policy goal if they can predict success. They will therefore join one "lobbying side"—independently of an individual group's resourcefulness—if other prominent officials (the White House or the party leadership in Congress) associate themselves publicly with the cause or if they see large resources mobilized by outside lobbying groups collectively. An interest group's individual material resources are hence not a good predictor of its lobbying success. The policy influence of any individual group cannot be derived from its material resources but depends on context, namely the mobilization of other groups.

This approach shares some similarities with Sabatier's (1998) "advocacy coalition" or Trumbull's (2012) "legitimacy coalitions." Advocacy coalitions consist of governmental and private actors working in tandem to promote a policy solution (Sabatier 1998, 103). By focusing on the role of government allies in pro-reform coalitions, so-called insider–outsider coalitions, this study will build on the insights of these studies. In the sequence of decision-making, mobilization of diffuse interests is here considered to be a necessary condition for public officials to become leading advocates of a policy proposal (Mahoney and Baumgartner 2015, 207). Government officials start to actively promote a policy solution as partners in advocacy with outside groups *after* or as a reaction to intense mobilization of interest groups and an assessment of overall political receptivity. Following this, I test the following hypothesis: *intense pro-reform mobilization leads to a bandwagon effect that strengthens the reform side of the debate and encourages public officials to actively side with the pro-reform coalition as "government allies."*

Conceptualization of the causal argument

Focusing on the question of how diffuse interests were able to have their preferences met in financial reforms, a necessary supply side factor such as the opened-up institutional context in times of crisis needs to be combined with the organization of societal groups as a coordinated coalition. This, in turn, provides sufficient resources and allows pro-reform coalitions to channel widespread public support, to align themselves with well-positioned elite allies. For process-tracing, I re-conceptualize the theory here as a mechanism with five distinct parts: (i) political opportunities open up a policy window for diffuse interests in terms of access and responsiveness; (ii) diffuse interest groups form a "countervailing force" to channel public opinion, deploy expertise, and exploit the (temporary) weakness of the opposition; (iii) policy entrepreneurs support diffuse interest groups; (iv) government allies defend diffuse interests, promoting the same policy goals; and (v) financial regulatory reform outcomes reflect diffuse interests. The context in which this mechanism is hypothesized to function is characterized by the presence of a legitimacy crisis that weakens the incumbent financial sector groups. (The full mechanism is illustrated in Figure 2.1.)

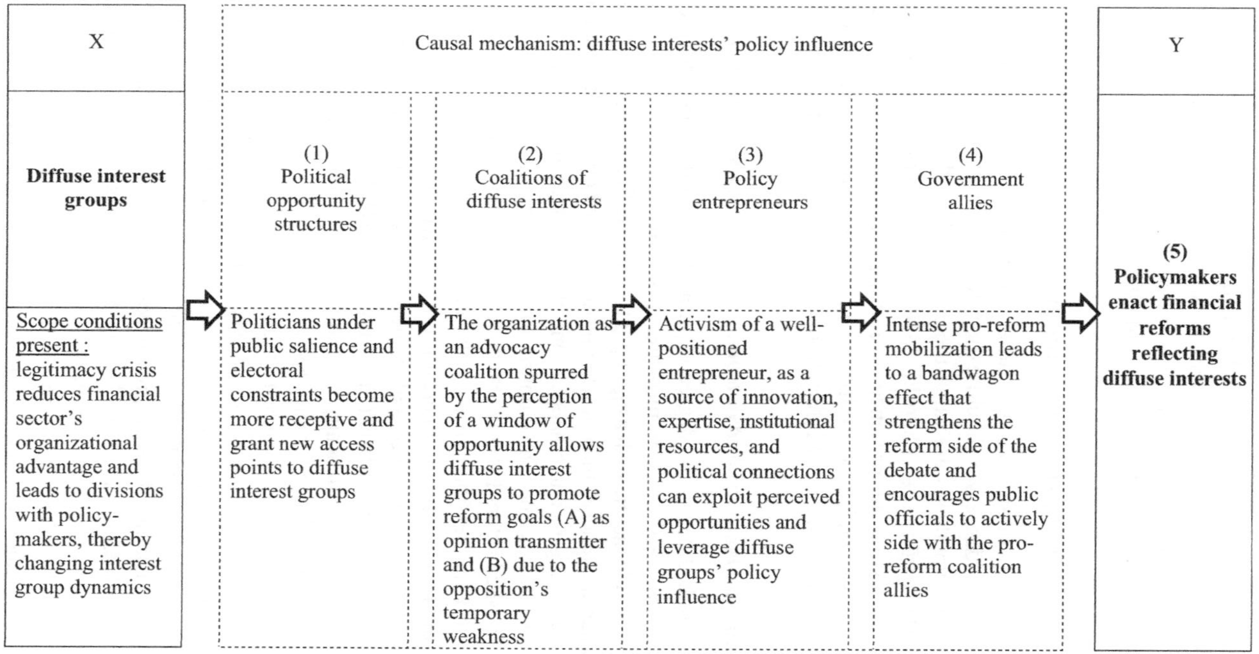
X
Causal mechanism: diffuse interests' policy influence
Y
Diffuse interest groups
(1) Political opportunity structures
(2) Coalitions of diffuse interests
(3) Policy entrepreneurs
(4) Government allies
(5) Policymakers enact financial reforms reflecting diffuse interests
Scope conditions present : legitimacy crisis reduces financial sector's organizational advantage and leads to divisions with policy-makers, thereby changing interest group dynamics
Politicians under public salience and electoral constraints become more receptive and grant new access points to diffuse interest groups
The organization as an advocacy coalition spurred by the perception of a window of opportunity allows diffuse interest groups to promote reform goals (A) as opinion transmitter and (B) due to the opposition's temporary weakness
Activism of a well-positioned entrepreneur, as a source of innovation, expertise, institutional resources, and political connections can exploit perceived opportunities and leverage diffuse groups' policy influence
Intense pro-reform mobilization leads to a bandwagon effect that strengthens the reform side of the debate and encourages public officials to actively side with the pro-reform coalition allies

Figure 2.1 A causal mechanism: How diffuse interests can influence financial regulatory politics[1]

Visualizing these relations in a scheme is, of course, only a reductionist way of modeling relationships among factors that are empirically much more complex. The relation between group behavior and political opportunities is probably best understood as a dynamic interaction: while opened-up institutional access and political receptivity of government officials encouraged initial interest group activities, it is the extensive mobilization of groups (in combination with the support of other prominent entrepreneurs) that made officials into active government allies. While diffuse interest groups can take advantage of political opportunities created by political elites, the reverse is also possible: collective action of lobbying groups can create incentives for elites to pursue their own policy goals.

Operationalization of process-tracing tests

Table 2.1 tries to operationalize the causal mechanism in case-specific predictions about what evidence we should expect to find for every single part of the mechanism if the hypotheses are valid, thereby avoiding "lazy mechanism-based storytelling" (Hedström and Ylikoski 2010, 54). The collection of empirical observations for testing the presence of empirical evidence for a hypothesized mechanism is theory-guided. If empirical evidence confirms the existence of each part of the mechanism, it can be inferred that the mechanism actually exists.

Measuring initial conditions and outcome: preferences and influence

The outcome studied here—the degree of influence of diffuse interest groups on regulatory reforms—is difficult to measure. It is hard to establish the direct cause and effect of any one factor, such as group advocacy, with any degree of certainty. Interview research, namely "interviewing those involved on all sides, asking them what they were trying to make happen, and then seeing what actually occurred" (Mahoney 2007, 38), is one viable option for measuring interest group influence. Accordingly, I asked actors for concrete actions, what they did, but I also included questions about who they thought were the most influential actors. Influence can also be measured by comparing interest groups' stated goals (as a proxy for their true policy positions), triangulated with contextual information and interviews with other actors involved in the debate (Mahoney 2007, 37). In the case studies, regulatory change will be systematically gauged against the advocacy goals of diffuse interest groups. The evidence for successful interest group lobbying can be one of the following: if a proposal by interest groups is actually translated into regulatory policy or if a regulatory proposal is removed from the agenda due to an interest groups intervention. If, for instance, an item survives the policy-agenda even though industry lobbying opposed to it, this evidence would be an empirical indicator for failed industry capture. Interest groups could, of course, see their preferences reflected in a policy decision without having done anything to bring about this policy outcome. While we should keep in mind that lobbying success does not mean that a group was influential, "it can give us a sense of who is winning and losing in policy debates, and allow us to get a handle on why this is so" (Mahoney 2007, 44).

Table 2.1 Conceptualization and operationalization of the causal mechanism

Conceptualization	Predicted evidence	Type of evidence (Examples)
Scope conditions present: legitimacy crisis neutralizes financial sector's organizational advantage and leads to divisions with policymakers, thereby changing interest group dynamics	Increased salience of financial reforms	*Media reporting about policy failure due to undue industry influence measured by systematic press survey as indicator for legitimacy crisis*
	Divisions among policymakers and industry or at least reservation towards industry groups	*Number of press articles about financial reforms as a measure of salience*
		Policymakers call industry groups' expertise into question, find industry's proposals not well suited to limit damage, dropping levels of communication, exchange of information about intended policy change at later stages as a measure of divisions based on account evidence, triangulating interviews with both actor groups and press articles
	De-legitimization forces industry to retreat and adapt its lobbying strategies	*Softening lobby positions of industry comparatively to pre-crisis level, refraining from veto, diverting attention to other stages in the policy cycle, measured using public position papers*
(1) Favorable opportunity structures: politicians under public salience and electoral constraints become more receptive and grant new access points to diffuse interest groups	Increased issue salience of reform measure; favorable public opinion	*Number of articles dealing with the CFPB as a measure of salience*
	Increased receptivity of decision-makers to diffuse groups	*Polls indicating support of CFPB as measure of public opinion*
		Increased receptivity (in comparison to pre-crisis levels) measured using account evidence from public documents and triangulating interviews with both policymakers and groups
	Qualitative shift in institutional environment for reforms	*Qualitative shift from expert committees (pre-crisis situation) to governmental agendas, allowing access for consumer groups*
(2) Diffuse interest coalitions: due to a perceived policy window, new coalitions mobilize, enhancing collective action capacity of diffuse interests [...]	Policy window triggers mobilization	*Crisis-induced mobilization measured by comparing pre-and post-crisis levels, using systematic media survey and secondary IPE literature*
	Coalition-building among diffuse groups as countervailing force	*Networking among groups in more or less formalized coalitions, incl. the mobilization of common organizational (financial, human) resources, measured using account evidence from interviews with advocates*
	Groups acting as opinion transmitters	*Groups as opinion transmitter measured by group activities (i.e. campaigns addressed at policymakers) and policymakers referring to public pressure*
	Fragmentation among industry groups	*Emergence of Baptist-bootlegger coalitions, measured using interviews*

(Continued)

Table 2.1 (Continued)

Conceptualization	Predicted evidence	Type of evidence (Examples)
(3) Policy entrepreneurs: activism of well-positioned entrepreneurs, as source of innovation [...], leverages diffuse groups' policy influence	Coalition-building among pro-reform groups and well-positioned policy entrepreneurs that can provide expertise, institutional resources etc. thereby leveraging diffuse advocacy groups' influence	Political actors are considered entrepreneurs when they have innovative ideas, expertise, are well-positioned and willing to invest resources (Kingdon 2010), measured using account evidence from interviews, newspaper articles and secondary sources
(4) Government allies: Intense pro-reform mobilization leads to a bandwagon effect that strengthens that side of the debate and encourages public officials to actively side with the pro-reform coalition as allies	Elected officials become active allies after initial intense group mobilization and support of other elite allies (Baumgartner and Mahoney 2015) Diffuse interest groups and their governmental allies cooperate closely and push for the same policy solutions in insider-outsider coalitions	Effect of increased mobilization on decision-makers can be measured by triangulating account and sequence evidence from interviews, newspaper articles and press statements Government allies: close cooperation, coordination in team-like structures, timely exchange of information between policymakers and interest groups which serve as source of expertise, measured triangulating account evidence from interviews with both actor groups
(5) Outcome: Policymakers enact financial reforms reflecting diffuse interests.	Financial regulatory reforms reflecting diffuse consumer interests rather than interests of most resourceful groups	Lobbying success can be measured by comparing interest groups' stated goals (as a proxy for their true policy positions), triangulated with contextual information (letters, statements, final positions produced) and interviews with actors involved in the debate reporting success or loss in relation to policy outcome Counter-evidence to capture: if an item survives the policy-agenda in spite of industry lobbying opposed to it

Preferences of the main policy-makers and interest groups involved can be extrapolated inductively by examining position papers, press statements, and consultation documents, as well as from interviews with senior elites. Consultation documents refer to comment letters to policy proposals that are usually subject to formal consultations held, for example, by European Commission Directorates General. These sources taken together provide a relatively systematic picture of groups' mobilization and preferences (Klüver 2009). The initial assumption is that policy-makers respond to public pressure from their constituents, in the form of interest groups. But policy-makers are not merely on the receiving end of group pressure; they may have strong preferences of their own. One can assume that policy-makers are rational actors whose preferences are determined by desires for re-election, as well as the "likelihood of success in achieving their policy goals" (Mahoney and Baumgartner 2015, 202).

Note

1 Following Beach and Pedersen (2013, 29) each part of the mechanism is conceptualized "as composed of entities that undertake activities" while only those elements of the mechanism are included that are considered necessary to produce the outcome. According to this approach, a causal mechanism should be conceptualized as follows: $X \rightarrow [(n1\rightarrow)]*(n2\rightarrow)]$ Y (read: X transmits causal forces through the mechanism composed of part 1 (entity 1 and an activity) and part 2 (entity 2 and an activity)) that together contribute to producing outcome Y under specific contextual conditions.

References

Baker, A. (2010) 'Restraining Regulatory Capture? Anglo-America, Crisis Politics and Trajectories of Change in Global Financial Governance', *International Affairs* 86 (3): 647–63.

Birkland, T. A. (1998) 'Focusing Events, Mobilization, and Agenda Setting', *Journal of Public Policy* 18 (1): 53–74.

Bouwen, P. (2004) 'Exchanging Goods for Acces: A Comparative Study of Business Lobbying in the European Institutions', *European Journal of Political Research* 43: 337–69.

Capoccia, G. and Kelemen, R. D. (2007) 'The Study of Critical Junctures: Theory, Narrative, and Counterfactuals in Historical Institutionalism', *World Politics* 59 (3): 341–69.

Clapp, J. and Helleiner, E. (2012) 'Troubled Futures? The Global Food Crisis and the Politics of Agricultural Derivatives Regulation', *Review of International Political Economy* 19 (2): 181–207.

Culpepper, P. D. (2011) *Quiet Politics and Business Power: Corporate Control in Europe and Japan*, Cambridge: Cambridge University Press.

Derthick, M. and Quirk, P. J. (1985) *The Politics of Deregulation*, Washington, DC: Brookings Institution Press.

Dobusch, L. and Quack, S. (2013) 'Framing Standards, Mobilizing Users: Copyright versus Fair Use in Transnational Regulation', *Review of International Political Economy* 20 (1): 52–88.

Dür, A., and Mateo, G. (2014) 'Public Opinion and Interest Group Influence: How Citizen Groups Derailed the Anti-Counterfeiting Trade Agreement', *Journal of European Public Policy* 21 (8): 1199–217.

Engelen, E. et al. (eds) (2011) *After the Great Complacence: Financial Crisis and the Politics of Reform*, Oxford, New York: Oxford University Press.

Greenwood, J. (2011) *Interest Representation in the European Union*, Basingstoke: Palgrave.

Haas, P. M. (1992) Introduction: Epistemic Communities and International Policy Coordination, *International Organization* 46 (1): 1–35.

Hacker, J. S. and Pierson, P. (2010) 'Winner-Take-All Politics: Public Policy, Political Organization, and the Precipitous Rise of Top Incomes in the United States', *Politics & Society* 38 (2): 152–204.

Hedström, P. and Ylikoski, P. (2010) 'Causal Mechanisms in the Social Sciences', *Annual Review of Sociology* 36 (1): 49–67.

Helleiner, E. and Pagliari, S. (2011) 'The End of an Era in International Financial Regulation? A Postcrisis Research Agenda', *International Organization* 65 (1): 169–200.

Keck, M. E. and Sikkink, K. (1998) *Activists Beyond Borders: Advocacy Networks in International Politics*, Ithaca, NY: Cornell University Press.

Kingdon, J. W. (2010) *Agendas, Alternatives, and Public Policies*, 2nd edition, Boston: Pearson.

Klüver, H. (2009) 'Measuring Interest Group Influence Using Quantitative Text Analysis', *European Union Politics* 10 (4): 535–49.

Kollman, K. (1998) *Outside Lobbying: Public Opinion and Interest Group Strategies*, Princeton: Princeton University Press.

Kriesi, H. (1989) 'The Political Opportunity Structure of the Dutch Peace Movement', *West European Politics* 12 (3): 295–312.

Levine, M. E. (1976) The Economic Theory of Regulation a Decade After Deregulation. Comments and Discussion, Brookings Papers on Economic Activity, Brookings Institution, Washington, DC, available at www.brookings.edu/bpea-articles/the-economic-theory-of-regulation-after-a-decade-of-deregulation (accessed September 2016).

Mahoney, C. (2007) 'Lobbying Success in the United States and the European Union', *Journal of Public Policy* 27 (1): 35–56.

Mahoney, C. and Baumgartner, F. (2008) 'Converging Perspectives on Interest Group Research in Europe and America', *West European Politics* 31 (6): 1253–73.

Mahoney, C. and Baumgartner, F. (2015) 'Partners in Advocacy: Lobbyists and Government Officials in Washington', *The Journal of Politics* 77 (1): 202–15.

Mattli, W. and Woods, N. (2009) In Whose Benefit? Explaining Regulatory Change in Global Politics, in W. Mattli and N. Wood (eds), *The Politics of Global Regulation*, Princeton: Princeton University Press, pp. 1–43.

McAdam, D. (1996) Conceptual Origins, Current Problems, Future Directions, in D. McAdam et al. (eds), *Comparative Perspectives on Social Movements: Political Opportunities, Mobilizing Structures, and Cultural Framings*, Cambridge, New York: Cambridge University Press, pp. 23–40.

McAdam, D. et al. (1996) Introduction: Opportunities, Mobilizing Structures, and Framing Processes – Toward a Synthetic, Comparative Perspective on Social Movements, in D. McAdam et al. (eds), *Comparative Perspectives on Social Movements: Political Opportunities, Mobilizing Structures, and Cultural Framings*, Cambridge, New York: Cambridge University Press, pp. 1–22.

McAdam, D. et al. (2001) *Dynamics of Contention*, Cambridge: Cambridge University Press.

Meins, E. (2000) 'Up or Down? Explaining the Stringency of Consumer Protection', *Swiss Political Science Review* 6 (2): 94–9.

Morgan, G. (2010) 'Legitimacy in Financial Markets: Credit Default Swaps in the Current Crisis', *Socio-Economic Review* 8 (1): 17–45.

Pagliari, S. (2013) Public Salience and International Financial Regulation: Explaining the International Regulation of OTC Derivatives, Rating Agencies, and Hedge Funds, Ph.D. dissertation, University of Waterloo, available at www.stefanopagliari.net/pagliari_-_phd_thesis_-.pdf (accessed September 2016).

Pagliari, S. and Young, K. L. (2013) The Wall Street–Main Street Nexus in Financial Regulation: Business Coalitions Inside and Outside the Financial Sector in the Regulation of OTC Derivatives, in M. Moschella and E. Tsingou (eds), *Great Expectations, Slow Transformations: Incremental Change in Financial Governance*, Colchester: ECPR Press, pp. 125–48.

Patashnik, E. M. (2008) *Reforms at Risk: What Happens After Major Policy Changes Are Enacted*, Princeton: Princeton University Press.

Pollack, M. A. (1997) 'Representing Diffuse Interests in EC Policy-Making', *Journal of European Public Policy* 4 (4): 572–90.

Price, R. (1998) 'Reversing the Gun Sights: Transnational Civil Society Targets Land Mines', *International Organization* 52 (3): 613–44.

Princen, S. and Kerremans, B. (2008) 'Opportunity Structures in the EU Multi-Level System', *West European Politics* 31 (6): 1129–46.

Sabatier, P. A. (1998) 'The Advocacy Coalition Framework: Revisions and Relevance for Europe', *Journal of European Public Policy* 5 (1): 98–130.

Salisbury, R. H. (1969) 'An Exchange Theory of Interest Groups', *Midwest Journal of Political Science* 13 (1): 1–32.

Schumpeter, J. A. (1934) *The Theory of Economic Development: An Inquiry into Profits, Capital, Credit, Interest, and the Business Cycle*, London: Transaction Publishers.

Sheingate, A. D. (2003) 'Political Entrepreneurship, Institutional Change, and American Political Development', *Studies in American Political Development* 17 (2): 185–203.

Smith, M. A. (2000) *American Business and Political Power*, Chicago, London: The University of Chicago Press.

Steinlin, S. and Trampusch, C. (2012) 'Institutional Shrinkage: The Deviant Case of Swiss Banking Secrecy', *Regulation & Governance* 6 (2): 242–59.

Tarrow, S. (1996) States and Opportunities: The Political Structuring of Social Movements, in D. McAdam et al. (eds), *Comparative Perspectives on Social Movements: Political Opportunities, Mobilizing Structures, and Cultural Framings*, Cambridge, New York: Cambridge University Press, pp. 41–61.

Tarrow, S. (2011) *Power in Movement: Social Movements and Contentious Politics*, 3rd edition, Cambridge, NY: Cambridge University Press.

Tilly, C. (1978) *From Mobilization to Revolution*, Reading, MA: Longman Higher Education.

Trumbull, G. (2012) *Strength in Numbers: The Political Power of Weak Interests*, Cambridge, MA: Harvard University Press.

Tsingou, E. (2008) Transnational Private Governance and the Basel Process: Banking Regulation and Supervision, Private Interests and Basel II, in A. Nölke and J.-C. Graz (eds), *Transnational Private Governance and Its Limits*, London: Routledge and ECPR, pp. 58–68.

Vogel, D. (1993) Representing Diffuse Interests in Environmental Policymaking, in R. K. Weaver and B. A. Rockman (eds), *Do Institutions Matter? Government Capabilities in the United States and Abroad*, Washington, DC: The Brookings Institution, pp. 237–71

Wilson, J. Q. (1980) *The Politics of Regulation*, New York: Basic Books.

Woolley, J. T. and Ziegler, J. N. (2011) The Two-Tiered Politics of Financial Reform in the United States, IRLE Working Paper 111-11. Berkeley: Institute for Research on Labor and Employment, University of California, available at irle.berkeley.edu/working papers/111-11.pdf (accessed September 2016).

Woolley, J. T. and Ziegler, J. N. (2014) Who Shapes Institutional Reform: A Process-Tracing Approach to the Politics of Financial Reform in the United States, 2008–2010, Paper presented at a workshop, Sciences Po, Paris, 22–23 May.

Young, K. L. (2012) 'Transnational Regulatory Capture? An Empirical Examination of the Transnational Lobbying of the Basel Committee on Banking Supervision', *Review of International Political Economy* 19 (4): 663–88.

Young, K. L. (2013) 'Financial Industry Groups Adaptation to the Post-Crisis Regulatory Environment: Changing Approaches to the Policy Cycle', *Regulation & Governance* 7 (4): 460–80.

Young, K. L. (2014) 'Losing Abroad but Winning at Home: European Financial Industry Groups in Global Financial Governance since the Crisis', *Journal of European Public Policy* 21 (3): 367–88.

Part II
The cases

3 Winner-take-all politics and diffuse interest groups

The US consumer regulator

Introduction

On July 21, 2010, US President Barack Obama signed the Dodd-Frank Wall Street Reform and Consumer Protection Act (Dodd-Frank Act) into law, including major consumer protection provisions which fundamentally changed the regulatory landscape for financial services. Dodd-Frank's preamble declares one object to be "to protect consumers from abusive financial services practices."[1] Under Title X, the reform law established a new federal regulator, the Consumer Financial Protection Bureau (CFPB). There is wide agreement among regulators, activists, and industry representatives that the consumer protection reforms introduced in response to the crisis go beyond mere "gesture politics."

The political debate surrounding the creation of the consumer agency was characterized by intense lobbying and mobilization by interest groups from two opposing camps. An emerging coalition of relatively resource-poor civil society actors, including consumer associations, trade unions, NGOs, grassroots groups, and small business groups, actively supported the new consumer regulator. They were opposed by a much more powerful financial lobby. Johnson and Kwak (2011, 198) write that the financial industry and its defenders "closed ranks" against the bureau. Arguably, the new consumer bureau attracted more hostility from industry groups than any other reform proposals after the crisis. Strong opposition came from the American Bankers Association (ABA), the US Chamber of Commerce, and the Mortgage Bankers Association (MBA). Against all odds, the civil society coalition formed among actors usually classified as weak, managed to win a major victory when the President signed Dodd-Frank into law—including a powerful new regulator for consumer financial products.

Despite the fact that massive industry lobbying had successfully slowed down the implementation process of US financial regulatory reform—with 60% of Dodd-Frank's rules not yet in place by July 2013, roughly 40% in place by July 2014 and final rules expected to be written by mid-2017[2]—the creation and implementation of the CFPB (despite the attempt of the Republican Party to block the confirmation of an executive director till July 2013 and a lawsuit filed in June 2012 challenging the CFPB's constitutionality on grounds that it violated the US Constitution's separation of powers principle which was revived by a federal appeals court in July 2015) was a unique win for consumer advocates. At the 2010 conference of the American Council on Consumer Interests, Ed Mierzwinski (2010, 596), consumer advocate at the US Public Interest Research Group (US PIRG), celebrated the bureau as a huge victory for the consumer movement: "Over the past year, the traditional consumer movement aligned itself with civil rights, labor, senior and other groups faced off against a phalanx of powerful special interests hell-bent on beating our big idea that consumers deserved an independent agency [...] They lost. We won." The outcome is puzzling, as we would normally expect more resourceful groups to have more political influence. In particular, the US banking industry is one of the most resourceful, powerful, and politically savvy actors in Washington, winning many of their political battles. The CFPB is therefore a case in point to study the power of weak interests in financial regulation. Why was the US banking industry not able to beat out consumer groups in the case at hand? What explains the fact that rather weak and peripheral actors prevailed over more resourceful and dominant actors?

In this chapter, I look beyond the impact of materially resources in influencing policy decisions. This chapter offers one of the first scholarly analyses of the successful creation of a new financial regulator with the sole responsibility to protect consumers (for other studies, see Kirsch and Mayer 2013 as well as Woolley and Ziegler 2011 and 2014). Analyzing consumer credit market reforms is particularly interesting because abusive consumer-lending practices—in particular in the mortgage market, but also in relation to credit cards and other subprime consumer credit product—allegedly contributed to the financial meltdown that started in 2007. In offering a close empirical analysis of a causal mechanism at work that allows diffuse interest groups to leave their imprint on financial regulatory reforms, the account here will be dealing with a side that is less well-known to researchers.

This chapter is organized as follows. It starts with a brief discussion of the main characteristics of the new regulatory agency that was established as part of the Dodd-Frank regulation in 2010. A considerable part of the consumer groups' positions is reflected in the consecutive drafts, while this is not the case for the positions taken by the industry groups. It then outlines the political struggles surrounding the creation of the new regulator, highlighting the position of the financial industry and consumer groups on the legislative proposal. The next section will interpret the policy process by applying the theoretically derived hypotheses to the empirical record of the case study by employing the method of process-tracing. The chapter will conclude by reflecting on the implications for our understanding of regulatory capture.

Regulatory change and group influence

Before the Dodd-Frank Act went into effect, the rulemaking authority to implement federal consumer financial protection laws was largely held by the Federal Reserve System ("Fed"). Prior to the reforms, consumer protection functions were scattered among different banking regulators. The system of consumer finance protection on the eve of the crisis was marked by regulatory gaps, allowing for ruthless lending practices which contributed to increased defaults and eventually to the meltdown of the US housing market. The consequence of lax regulations was a "downward spiral in lending standards" with lenders shopping for the weakest state laws and non-depository institutions trying to escape regulation entirely (Engel and McCoy 2011, 166). In their analysis of the crisis, Cooley et al. (2011, 76) conclude that consumer protection laws which were in place prior to the crisis, were "ineffective." In sum, federal preemption but also the fragmentation of the US consumer financial protection regulatory system led to loopholes, regulatory arbitrage, and lax regulations.

In order to address the regulatory failure of the past, the Dodd-Frank Act centralized consumer protection regulations at one single agency, which is well funded, and is under the leadership of a single director. It thereby translated key demands of consumer groups into policy.[3] The Bureau passed in Title X of the reform law as an independent regulatory agency with the sole responsibility of protecting consumers of financial products. While the CFPB is administratively located within the Fed, the Board of Governors cannot interfere in its operations. In charging one single agency with consumer protection responsibilities, the reform succeeded in replacing a patchwork of seven different agencies, thereby consolidating and strengthening the regulation of consumer financial products. Not only does the CFPB consolidate the consumer protection functions of various agencies, it also consolidates consumer protection legislation previously found in a number of different statutes (such as the Truth in Lending Act and the CARD Act of 2009). The new bureau also hosts a national consumer complaint hotline as a single toll-free number for consumers to report problems as well as a new Office of Financial Education to promote financial literacy. Funding and powers of the new bureau are comparable to those of other federal financial regulators (Wilmarth 2012, 904; Pridgen 2013, 7). Taken together, the new bureau's powers should "serve as counterweight within the government to a set of regulatory agencies that have historically seen the world from the perspective of the banks they regulate rather than the costumers served by those banks" (Johnson and Kwak 2011, 200).

Some might object that the new regulator for consumer products was merely window-dressing in the financial overhaul. A reason to think that this was not the case is the amount of resources the industry invested to defeat the new bureau. Industry groups had clearly preferred the status quo, and the regulation passed in spite of industry's attempts to block it. The CFPB was also not window-dressing but real reform. Indeed, a broad range of experts, including consumer lawyers, industry groups, and consumer associations, widely acknowledged the new bureau as a powerful new regulator (Pridgen 2013; Caggiano et al. 2011). Most importantly, the CFPB considerably increased compliance costs for the financial services industry and reduced its autonomy in the provision of consumer financial products (Aptean 2016; American Banker 2012).

In the final bill the pro-reform advocates met their major policy aims: in accordance with activists' wishes the new bureau has significant authority on rules supervision and enforcement over banks and non-banks, market-wide coverage, a single director, its funds are not subject to the congressional appropriations process, and it allows states to adopt stricter consumer protection rules. Table 3.1 summarizes the main features of the CFPB as signed into law in July 2010. The Dodd-Frank Act delegated three types of authority to the new bureau: the CFPB conducts rule-making, supervision, and enforcement for federal consumer financial protection laws. The CFPB is the first federal regulator that not only has the ability to write rules for non-banks, but it also has the ability to supervise and examine non-banks. It is a first in the history of non-banks that they are subject to examination by federal regulators. This makes the CFPB a much powerful regulatory for consumer financial services than the Federal Trade Commission with its sole authority over non-bank entities (Pridgen 2013). Consumer advocates thereby saw a major policy goal reflected in the final legislation.[4] With regards to small banks (under $10 billion), industry lobbyists negotiated a semi-carve-out. The new Bureau has the authority to oversee very large banks, thrifts, and credit unions with assets over $10 billion, as well as non-bank businesses (companies that can offer consumer financial products or services without having a bank, thrift, or credit union charter). Consumer advocates counted the semi-carve as a partial victory, since the CFPB still kept its rule-writing authority over small banks. With a single director as head of the agency (instead of a five-person board), consumer advocates saw another key demand translated into policy. With regards to funding, the agency has independent funding, specified as a percentage of the Fed's budget, and is not subject to the appropriations process. The fact that the CFPB receives its funding outside of the appropriations process was an important aspect for consumer advocates, since it avoids "a mechanism for imposing undesirable political pressure" (Cooley 2010, 79).

Another important provision is that the Dodd-Frank Act curbs federal preemption which had previously prevented effective pro-consumer state legislation. The law functions as a federal "floor" (not a ceiling) which allows states to raise the level of consumer protection, one of the key demands of consumer advocates. Title X expands state authority by allowing states to adopt stricter consumer protection laws on top of the federal regulations. The law does, however, preserve the possibility of OCC preemption of state laws for national banks and federal thrifts (Cooley et al. 2011, 79; Engel and McCoy 2011, 255). Preemption was a loss to industry groups that had lobbied for the CFPB to have preemptive authority, arguing that "one rule at the national level is easier to comply with than 50 rules at the state level."[5]

Among the legislative compromises that had to be made by consumer groups, according to one activist, "none materially weakened the bureau."[6] For example, the Bureau's rulemaking authority is somewhat restricted by the provision that a two-thirds majority of the Financial Stability Oversight Council (FSOC) can set aside CFPB rules if they threaten the safety and soundness of the financial system (Cooley et al. 2011, 78). Moreover, despite lobbying efforts of consumer groups, the CFPB does not have the power to regulate credit insurance or auto dealers. Another loss, especially to community groups, was that the Community Reinvestment Act (CRA) was not transferred to the CFPB's authority.

Table 3.1 Main features of the CFPB under the Dodd-Frank Act as signed into law in 2010

Regulatory policy	*Reform measures in line with consumer groups' demands*
Structure/Head	Agency established within the Federal Reserve System; single director appointed by the President for five-year term
Funding	Transfer of 10–12% of the Federal Reserve System's budget
Coverage/Authority	Broad powers over all persons, other than those explicitly carved out from the Bureau's authority, engaged in the provision of a consumer financial product or service
Examination and enforcement power over smaller financial institutions	Smaller financial institutions (with assets of $10 billion or less) will continue to be subject to the examination and enforcement authority of their current regulators
Relationship to state law (federal preemption)	Would only preempt state laws to the extent of their inconsistency, state laws providing greater consumer protection are not to be considered inconsistent with federal law
	Compromises/losses for consumer groups
Oversight by the Financial Stability Oversight Council	Financial Stability Oversight Council with ability to set aside CFPB regulations if the regulation "would put the safety and soundness of the banking system or the stability of the financial system at risk"
Notable carve-outs	Carve-out for auto dealers and small businesses
Authority over consumer laws	Community Reinvestment Act (CRA) exempt from CFPB authority

The Independent Community Bankers Association (ICBA) argued that a transfer of authority over the CRA to the new agency would risk safety and soundness examinations to be trumped by consumer protection considerations (MacPhee 2009). Despite these compromises, the final legislation was clearly a victory to consumer advocates, who saw their main advocacy goals translated into regulatory reform. The next section will provide a brief overview of how the legislative struggle that lead to this outcome unfolded.

The legislative struggle for the CFPB

To define the temporal context in this analysis, we have chosen the financial crisis that originated in 2007, since it is a clear starting point that sets the causal mechanism in motion. The case study analysis therefore starts here, with a brief chronology of the passage of the reform law starting in early 2009, when legislative reform debates started to unfold.

In June 2009, the Treasury included a proposal of a new consumer agency in its 90-page White Paper, entitled "A New Foundation: Rebuilding Financial Supervision and Regulation," which served as a blueprint for financial reform. The White Paper proposed five objectives for financial reform, including a Consumer Financial Protection Agency (CFPA) (Department of the Treasury 2009). In September, the legislative debate subsequently moved to the House of Representatives, which passed its bill in early December 2009. The main venue of discussion was the House Financial Services Committee, chaired by Representative Barney Frank. The Senate Banking Committee chaired by Senator Christopher Dodd, discussed the bill in February and March 2010. The Conference Committee finalized its report on June 29, 2010. The bill subsequently moved separately to both the House and Senate floors, where it was voted on in June by the House and mid-July by the Senate.[7] On July 21, President Obama signed the Dodd-Frank Wall Street Reform and Consumer Protection Act into law.

At several stages during the legislative process, passage of the CFPB was at the tipping point. In order to secure a bipartisan deal, Senator Dodd had set out to a compromise that would have strengthened the consumer protection division of an existing federal agency, instead of creating a stand-alone bureau (Palletta 2010). According to Senator Bob Corker, the CFPB's creation was "the most contentious issue" and was "the elephant in the room" during the Senate's negotiations that prevented any bipartisan agreement on the bill (Rowley and Lerer 2010). On March 15, 2010, the Senate Banking Committee proposed a new bill, the "Restoring American Financial Stability Act (RAFSA) of 2010" (S. 3217) including a new independent consumer agency housed at the Federal Reserve, "an idea that had emerged from [Dodd's] failed negotiations with Corker" (Kirsch and Mayer 2013, 93). After the Senate Committee reported the bill, Republicans blocked the legislative proposal before it eventually reached the Senate floor in April. Under Senate rules, the Democrats needed 60 votes to overcome a Republican filibuster and move forward with debate (*New York Times* 2010a, 2010b). On May 5, Senator Shelby introduced amendment S.3826 on the Senate floor that would have weakened CFPB's powers and removed its independence, by placing the bureau under FDIC's control and barring it from examining or regulating depository institutions (Wilmarth 2012, 888). However, the amendment was defeated by the Democratic majority in the Senate. Eventually, on May 20, 2010, the Senate, by a vote of 59 to 39, approved a comprehensive financial reform bill, including Title X, a Bureau of Consumer Financial Protection within the Fed. The Senate's vote paved the way to convene the Conference Committee to reconcile the two different bills and settle on a compromise.

The proposal of an independent consumer regulator pitted two coalitions against each other. From the beginning, business groups—mainly the American Bankers Association, the Mortgage Bankers Association of America, and the American Chamber of Commerce—opposed the legislative proposal of a new consumer regulator. These groups are well organized and possess ample material resources. According to the Center for Responsive Politics, the financial industry mobilized and spent $224.6 million on lobbying in 2009, more than any other sector except for the health sector which spent $263.6 million during the same time period (Renick Mayer 2009). The US Chamber set up a "stoptheCFPA. com" website[8] and started an advertising campaign of at least $2 million aimed at defeating the new bureau. When he testified before the Senate Committee on Banking, Edward Yingling (2009), then president of the ABA, complained that the CFPB would undermine innovation, limit consumer choice, complicate existing regulatory structures, and disproportionately burden small banks and credit unions. The Bankers Association's public outcry against a consumer agency and the appearance of the then president of the ABA to testify in front of a Congressional Committee made clear that preventing the enactment of a consumer bureau was of high legislative priority to the industry.

The new consumer regulator was actively promoted by a new pro-reform coalition, acting as a countervailing force to industry interests. About the same time the administration brought forward its reform proposals, a new coalition of about 250 civil society organizations started to actively support the creation of a consumer regulator. The US Public Interest Research Group (PIRG), together with other NGOs and the largest labor groups, including the AFL-CIO and the SEIU, established a new and unprecedented coalition of labor, civil rights, small businesses, and senior organizations, which formally went public in May 2009 as "Americans for Financial Reform" (AFR). The formation of such an alliance in the financial services sector, representing "a cohesive non-industry voice," was a unique event in American history (Woolley and Ziegler 2011, 23). Some scholars refer to the mobilization that took place in response to the crisis as the "fourth wave of consumer activism" (Cohen 2010, 235).

In terms of material resources, the pro-reform coalition was clearly outmatched by the opposing financial industry lobby. Funding for pro-reform groups became available from progressive foundations, with AFR raising about $1.4 million in the first year, only a fraction of the financial industry's lobbying budget.[9] Nevertheless, consumer and labor groups, representing diffuse interests, saw their preferences translated into public policy, in spite of more resourceful and influential opponents. As one consumer activist commented on the legislation: "Compared to a world where we could not make a single advance on consumer regulation for decades, this is a big change."[10] How did diffuse consumer interests come to be reflected in the reform outcome?

Advocacy for a new consumer finance regulator

Contextual conditions: the post-crisis financial regulatory environment

Regulatory reform emerged in a post-crisis environment which saw the legitimacy of the financial industry and its practices being strongly contested in the public sphere. The heightened media attention raised by the crisis increased the perception of undue industry influence. Major newspapers published reports and articles where the financial sector was shown in an extremely unfavorable light.

The *New York Times* repeatedly cited the Center for Responsive Politics and the Sunlight Foundation quoting reports on the financial sector's spending on lobbying (*New York Times* 2012; Wyatt and Lichtblau 2010; Protess 2011). CNN Money released an article citing PIRG's statistics as well as a Public Citizen's report about financial institutions hiring some 1,000 lobbyists since 2009 (Liberto 2010). More information came to light about how bad industry practices were. The non-profit Wall Street Watch project attracted public attention with a critical report on the financial sector's political influence called "Sold Out." The non-profit public broadcasting service PBS portrayed a similar message in a documentary it released called "The Warning," which was but one of a whole series on industry malpractices that PBS showed throughout 2009.

Previous regulatory deficits became the subject of public outrage pushing financial regulatory reform into the arena of "noisy politics," to use Culpepper's terminology. As mentioned above, heightened salience is an important dynamic, since it can be a strong motivator for elected officials to act against the narrow interests of an industry. Young (2013) could show empirically that financial regulation became highly salient with the wider public during the early reform period, from mid-2008 till mid-2009 by assessing the amount of news coverage in the general interest press as well as in the regulatory policy community. The subprime mortgage crisis also directed attention to shortcomings of the existing consumer protection framework, bolstering the demands by pro-reform advocates. There is little doubt, that problems with the consumer protection framework, including widespread predatory lending practices, were evident at the time of the Obama administration's reform effort. The pre-crisis regulatory system had largely been criticized by scholars and consumer advocates for being dispersed and putting too little focus on consumer protection. Analysts have pinpointed failures in consumer protection as "the detonators and amplifiers" in the crisis and subsequently demanded more effective consumer protection in provision of financial products and services (Melecky and Rutledge 2011). This analysis was largely based on the experience of the US housing bubble, which was made possible by deteriorating mortgage origination and underwriting standards. Accordingly, the Senate report on the Dodd-Frank Act concluded in April 2010, that "the current system of consumer protection suffers from a number of serious structural flaws that undermine its effectiveness, including a lack of focus resulting from conflicting regulatory missions, fragmentation, and regulatory arbitrage" (US Senate 2010).

In light of the devastating consequences of the financial crisis, policy-makers started to call industry groups' expertise into question, as Representative Brad Miller remarked in a statement in March 2009 about intended mortgage reform: "The political climate has changed. The foreclosure crisis has wreaked havoc on middle-class families and our economy as a whole. The industry's arguments [...] are not at all convincing" (Harney 2009). Commenting on the legislative proposal of a new consumer agency, Miller argued in favor of stricter consumer protection and against the rationale of increasing access to credit the industry had promoted for years: "Our economy is in a deep hole dug by the financial industry. For years they defended every consumer lending practice, regardless of how predatory the practice appeared on its face, as necessary to make credit available to ordinary Americans. And the result was eye-popping profits for the industry and millions of middle-class Americans hopelessly in debt, trapped by indefensible fees and penalties explained in legalese in tiny print. We can't let that happen again" (cited in Durbin 2009b).

With their reputation highly damaged and under the lasting impression of the crisis and moral outrage about banks' misbehavior, financial lobby groups had partly lost their political leverage. The financial sector was the culprit of the crisis. The following de-legitimization was clearly felt by those lobbying on its behalf, as one interviewee for this research project put it, "with the crisis the industry was not in a position of strength because we had made mistakes and the policy makers were looking to strengthen the regulatory framework around that. So it is difficult for an industry who is culpable [...] to come in and say here is what we think you should do to fix it."[11]

Increased issues salience in the regulatory reform context was accompanied by qualitative shifts in policy-making that displayed increasing divisions among policy-makers and the private sector. In his Wall Street speech in April 2010, the President made clear that he regarded consumer protection as an essential element of the financial reform, thereby risking "increasingly fractious relations" with the financial industry (Cooper 2010). In April 2010, The *New York Times* highlighted the President's stance against the financial industry:

> Addressing leaders of New York's financial giants, including Goldman Sachs, Mr. Obama described himself as a champion of change battling "battalions of financial industry lobbyists" and the "withering forces" of the economic elite. With his poll numbers sagging, the choreographed confrontation seemed aimed at tapping the nation's antiestablishment mood as well as muscling financial regulation legislation through Congress.
>
> (Baker and Herszenhorn 2010)

Several examples from our interviews illustrate that the regulatory dialogue among industry groups and government officials had suffered from considerable cracks since the crisis. One indicator of such a crack is that financial groups learned about legislative proposals and intended policy changes much later than in the past, largely excluding industry groups from the agenda-setting phase of the decision-making process. Interviews conducted with industry groups in Washington corroborate a story that their knowledge of the particular content of the proposed consumer agency prior to the Treasury's blueprint in June 2009 was either unknown or extremely fuzzy. Some industry representatives reported that they saw themselves "cut out of the process" during early legislative debates.[12] About the Treasury's White Paper, one industry representative remembered talking to Treasury officials but having "very little impact on the administration's thinking on the consumer side of the law." He also described how the regulatory dialogue had noticeably changed after the crisis, saying that regarding the policy proposal to establish a new consumer watchdog, industry associations "had almost no contact with the administration," which he characterized as "extremely unusual." When financial industry participants were invited to the White House, the administration would listen, but not negotiate, as one lobbyists reported: "I was invited to the White House a lot at the beginning. There were people who would always talk to me and we had very good conversations. I can't say that they wanted to negotiate with us in any way." Finally, when the White Paper was issued in June 2009, including a detailed provision on the creation of a consumer agency, industry groups were surprised about its content.[13] Another interviewee from the industry side remembered lobbying on regulatory reform to have been "very frustrating" and "difficult." About the legislative process, he recalled: "We were able to have a little bit of consultation with Barney Frank, while the House was putting together its bill, but not a lot, and very little with Chris Dodd, I am not sure we had any."[14] Banking lobbyists' policy influence was largely curtailed in the immediate aftermath of the crisis. According to this industry lobbyist: "When I was trying to get something done for the biggest banks, there was not a lot I could do."[15]

A senior level government official, directly involved in the drafting of the White Paper confirmed that relations with industry groups were less cozy than before the crisis: "We did not share our views with [financial sector groups]. Partly that was a response to what many of us thought was an excessive involvement of the financial sector in prior attempts to regulate the market. We had meetings with them all spring on various aspects of reform to solicit their views, but we did not invite them into write anything, to draft anything, or to shape our policy and that was very much a conscious choice."[16] A Senate staffer confirmed that in the context of the crisis and increased public attention, banking lobbyists had lost their political leverage: "The banking lobby is not well loved by the public in general, but usually because the issues are not so out front and center as the financial crisis [...]. The public doesn't quite get as engaged on these issues on a normal basis."[17] In general, industry views seem to have mattered less to policymakers in the immediate aftermath of the crisis.

Adapting to the new regulatory environment, financial industry groups also changed their lobbying strategies, refraining from outright vetoes. Albeit the banking lobby opposed a new regulatory agency, Edward Yingling, then president of the ABA, testified in front of the Senate Banking Committee in July 2010, saying that "the banking industry fully supports effective consumer protection." Instead of seeking to veto regulatory change, he also offered "to work with the Administration and Congress to achieve meaningful regulatory reform to improve consumer protection." Given the ABA's long history of strictly opposing regulation, "Yingling did an about-face when he testified before Congress," as one commentator put it (Huffington Post 2010). Recognizing the changed political climate, the ABA had clearly started to soften its lobbying position. These changes in interest group dynamics, as suggested here by anecdotal evidence from interviewees, are significant because they indicate that financial lobbyists saw their views largely ignored and had much less influence during the regulatory reform debate than during pre-crisis times. How did this context, which derailed traditional mechanisms of capture, affect the political opportunity structure for diffuse interest groups?

Political opportunities: access and receptivity

Under public pressure, policy-makers' reluctance to engage with the financial industry in the aftermath of the crisis was accompanied by increased receptivity to pro-reform demands from diffuse interest groups. First and foremost, in a qualitative shift in the policy-making environment from previously relatively obscure technocratic bodies to the top legislative agenda of the administration, Congress and its committees opened new access points for a broader range of interest groups. Starting in early 2009, consumer representatives repeatedly testified in front of Congressional committees. Increased access was also accompanied by increased receptiveness of policy-makers to demands coming from newly mobilized actors.

Consumer groups had very limited capacity to push their advocacy goals during the housing boom that pre-dated the crisis, precisely because policy-makers were not inclined to listen to their demands. The political environment changed dramatically in the fall of 2008, when public anger arose over the industry being bailed out at taxpayers' expenses. Overall, political receptivity to consumer demands increased in the wake of the crisis which had brought overwhelming evidence to the fore, so that consumer claims gained credibility and could no longer be ignored by policy-makers. As public pressure grew, demands by pro-reform groups attracted attention among policy-makers. In March 2009, Sheila Bair, Chair of the US Federal Deposit Insurance Corporation, acknowledged the need for stronger consumer protection: "There can no longer be any doubt about the link between protecting consumers from abusive products and practices and the safety and soundness of the financial system."[18] With democratic majorities in both houses, there was a greater receptivity in Congress towards consumer bills in general and consumer groups also found a sympathetic interlocutor in Congress. Democrats in Congress decided early on to endorse regulatory reform. In October 2008, Representative William Delahunt and Senator Richard Durbin picked up the idea and introduced a bill entitled the Consumer Credit Safety Commission Act of 2008, H.R. 7258 and S. 3629, into Congress. The bill created a Consumer Credit Safety Commission with responsibility to promulgate consumer credit safety rules that ban abusive, deceptive, and predatory practices.[19] Although the bill was never enacted into law, it signaled the increased political willingness to enact consumer-friendly legislation in Congress to advocates.

The changing political climate was clearly felt by consumer advocates, as one interviewee reported, "I was a consumer lawyer for many years […].We testified for years how bad the lending practice is. We were completely ignored. Suddenly it was a national crisis, more than just poor and minority communities."[20] Members of Congress increasingly responded to demands coming from consumer groups to restrict subprime lending and increase consumer protection. Another representative of a consumer association described virtually the identical process: "People had been trying for a long time to bring reforms about with more or less good bills, with no success because there was this political and ideological opposition to regulating the markets which after all were providing such fabulous results for American consumers […]. Now in the aftermath of the boom there was less confidence that the markets produced fabulous results and there was a much more receptive environment that we have to act on the lessons we have learned through this crisis."[21] This consumer representative from the Consumers Union shared the same view, reporting about spring 2009: "For a long time, there were few consumer groups that had seen the inside of the White House or the Treasury. Now sometimes you go to these meetings, and they say, 'tell us what's on your mind'. And then *they* start taking notes" (Interview, cited in Kirsch and Mayer 2013, 47; italic in original). A Congressional staffer confirmed this interpretation, saying that in the midst of the turmoil of the financial crisis, "it had gotten more difficult to ignore them"—even for members of Congress who had not necessarily been champions of consumer protection issues.[22] Taken together, this anecdotal evidence suggests that the crisis had transformed the political context changing the lack of support of consumer issues or indifference towards consumer finance protection in Congress to a much more receptive environment.

Also regulators became more receptive to consumer demands, as a representative of an US consumer group put it, "consumer groups had been talking to the Federal Reserve about mortgage problems and subprime-lending for 10 years and the Federal Reserve did nothing until the crash came; then politics was right."[23] With respect to political receptivity of financial regulators, another advocate recalled: "Up until 2008, folks like me; you sit in a room with them and they just want to get over with this. Now you're actually meeting with them and they are interested in talking. State regulators and the Fed [became] more consumer-friendly than they ha[d]ever been."[24] Industry representatives also testified to the increasing receptivity of politicians and regulators to pro-consumer advocacy groups during the legislative process, as one banking lobbyist put it, "as we were at a position of weakness, they had a position of strength."[25]

Increased political receptivity of decision-makers to the concerns and demands of consumer groups can be explained in the light of heightened issue salience and public opinion trends clearly favorable to regulatory reform. Now, not only had financial regulation become highly salient with the public—but the consumer bureau became highly salient with the wider public as well. By way of illustration, the increase in issue salience is visible by simply tracing the use of the term "consumer financial protection" in the financial press (Figure 3.1). Although the spike in attention clearly follows the Obama administration's introduction of the White Paper for financial reform at the beginning of June 2009, with public opinion reflecting the governmental agenda rather than the other way round, the amount of press coverage nevertheless shows the increased publicity generated by financial regulatory reforms.

The bureau's increase in public salience is also evident in the increase in Internet searches in the US for the term "Consumer Financial Protection Agency," as illustrated in Figure 3.2. The number of searches based on google search trends shows that the new consumer agency did generate no public interest until June

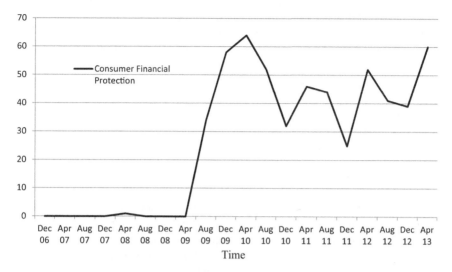

Figure 3.1 Number of articles mentioning "consumer financial protection" in the *Financial Times* and the *Wall Street Journal*.

Source: Factiva.

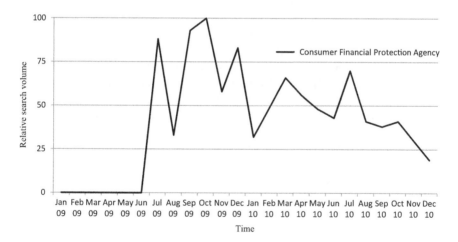

Figure 3.2 Internet searches for "Consumer Financial Protection Agency." [26]

Source: Google trends, available at www.google.com/trends/, accessed April 29, 2015.

2009, when the Treasury included a proposal of a consumer agency in its blueprint for reform. Public interest then fell again, until a brief period of heightened attention between September and December 2009, when the reform legislation was debated in the House of Representatives. A second spike in attention is visible in July 2010, when the President signed Dodd-Frank including the new regulator into law. The increase in google searches indicates the heightened public interest generated by an obscure financial reform issue such as a new regulatory agency.

Polling data released by the Consumer Federation of America in September 2009 gives us clues about why the topic was very popular with decision-makers in general, with 57% of those polled supporting the idea of creating a new federal agency to protect consumers. According to the survey, support was highest among adults under 35, blacks, Hispanics and low-income individuals (Limbach 2009). In October 2009, a survey by Lake Research Partners confirmed that even in conservative democratic districts and swing states a majority of voters were in favor of a new agency. And when asked how a vote by their representative on the new consumer regulator would affect their vote, 41% of respondents said that a vote against the agency would make them less likely to re-elect their representative (only 14% said it would make them more likely) (Americans for Financial Reform 2009b). A public opinion poll carried out by Gallup Poll in August 2010 with about 1,000 respondents, offers evidence of public opinion in favor of stricter financial regulation. A majority of Americans (61%) held a positive opinion of the Dodd-Frank Act. Wall Street regulatory reform was in fact the most popular among five pieces of legislation Congress had passed (including the 2009 economic stimulus package and healthcare reform) (Gallup 2010). Opinion polls also indicated that the public was generally in favor of a new consumer protection agency. Another public opinion poll carried out by Consumers Union in July 2011 with about 1,000 respondents indicated that the CFPB enjoyed support from a large majority of respondents (74%) (Consumers Union 2011). Public opinion likely had an impact on policy choices, as the *Wall Street Journal* put it in a comment on the US Financial Reform Act: "the CFPB became a symbol of the legislation, and many Democrats saw it as a way to sell the financial regulatory overhaul to voters" (Palletta 2010). To say that public opinion mattered to policy decisions does not mean that the role of interest groups can be neglected or that groups were mere epiphenomena. Interest groups can be important actors in linking public opinion to decision-makers. The next section will pay closer attention to this hypothesized part of the causal mechanism.

To sum up, the crisis had at least partly redistributed political leverage from financial interests to consumer advocates. Qualitative changes in the post-crisis institutional context allowed increased access of consumer groups advocating for reform. This shift was, as predicted by our second expectation, accompanied by increased overall political receptivity for consumer groups' reform demands in the context of heightened public attention.

Mobilization of diffuse interests

Another development that bolstered the influence of diffuse interest groups was their ability to forge coalitions among themselves. The perception of opened-up political opportunities after the subprime mortgage crisis was an important trigger for collective action among diffuse interest groups. Although civil society groups had well-established connections among themselves, in May 2009 relations were formalized under the umbrella of "Americans for Financial Reform," including 250 consumer associations, trade unions, NGOs, and grassroots groups who pulled together common financial and human resources. Funding for pro-reform groups became available from progressive foundations for a start-up like AFR promoting regulatory reform.[27] Heather Booth, an organizer for progressive issues for over forty years, was brought on board as Director and an office location on Washington's K Street was established. In February 2009, pro-reform advocates convened a first preliminary meeting in Washington, D.C. to form a coalition for financial reform. The meeting among 75 people representing a broad range of public interest groups took place at the AFL-CIO headquarters in Washington (Warren 2014, 132). Once relations were formalized, regular meetings started to take place. Executive committee meetings among core groups would interact twice a week by phone, and members of the steering committee would meet on a weekly basis. Oftentimes groups would interact every day.[28]

Early on, consumer groups decided to focus their reform campaign on the establishment of a consumer protection agency. The agency became the rallying point that all groups, despite their different advocacy goals, could agree on as a top legislative priority.[29] To set up a consumer agency that would then be able to subsequently deal with all consumer protection regulations from its unique consumer viewpoint, was also a compelling narrative.[30] One of the first actions of the leaders of seven of the country's leading consumer groups which would later become AFR, was the release of a joint statement in December 2008, giving clear instructions for the reinstatement of an Office of Consumer Affairs in the White House, about one year before the idea was formally introduced into Congress (Consumers Union 2008). The reform agenda was then sent to President-elect Barack Obama. Consumer advocates quickly recognized that the coalition would be more successful if it was broader than the consumer community and started to bring labor unions and civil rights groups on board. In the fall of 2008, then, representatives of consumer groups and labor came together, to talk about putting together a coalition. At a first meeting, Steve Abrecht, a senior official at the SEIU, Gary Kalman, Legislative Director at US PIRG, and Ed Mierzwinski, Consumer Program Director at US PIRG, decided to take first steps to bring together consumer, investor, and community groups to lobby for financial reforms. In July, the AFR issued its first position paper, proposing a new consumer financial product safety agency as well as an Office of Consumer Affairs in the White House to "give consumers a voice in the administration and provide some balance to the influence enjoyed by Wall Street" (Americans for Financial Reform 2009a).

Table 3.2 gives an overview of the key groups forming the broad coalition, including community groups, the largest US labor groups, important consumer groups, and a number of NGOs. Working together as a coalition clearly helped groups to tackle the massive reform load. According to one organizer: "We realized the more people we would have to join in this fight; the easier it would be to divide up the work and to achieve our objectives. No one organization could have done Dodd-Frank all by itself. It was too vast." Groups started to divide up the work among themselves: "We literally took the bill and organizations signed up to

Table 3.2 Selected actors supporting the CFPB as "Americans for Financial Reform"

Name	Founded	Number of members	Type of organization
AARP (American Association of Retired Persons)	1958	37 million	Non-profit membership organization for people aged 50 or over
American Federation of Labor and Congress of Industrial Organizations (AFL-CIO)	1955	1.4 million members	Largest federation of unions in the US
Consumer Federation of America (CFA)	1968	300 non-profit organizations	Association of non-profit consumer organizations to advance the consumer interest
Center for Responsible Lending (CRL)	2002	–	Non-profit consumer group fighting predatory lending practices
Consumers Union (CU)	1936	8 million subscriptions to newsletters	Independent, non-profit organization
National Association of Consumer Advocates (NACA)	–	1,500 attorneys	Non-profit association of attorneys and consumer advocates
National Consumers League (NCL)	1899	–	Consumer organization
National Community Reinvestment Coalition (NCRC)	1990	600 member organizations	Association that promotes access to basic banking services
Public Citizen	1971	80,000 members	Consumer rights group, non-profit organization
Service Employees International Union (SEIU)	1921	1.9 million members	Labor union
US Public Interest Research Group (US PIRG)	1970	26 state PIRGS	Federation of state Public Interest Research Groups

take the lead on the various aspects or titles in the bill. […] When we had to write a letter for or against a particular provision, the lead organization would generally produce the letter and ask the other organizations to sign on. That is the only way we could have done such a massive bill."[31] Lobbyists from the financial industry side attributed the success of consumer groups partly to the fact that "they organized effectively."[32]

AFR enabled consumer advocates to present a united front, including consumer associations, labor and public interest, and community groups. Albeit critical moments where the coalition's cohesion was in jeopardy, the groups did not split. The community reinvestment groups stayed in the coalition after a reform of the CRA was stalled by opposition of community banks. Originally, the Administration's proposal had included a transferal of the CRA to the authority of the new consumer agency, thereby echoing the wishes of the National Community Reinvestment Coalition (NCRC) (Americans for Financial Reform 2010). The decision to eliminate the CRA from the law was a strategic choice by Chairman Barney Frank in an effort to avoid another layer of opposition. The plan was to "have them [small banks] not like it but make them not hate it."[33] Despite this setback for community groups, the NCRC decided to stay part of the coalition.[34]

The broad coalition among civil society organizations was made possible by the advocates' perception of a policy window, as one coalition member recalled: "We always wanted to do this coalition. The financial collapse created this window. Suddenly it was a national crisis, more than just poor and minority communities."[35] Advocates realized that in order to win real reforms they had to take advantage of the public anger about costly bank bailouts and political opportunities that presented themselves for regulatory change. One coalition member reported: "Everybody understood the opportunity and that this was a moment to be seized, there was a collective willingness to spend energy and resources."[36]

Pro-reform groups were keenly aware of the fleeting nature of their opportunity to set up a new and powerful consumer agency. They knew that their best opportunity was in the first years of the administration, when the Democratic Party had a majority in Congress. After the midterm elections of 2010, the cushion in Congress would be smaller. The stars were aligned, so to speak, and reform advocates had to take advantage of this. According to one consumer representative: "The politics was right: we had a new presidency who had previously during the campaign expressed support for this; I knew Barney Frank and Chris Dodd, the chairs to the committees. That kind of alignment does not happen very often and when it does you got a go for it."[37] After the 2008 election, the Democratic Party enjoyed a comfortable margin in the House to pass reform legislation (with a majority of 51% required). The election also brought a filibuster-proof Democratic majority to the Senate (sixty Democratic votes). If all sixty Senators were to vote for a reform bill, pro-reform advocates could overcome the expected Republican filibuster. Indeed, during the final passage of the Dodd-Frank Act, the sixty votes in the Senate did enable the Democrats to pass the bill with all but three Republicans in opposition.

The perception of opened-up political opportunities after the subprime mortgage crisis as a trigger for collective action among diffuse interest groups was reinforced by the early passage of the Credit Card Accountability, Responsibility and Disclosure Act (short Credit CARD Act) before Dodd-Frank in May 2009. The CARD act had broken the ground as a first success indicating to consumer advocates that a policy window had opened that allowed for the passage of broad consumer-friendly regulations. In response to mounting debt levels and industry malpractices, Congress improved credit card contract regulation in May 2009 by passing the CARD Act. The Center for Responsible Lending called the Act "the most significant federal consumer financial reform in decades" (Wolff 2012).[38] With many consumers heavily indebted with credit card fees, it had become clear to policy-makers that credit card reform had broad populist appeal. Commenting on the credit card reforms, the *New York Times* wrote: "Members of Congress and the Obama administration have seized on the discontent to push reforms that the industry succeeded in tamping down when the economy was flying high" (Martin 2009). Passing a new regulation of credit cards was also a pragmatic policy response that would legitimize reform actions and follow the path of least resistance as one policy insider reported: "Early 2009, the financial crisis was still raging, people wanted blood from the banks, and this was just an easy thing to drive through. Other bills that were out there [...] were more controversial [...] for the big banks and so were harder to get through. But credit cards—who could argue against credit cards?"[39]

To the consumer lobby, the passage of the CARD Act was breakthrough legislation after years of congressional and regulatory inaction. It was a strong signal that the crisis had opened a policy window where it would be easier to push for consumer protection regulations. For many years consumer groups tried to bring unfair and abusive practices of the credit card industry to light. But it was only in the wake of the financial crisis which brought overwhelming evidence to the fore, that consumer claims gained credibility. Groups such as the National Consumer Law Center (NCLC) had lobbied for years for better protection for consumers, among others, from "fee-harvester" credit cards. In midst of the turmoil of the mortgage crisis, advocacy groups tried to use the momentum and intensified their lobbying for fair credit card practices. The groups including US PIRG, ACORN, the CFA, the NCLC, the National Association of Consumer Advocates (NACA), and also labor groups such as the AFL-CIO and civil rights groups, came together as an informal coalition. Reflecting on the credit card campaign, a leading consumer advocate remembered that "winning this bill was as big and powerful a victory as we ever have had against a powerful opponent." Passage of the bill was perceived as "an early warning" that the consumer lobby could win when the industry was vulnerable and when it seized the moment of a democrat majority in both houses in Congress.[40] Passage of the CARD Act greatly encouraged pro-reform advocates and the members of the CARD coalition would eventually become the core of AFR.[41]

Further evidence that collective action among diffuse interest groups was spurred by perception of political opportunities following the financial crisis, is provided by the fact that earlier attempts to forge coalitions did not succeed. Shortly before the crisis, in 2007, earlier efforts of coalition building among advocacy groups with similar policy goals under the umbrella of non-profit organization named Americans for Fairness in Lending (AFFIL), had failed. The funding that had become available in form of cy pres funds from a class action suit[42] was a good opportunity to found a new coalition; and national consumer, civil rights, faith-based, non-partisan, and grassroots organizations were eager to join in. Most of the twenty groups brought together under the AFFIL umbrella would later form the core of AFR: CRL, Consumer Action, CFA, CU, NCLC, and US PIRG. AFFIL launched a national campaign to raise public awareness of predatory lending and the need for stronger consumer protection regulations and fairer lending practices. Ad campaigns framing predatory lending as an "American Tragedy"[43] were supposed to change the way the public perceived predatory lending.[44]

In 2008, AFFIL also engaged in the credit card campaign that led to the CARD Act. With AFFIL's funds largely consumed after three and a half years, and the coalition slowly falling apart, the board decided to make its remaining staff available to AFR and so the two organizations merged in September 2009.

Mobilized diffuse groups were also influential because of public opinion favourable to their cause. Newly mobilized groups were key actors in transmitting public opinion to decision-makers; as one staffer put it bluntly, "AFR was able to be influential [...] they had special clout, because they were able to tap into public sentiment."[45] One of the first steps of the coalition had been to provide support for local grassroots groups and their activities, in order to enable those groups to engage with their members of Congress.[46] The AFR pro-reform groups were very active in lobbying Congress and top governmental officials throughout the long process that led up to the passage of the Dodd-Frank bill. Members of the coalition regularly gave testimony before Congressional committees pushing for a single regulatory agency. Between March and June 2009, members of the coalition testified in several House and Senate committee and subcommittee hearings providing a coherent "causal story" of policy failures in the run-up to the subprime crisis. During the passage of Dodd-Frank, at least twelve different AFR members strongly supported the CFPB in testimony before the House and the Senate in hearings between June and September 2009 (Kirsch and Mayer 2013, 74). In June 2009, several AFR members gave testimony before the Financial Services House Committee. Ed Mierzwinski of US PIRG and Travis Plunkett of the Consumer Federation of America testified in June 2009 that a "robust, independent, federal Consumer Financial Protection Agency" was needed to address the "failure of federal regulators to stop abusive lending." The Center for Responsible Lending argued that "[a]n independent consumer protection agency, dedicated and empowered to keep the markets free of abusive financial products, committed to transparency [...] would help to restore consumer trust and confidence, stabilize the markets, and put us back on the road to economic prosperity" (Keest 2009). All witnesses representing AFR agreed that the CFPB would effectively respond to the underlying causes of the crisis. Consumer activists' goal was to "lay out a convincing narrative about the causes of the mortgage meltdown [...] to show that creating a consumer financial protection agency was the right policy response" (Kirsch and Mayer 2013, 74).

Since they had disseminated information about abusive lending practices in an effort to create momentum for reform, pro-reform groups now played an important role for the pro-reform advocates within the administration. A database of collected stories about abusive lending served as important source of information for Congress. Groups like the Consumers Union and the Center for Responsible Lending collected testimonies by people wronged by abusive industry practices on their websites, asking people to share their "horror lending stories."[47] One consumer advocate recalled: "What we brought to the table: stories. During the height I got 30 calls a day from the press [saying] 'I want a story from a person in Baltimore whose home was foreclosed'. We were very good in activating those people and getting them engaged."[48] Another consumer advocate reported:

"I would get a Congressional office asking about stories. We will ask the person who submitted the story if they are comfortable sharing their story with the White House or Congress, and have availability to come to D.C. and talk about it. That is very effective." Due to the cumulative actions of interest groups, "these predatory lending stories were coming out all over the place," in the perception of one Congressional staffer.[49] Another Congressional staffer, directly involved in drafting the legislative language, confirmed that consumer groups with their actions fighting for consumer protection and bringing personal stories of wronged consumers to the fore had helped to set the stage for reforming abusive practices.[50] A comment by a senior-level official involved in drafting the legislation clearly testifies to the role of pro-reform groups as a link between public opinion and policy-makers. He reported that newly mobilized groups "helped in bringing attention to the issues and trying to get the public focused on the key questions […]. It definitely helped shape the debate and helped us to generate enthusiasm for what we were trying to do." Widespread public support in favor of stricter regulation also helped policy-makers to overcome the opposition of the industry, as one senior level official put it, "it was harder for the financial services lobbyists to push back against us, because we had on our side more public support."[51] Due to this changed political dynamics, industry groups had to refrain from blocking the legislative proposal for a new consumer agency. In the regulatory policy-making process of the crisis, the industry could not act as a straightforward "veto player." While financial industry groups were strictly opposed to a new regulator, they nevertheless saw stricter consumer regulations as largely inevitable.[52] A comment by a Congressional staffer about the legislative process in the House confirmed the weakened stance of the industry: "We gave [financial sector groups] the opportunity to constructively draft the bill but not to *not* do it."[53]

The influence of mobilized diffuse interests was not only due to favorable public opinion but also due to a split among two central financial sector groups. Deprived of their veto capacity, and although nearly the entire financial industry was opposed to a consumer protection bureau, the united front began crumbling during the passage of the House bill. Barney Frank, Chairman of the House Financial Services Committee, struck a deal with the ICBA, exempting small banks from CFPB oversight. This neutralized the smaller community bankers, divided the industry, and considerably weakened the overall industry's attempt to block passage of the CFPB or promote alternative proposals. From the industry groups' point of view, the deal was a huge loss. Consumer advocates counted the semi-carve-out for small banks under $10 billion as a partial victory, since the CFPB still had rule-writing authority over small banks. Small banks were only exempted from CFPB supervision and enforcement, which was to be conducted by prudential regulators instead. At the final stage of passage, during the joint conference committee, industry opposition proved unexpectedly weak, and no further amendments were offered that would have weakened the CFPB.[54]

As predicted, the active involvement of pro-reform groups was spurred by the financial crisis and based on the perception of a "window of opportunity" for reform. As a "countervailing force" to financial industry interests, the pro-reform coalition was able to restrain the industry's policy influence. Diffuse interest groups acted as transmitters of public opinion, putting increasing pressure on policy-makers to actively pursue regulatory change, even counter to the interests of the more powerful financial lobby. Facing increased actor plurality and changed interest group dynamics, industry groups saw themselves forced to refrain from vetoing the policy process which eventually led to a split of the opposition and a further weakening of the sector. The next section will discuss how consumer groups' policy influence was leveraged by another crucial factor: policy entrepreneurship.

Policy entrepreneurship

Another factor that boosted the influence of diffuse interest groups was the fact that a skilled policy entrepreneur served as source of an innovative idea and subsequently invested time and resources into the reform cause. Pro-change advocates found a strong and well-positioned policy entrepreneur in Harvard law professor and consumer advocate Elizabeth Warren, who had published the initial idea for a consumer protection agency in articles in 2007 and 2008. With the proposal of a new "Financial Product Safety Commission," Warren put forward an important innovative idea. In the 2007 article, Warren wrote: "Just as the Consumer Product Safety Commission (CPSC) protects buyers of goods and supports a competitive market, we need the same for consumers of financial products—a new regulatory regime, and even a new regulatory body, to protect consumers who use credit cards, home mortgages, car loans, and a host of other products" (Warren 2007).[55] The article entitled "Unsafe at any rate" made reference Ralph Nader's book *Unsafe at Any Speed* which was published in November 1965. Nader identified automobiles as cause for accidents and generated substantial publicity resulting in stronger consumer protection legislation. In a second article, published in November 2008, Warren and her co-author Bar-Gill laid out their reform solution to problems in the consumer credit market in more detail. They suggested "a single federal regulator [...] to be put in charge of consumer credit products" (Bar-Gill and Warren 2008, 98). At the time of publication, wider public attention to Warren's articles was only moderate.

Warren not only was an innovator, but also had another attribute indispensable of a successful policy entrepreneur: she was politically savvy. With the relevant political connections, she was able to shape political debate and build coalitions supporting her idea. Warren became a highly visible political figure in November 2008 as Chair of the Troubled Asset Relief Program Congressional Oversight Panel (COP), which was charged with reviewing the current state of financial markets and the regulatory system. The first COP "Special Report on Regulatory Reform," issued in January 2009, included Warren's proposal of a single federal regulator for consumer credit products.[56] Throughout the reform debate, Warren served as a key expert. One Congressional staffer remembered "a couple of instances where Warren was in Barney's office and we talked to her—her acceptance was important, her assessment was important."[57] Warren was also viewed of as an influential policy entrepreneur by interviewees from the industry side. One lobbyist reported that Warren was "a very effective" and "articulate" spokesperson, which gave the AFR coalition "additional clout."[58] In September 2010, Warren became part of the administration as Assistant to the President and Special Advisor to the Secretary of Treasury for the CFPB. In her position as Special Advisor to the Treasury at the CFPB, she became an important public entrepreneur on the political stage who defended the new consumer agency in Congressional hearings and various sub-committee meetings of the House of Representatives.[59] Warren also repeatedly denounced industry lobbying on TV shows such as *The Daily Show with Jon Stewart* and *The Colbert Report*, saying that industry's aim was to "to stick a knife in the ribs" of the new bureau (Warren 2011). Warren made her policy solution match politicians' needs to respond to public pressure. She had introduced the idea of a Consumer Finance Safety Commission with a metaphor comparing safety regulations for toasters to those for consumer financial products. "It is impossible to buy a toaster that has a one-in-five chance of bursting into flames and burning down your house. But it is possible to refinance an existing home with a mortgage that has the same one in-five chance of putting the family out on the street" (Warren 2014, 1). In spring 2009, the metaphor reoccurred in the letter by the three Senators Durbin, Kennedy and Schumer to Treasury Secretary Geithner: "[T]here is no reason for us to have regulations that prevent toasters from exploding into flames, but no protections to prevent mortgages and credit cards from doing the same" (Durbin 2009a). On March 19, President Obama employed the same metaphor when he appeared on *The Tonight Show with Jay Leno*, clearly indicating presidential support for consumer protection reforms. Due to Warren's entrepreneurship, her policy proposal of a Consumer Finance Safety Commission had slowly moved from the periphery to the center stage of politics.

Most importantly, Warren's idea of a new consumer regulator found its way into the work of a brainstorming group, a small group, including experts on financial institutions, law professors, and economists, the President had charged with the task of drafting a first reform bill in January 2009.[60] One member of the group, Assistant Secretary of the Treasury Michael Barr, personally knew Warren and was familiar with her academic work. Warren's idea clearly served as important inspiration for the brainstorming group. According to one member of the group: "The president had either read her article or at least knew about it or talked to her about it [...]. So the idea of doing a consumer bureau was not an alien one."[61] Reforms of the framework for consumer protection regulations, including a new agency, were a central part of the group's discussions throughout the spring of 2009 and were debated with Secretary Geithner, National Economic Council Director Larry Summers, and eventually with the President all spring long.[62] Based on their conclusions, the brainstorming group proposed an independent Consumer Financial Protection Bureau, and later that year, in June 2009, the Treasury included the proposal of a new agency in the White Paper.

Warren was also instrumental in rallying initial support for a single regulator among consumer, labor, and other interest groups. Warren's proposal enjoyed widespread support among consumer advocates who had been working with Warren since the 1990s.[63] Warren also joined the consumer groups' credit card campaign which led to the passage of the CARD Act in May 2009. First discussions among consumer advocates and Warren about the policy proposal of a consumer regulator started to take place in the summer of 2008, before Obama was elected President. When pro-reform advocates convened a first preliminary meeting in Washington, D.C. to form a coalition for financial reform in February 2009, Warren introduced the idea of a consumer finance protection agency to the audience, knowing that "if the groups represented by the people in this room didn't get behind the proposal, there was zero chance of getting it through Congress" (Warren 2014, 135). In light of the unsuccessful campaign in the 1970s under the leadership of Ralph Nader some civil society groups voiced concern about lobbying for a single consumer agency. But overall, Warren was able to make a good case and get broad-based consensus in favor of the idea.

In March 2009, two years after Warren's first article was published, and in the midst of the turmoil caused by the financial crisis, advocates of a consumer agency undertook another attempt to enact legislation. According to Warren's account, she met with Senator Ted Kennedy (D-MA) in early 2009, urging him to push for the agency (Warren 2014, 138). The two had known each other since the fight for bankruptcy law reform in 2005. In March, Kennedy, Senator Dick Durbin (D-IL), and Senator Chuck Schumer (D-NY) introduced the Financial Product Safety Commission Act of 2009 into Congress (S. 566), proposing the creation of a regulator with sole responsibility to protect consumers according to Warren's blueprint.[64] Consumer groups and labor unions supported the bill including the Consumer Federation of America, the Center for Responsible Lending, the Leadership Conference on Civil Rights, NAACP, La Raza, AFL-CIO, SEIU, National Consumer Law Center, Consumers Union, Public Citizen, and US PIRG. Representatives Bill Delahunt (D-MA) and Brad Miller (D-NC), a champion of the consumer movement, who had sponsored state mortgage reform legislation that passed in 1999, also championed the consumer agency and became co-sponsors of the bill. In April 2009, Senators Kennedy, Durbin, and Schumer wrote a letter to Treasury Secretary Tim Geithner, urging him to include their proposed Financial Product Safety Commission in the Administration's plan for financial reforms (Durbin 2009a). Also in April 2009, Warren, according to her own account, successfully convinced Barney Frank, the influential Chairman of the House Financial Services Committee, that the consumer agency was a politically viable idea (Warren 2014).

To sum up: had it not been for this support from a powerful entrepreneur, the consumer agency would most likely not have seen the light of day. The academic work of Harvard professor and credit expert Elizabeth Warren served as an important source of innovation, putting forward the idea of a new agency to protect consumers. Warren was not only an expert and innovator on consumer finance and housing issues, but was also politically well connected, able to successfully build supportive political coalitions for her idea and to exploit opportunities opened up by the credit crisis and the excessive industry influence over regulation that it brought to the fore. Warren was also an important actor to help diffuse interests in their efforts to organize as pro-reform coalition.

Government allies

To bring about substantial reforms, consumer groups worked closely with government allies inside the administration and Congress. The Obama administration became an important government ally and played a lead role in promoting the regulatory reform favored by consumer advocates. The White House publicly entered the picture in June 2009 with the White Paper that proposed five objectives for financial reform, including a "Consumer Financial Protection Agency (CFPA), with the authority and accountability to make sure that consumer protection regulations are written fairly and enforced vigorously" (Department of the Treasury 2009, 7). Before the White House issued its blueprint for financial reform in June 2009, which included the CFPB, consumer groups (that would later become AFR) had become a central interlocutor for the brainstorming group, the administration, and the Treasury Department. Consumer groups had routinely met with Treasury officials to give advice and express support for a strong consumer regulator. Individual consumer groups (which at that point were not yet organized into a coalition) enjoyed access to informal consultations and had effective connections with Treasury staff—such as Eric Stein, who had become the top deputy of the Assistant Secretary of the Treasury Barr after a career at one of the leading consumer organizations, the Center for Responsible Lending. Prior to his function at the Treasury, Barr himself had been involved in community development policies, where interactions with consumer, housing, and community groups had largely shaped his views. Close relations among consumer advocates and policy-makers persisted throughout the passage of financial reforms. Barr became responsible for consumer financial protection policy, including the enactment of the Credit CARD Act of 2009 and the CFPB. When, in June 2009, the White House published its White Paper, Barr and his top deputy Stein were in charge of drafting the legislation that was implemented from the blueprint. During the legislative process, meetings between the Assistant Secretary of the Treasury and the AFR coalition took place on a regular basis.[65] Within the administration, Barr and Stein became the "behind-the-scenes heroes" for the consumer advocates in drafting strong language and pushing for the consumer agency (Warren 2014, 162).

From the beginning, the issue of a consumer regulator had strong presidential support. As key government ally to consumer advocates, Obama played a lead role in promoting regulatory reform. Personally enthusiastic about reform, Obama highlighted the new consumer regulator in several speeches and as a guest on *The Daily Show with Jon Stewart* and *The Tonight Show with Jay Leno*, clearly indicating his support. In a speech given on 9 October 2009, Obama stated his continuing support for the new agency, actively siding with consumer activists: "We need a Consumer Financial Protection Agency that will stand up not for big banks, not for financial firms, but for hardworking Americans. [...] we need regulatory reform that will reward innovation and competition instead of short-cuts and abuses. [...] we can't let special interests win this fight." The President called claims made in a campaign ad sponsored by the Chamber of Commerce about the new agency being harmful to small businesses "completely false."

Recognizing the changed political dynamics, key political leaders joined the bandwagon and became governmental allies to actively push for a single consumer regulator. Most importantly, the Democratic leaders of the committees that handled financial reform—Representative Barney Frank, chairman of the House Financial Services Committee, and Senator Christopher Dodd, chairman of the Senate Banking Committee—became active allies defending diffuse interests in the policy process. Extensive mobilization of pro-reform groups in combination with the support of elite allies, including the President, made elected officials into allies advocating for diffuse interests in financial reforms. Collective material resources mobilized by outside groups in favor of regulatory reform signaled to policy-makers that a strong pro-reform lobby was in place. One Congressional staffer testified to the relevance of this outside mobilization, saying that the "united front [...] was quite important. It gave the consumer and civil rights community [...] the ability to expand the battlefield."[66] Moreover, strong presidential support for reform had already signaled to the committee leadership that the chances of passage would be good. A respondent from the industry side confirmed this assessment: "The crisis gave [consumer groups] a great atmosphere politically and then they had a White House and Treasury Department that was very sympathetic to them. That combination gave them a lot of clout."[67]

Both committee leaders—Frank and Dodd—subsequently became important allies to the pro-reform groups to push for reform. Both stood firm against nearly all weakening amendments and joined in support of strengthening ones. During the advocacy process for the new consumer regulator consumer groups on the outside and officials at the inside worked in tandem. Insider–outsider coalition with the consumer agency as shared policy goal emerged. Several examples illustrate the close working relationships among the AFR coalition and Congressional staff in the key committees. When legislative action moved to the House Financial Services Committee in the fall of 2009, consumer groups under the AFR umbrella started to cooperate with Frank and his staff. Frank expressed his support for the idea of a consumer agency in one of the first meetings with the AFR coalition.[68] The following passages stem from interviews with outside lobbying organizations and staff members in Congress. One reform advocate gave an explanation of the degree of cooperation and planning among the administration and consumer groups which testifies to the advocates' exceptional access to the policy process: "We had been talking to the Treasury people, then the President came out with his blueprint, and it included the CFPB. So that summer [2009] we had all these meetings and negotiations with Treasury and then with Frank. We worked with them and advised them on the blue print and then we worked with them on a strategy to draft the legislation that was implemented from the blueprint."[69]

Remarking on the cooperation with Senator Dodd's staff, another AFR organizer described the interest groups' close relation with governmental allies in Congress this way: "We had a big meeting with Dodd and his whole staff [...]. We had three meetings with him and his whole staff in the course of the campaign, once at the start, once before the end, and once in the middle. We met with the staff [...] all the time."[70]

From inside Congress, the advocacy process looked similar. Congressional staffers interviewed for this study on the House and Senate side reported that they relied on consumer groups' expertise for drafting legislation. On mortgage reform, Barney Frank's staff reported that they relied on expertise from the Center for Responsible Lending, saying that they "got language when [they] needed it."[71] On the issue of preemption, staffers cooperated closely with the Consumer Federation of America. Within the coalition that AFR had brought together, one could find "experts on any given issue [...] with invaluable [knowledge] in technical areas," as a Congressional staffer reported.[72] Each of the groups brought a specific area of expertise on consumer financial issues to the table, so that Congressional staffers knew who to reach out to on the consumer side. As one Senate staffer recalled: "There was somebody who knew about credit cards and debt collection and there was somebody who knew about housing. One or two experts in a couple different organizations would be the folks that we would call up and say, 'Hey we're working on this bill, what do you think needs to be in it, can you take a look, what lawyers, what professors can we talk to?'"[73]

Another member of the Congressional staff reported that groups such as the Center for Responsible Lending and the Consumer Federation of America were "influential" and "credible partners" in drafting mortgage reform legislation, saying that he "could deal with those guys as discretely [...] as with the ABA."[74] According to staffers, consumer advocates were not "heavy lobbyists," but knowledgeable people who could draft legislative language when needed. One Congressional staffer saw AFR as "a collection of interest groups, many of which lend incredible know how to drafting [legislation] [...] many individuals and organizations within AFR that had the expertise [on consumer financial issues]."[75]

To sum up, pro-reform advocates on the outside had well-established working relationships with sympathetic government allies on the inside, namely, the President as well as the two key committee chairs Barney Frank and Chris Dodd who pushed the legislation through Congress. Extensive mobilization of pro-reform groups in combination with presidential support was instrumental in making the idea more attractive to committee leaders. The most accurate depiction of working relations among advocates and friendly policy-makers is that of members of a team, with advocacy groups serving as an important source of expertise in the drafting phase of the legislation.

Conclusions

What can this episode tell us about the politics of financial reform after the crisis? The puzzle addressed in the case study of the CFPB is that the regulatory change runs counter to the interests of the influential and resourceful financial industry associations. The in-depth analysis of the creation of a new consumer regulator in the US has shown that diffuse interests can be politically influential, even in a policy field that has been characterized as exclusively dominated by organized industry interests such as financial regulation. While consumer groups gained more access to the national policy-making process, industry groups saw their policy access curtailed. These findings call Olson's logic of collective action into question, which predicts that regulatory outcomes correspond to the preferences of the concentrated and well-organized industry interests, usually putting consumers at a disadvantage. Explanations of post-crisis regulatory policy-making need to go beyond concentrated interest-group pressure and take a closer look at interest group dynamics involving greater actor plurality. Through careful process-tracing, we demonstrate that financial reforms are best explained through a theoretical framework which takes into account the role of diffuse interest groups and their relations to legislators.

The results of applying the theoretically derived hypotheses to the empirical record of the case at hand are summarized in Table 3.3. The new consumer regulator in the US supports the thesis that the post-crisis financial reform policies were shaped by the mobilization of non-financial industry groups rather than captured by financial industry interests (Helleiner and Pagliari 2011a). This chapter tried to demonstrate that the story of post-crisis regulatory reform in the US was one of diffuse interest coalitions as a countervailing force to industry interests, policy entrepreneurship, and governmental allies, as much as—if not more than—a story of concentrated industry capture. The importance of coalitions is particularly apparent in the formation of the broad-based civil society coalition under the "Americans for Financial Reform" umbrella that came together to advocate for a new consumer regulator, opposing financial industry interests. The engagement of this unprecedented coalition of non-financial groups in the reform debate increased actor plurality and reduced industry dominance throughout the legislative process. The pro-reform coalition effectively exploited a split in industry opposition. The cooperation with a well-positioned and savvy policy entrepreneur was another key factor in determining reform outcomes. Harvard law professor and consumer finance expert Elizabeth Warren played a central role as innovator who provided the idea of a new consumer regulator and subsequently built a political coalition in support of reform.

Other important drivers of regulatory change representing diffuse interests were governmental allies, including the President and committee chairmen, who pushed the proposal for a new consumer watchdog through Congress. Notably, Representative Frank and Senator Dodd, the committee chairmen responsible for financial reform, became active proponents of the consumer cause and cooperated closely in team-like structures with the newly mobilized consumer advocacy coalition. Insider–outsider coalitions with the consumer regulator as shared policy goal emerged. Newly mobilized groups served as an important transmitter of public opinion to policy-makers as well as an important source of specialized expertise throughout the drafting process of legislation. The legislative outcome was a winner-take-all result with consumer groups winning the day and only minor carve-outs for small community banks.

Table 3.3 Summary of findings

Propositions	Findings
Scope conditions present:	**Yes.** Financial lobbyists saw their views largely ignored and had much less influence during the regulatory reform debate than during pre-crisis times.
1 **Favorable opportunity structures:** politicians under public salience and electoral constraints become more receptive and grant new access points to diffuse interest groups.	**Yes.** Congress and its committees opened new access points for a broader range of interest groups. Due to substantial public pressure, demands by pro-reform groups attracted political attention.
2 **Diffuse interest coalitions:** the organization as advocacy coalition spurred by the perception of a window of opportunity allows diffuse interest groups to promote reform goals.	**Yes.** Formation of AFR as a countervailing force to the financial industry, based on the perception of a "window of opportunity." AFR as beneficiary of favorable public opinion and of a lack of unity among industry groups.
3 **Policy entrepreneurs:** activism of entrepreneurs as sources of innovation, expertise, institutional resources, etc., thereby leveraging advocacy groups' influence.	**Yes.** Consumer credit expert Elizabeth Warren plays central role as an innovator who introduces the idea of a consumer agency; she is also politically savvy and defends the idea in the reform debate.
4 **Government allies:** Joining the bandwagon public officials actively side with mobilized diffuse interests to promote same policy solution in team-like structures.	**Yes.** Insider–outsider coalition with well-established working relations among advocates and key government allies, Committee chairs Barney Frank and Chris Dodd, with advocates as source of expertise.
5 **Outcome:** Policy-makers enact financial reforms reflecting diffuse interests.	**Yes.** Winner-take-all outcome for consumer groups.

To sum up, regulatory capture theories as the dominant theoretical lens used to explain US financial reforms after the 2008 crisis, clearly helped identify the causes for the incrementality of the overall reform law in spite of the major shock the crisis had caused. My goal, however, has been to show that this is only half of the story, and that diffuse interests did not go unrepresented in the American financial regulatory overhaul. The findings presented here correspond to Trumbull's argument that diffuse interests are commonly represented in public policy, even in the field of financial regulation (Trumbull 2012). Ultimately, the story of the struggle between consumer advocacy groups and financial industry groups in the case of the CFPB suggests that coalition-building among diffuse interest groups and with important elite allies on the outside and the inside of government considerably affects that group's ability to shape regulatory policy, allowing groups to bear on policy decisions independently of an individual group's material resources. Accordingly, the case study of the CFPB confirms Trumbull's proposition that researchers seeking to understand the outcome of interest group conflicts must look beyond the simple variable of material resourcefulness.

Notes

1 Dodd–Frank Wall Street Reform and Consumer Protection Act, Pub. L. No. 111-203, 124 Stat. 1376 (2010), Preamble (describing the purposes of Dodd-Frank).
2 Updated versions of Dodd-Frank Progress Reports by Davis Polk are available at www. davispolk.com/ Dodd-Frank-Rulemaking-Progress-Report or the website of the US Securities and Exchange Commission at www.sec.gov/spotlight/dodd-frank.shtml.
3 Interviews with consumer advocates in Washington, D.C., conducted in September 2013 and in February and March 2014.
4 Interview 65a with representative of consumer association, Washington, D.C., August 5, 2011.
5 Interview 100 with financial industry lobbyist, Washington, D.C., September 16, 2013.
6 Interview 89 with consumer advocate, Washington, D.C., September 16, 2013.
7 The Administration's CFPA Act; H.R. 4173, Title IV, as it passed the House, and S.3217, Title X, as it passed the Senate.
8 The website is no longer operational and redirects to http://www.cfpbspotlight.com/.
9 Interviews, Washington, D.C., interview 10 with consumer advocate, September 28, 2013; Interview 2 with trade union representative, February 10, 2014.
10 Interview 3a with consumer advocate, Washington, D.C., September 6, 2013.
11 Interview 100 with a financial industry lobbyist, Washington, D.C., September 16, 2013.
12 Interview 113 with a banking lobbyist, Washington, D.C., February 25, 2014.
13 Ibid.
14 Interview 1 with a banking lobbyist, Washington, D.C., September 20, 2013.
15 Interview 113 with a banking lobbyist, Washington, D.C., February 25, 2014.
16 Interview 5 with a government official, March 10, 2014.
17 Interview 34 with a Congressional staffer, Washington, D.C., March 7, 2014.
18 Statement of Sheila Bair, Chair of the Federal Deposit Insurance Corporation, on Modernizing Bank Supervision and Regulation before the US Senate Banking Committee on Banking, March 19, 2009.
19 www.govtrack.us/congress/bills/110/s3629#summary/libraryofcongress
20 Interview 82a with a consumer lawyer, Washington, D.C., September 18, 2013.
21 Interview 115 with a consumer advocate, Washington, D.C., March 18, 2014.
22 Interview 14 with a Congressional staffer, Washington, D.C., March14, 2014.
23 Interview 3a with a consumer representative, Washington, D.C., September 6, 2013.
24 Interview 82a with a consumer lawyer, Washington, D.C., September 18, 2013.
25 Interview 100 with a financial industry lobbyist, Washington, D.C., September 16, 2013.
26 The new agency went from being dubbed the "Consumer Financial Protection Agency" (and before that, the "Financial Product Safety Commission") to the "Consumer Financial Protection Bureau," "Agency" was, however, the predominant terminology used throughout the legislative debate.
27 Interview 10 with a consumer advocate, September 28, 2013; interview 2 with a trade union representative, February 10, 2014, Washington, D.C.
28 Interview 10 with a consumer advocate, Washington, D.C., September 28, 2013.
29 Interview 82a with a consumer lawyer, Washington, D.C., September 18, 2013.
30 Ibid.

31 Interview 3a with a consumer representative, Washington, D.C., September 6, 2013.
32 Interview 113 with a banking lobbyist, Washington, D.C., February 25, 2014.
33 Interview 114 with a Congressional staffer Washington, D.C., March 17, 2014.
34 Interview 65b with a consumer advocate, Washington, D.C., February 13, 2014.
35 Interview 82a with a consumer advocate, Washington, D.C., September 18, 2013.
36 Interview 23 with a consumer advocate, Washington, D.C., September 12, 2013.
37 Interview 79 with a consumer advocate, Washington, D.C., September 13, 2013.
38 After passage of Dodd-Frank in July 2010 the CFPB was charged with implementing the Act. The new law mainly deals with four categories where consumer protection provisions were enhanced: provisions affecting rates; billing practices; fees; and protections for young costumers (Pridgen 2013, 24).
39 Interview 34 with a Congressional staffer, Washington, D.C., March 7, 2014.
40 Interview 65b with a consumer advocate, Washington, D.C., February 13, 2014.
41 Interview 82a with a consumer lawyer, Washington, D.C., September 18, 2013, interview 65b with a consumer advocate, Washington, D.C., February 13, 2014.
42 Cy pres are funds in class action cases and some other types of legal proceedings that cannot be distributed to the class members or intended beneficiaries of the fund. Typically, courts can distribute these remaining residual funds to appropriate non-profit organizations.
43 americansforfairnessinlending.wordpress.com/
44 Interview 65b with a consumer advocate, Washington, D.C., February 13, 2014.
45 Interview 34 with a Congressional staffer, Washington, D.C., March 7, 2014.
46 Interview 23 with a consumer advocate, Washington, D.C., September 12, 2013.
47 The website is available at www.responsiblelending.org/about-us/contact-us/share-story.html.
48 Interview 82a with a consumer lawyer, Washington, D.C., September 18, 2013.
49 Interview 34 with a Congressional staffer, Washington, D.C., March 7, 2014.
50 Interview 14 with a Congressional staffer, Washington, D.C., March 14, 2014.
51 Interview 34 with a Congressional staffer, Washington, D.C., March 7, 2014.
52 Interview 1 with a banking lobbyist, Washington, D.C., September 20, 2013.
53 Interview 114 with a Congressional staffer, Washington, D.C., March 17, 2014.
54 Interview 65b with a consumer advocate, Washington, D.C., February 13, 2014.
55 Warren's article in democracy was reprinted in fall 2008 in the *Journal of Consumer Affairs* entitled "Product Safety Regulation as a Model for Financial Services Regulation."
56 The full COP report is available at www.un.org/ga/president/63/commission/regulatoryreform.pdf.
57 Interview 66 with a Congressional staffer, Washington, D.C., March 24, 2014.
58 Interview 113 with a banking lobbyist, Washington, D.C., February 25, 2014.
59 Warren gave testimony about the CFPB to Congress in May 2011 and to the House Financial Services Committee in June 2009 and March 2011.
60 The group included Michael Barr, Diana Farell, Cass Sunstein, Patrick Parkinson, Neal Wolin (Kaiser 2013)
61 Interview 5 with a government official, Washington, D.C., March 10, 2014.
62 Ibid.
63 Interview 65b with a consumer advocate, Washington, D.C., February 13, 2014.
64 The full text of the bill is available at: www.govtrack.us/congress/bills/111/s566/text.
65 Interview 34 with a Congressional staffer, Washington, D.C., 7 March 2014 and interview 65b with a consumer advocate, Washington, D.C., February 13, 2014.
66 Interview 66 with a Congressional staffer, Washington, D.C., March 24, 2014
67 Interview 113 with a banking lobbyist, Washington, D.C., February 25, 2014.
68 Interview 65b with a consumer advocate, Washington, D.C., February 13, 2014.
69 Ibid.

70 Interview 10 with a consumer advocate, Washington, D.C., September 28, 2013.
71 Interview 66 with a Congressional staffer, Washington, D.C., March 24, 2014
72 Interview 114 with a Congressional staffer Washington, D.C., March 17, 2014. Cross-verification of evidence confirms this fact which may be considered "cheap talk." Information from various members of the Congressional staff, consumer advocates, and industry lobbyists who saw themselves "shut out" testifies to the correctness of the assessment.
73 Interview 34 with a Congressional staffer, Washington, D.C., March 7, 2014.
74 Interview 66 with a Congressional staffer, Washington, D.C., March 14, 2014.
75 Interview 114 with a Congressional staffer Washington, D.C., March 17, 2014.

References

American Banker (2012) 'CFPB Should Stand for "Choking Financial Professionals and Businesses"', 13 July, available at www.americanbanker.com/bankthink/CFPB-Stands-For-Choking-Financial-Professionals-and-Businesses-1050898-1.html (accessed September 2016).

Americans for Financial Reform (2009a) 'Restoring Oversight and Accountability to the Financial Markets', available at ourfinancialsecurity.org/2009/07/position-papers/ (accessed September 2016).

Americans for Financial Reform (2009b) 'Recent Polling Data on Financial Reform Legislation', available at ourfinancialsecurity.org/2009/10/recent-polling-data-on-financial-reform-legislation/ (accessed September 2016).

Americans for Financial Reform (2010) 'NPA and NCRC Urge Frank to Support Community Reinvestment Act', available at ourfinancialsecurity.org/2010/09/npa-and-ncrc-urge-frank-to-support-community-reinvestment-act/ (accessed September 2016).

Aptean (2016) 'CFPB Compliance Drives Increased Costs', 19 April, available at www.aptean.com/company/news/2016/cfpb-compliance-drives-increased-costs (accessed September 2016).

Baker, P. and Herszenhorn, D. M. (2010) 'Obama to Wall St.: "Join Us, Instead of Fighting Us"', 22 April, available at www.nytimes.com/2010/04/23/business/economy/23obama.html (accessed September 2016).

Bar-Gill, O. and Warren, E. (2008) 'Making Credit Safer', *University of Pennsylvania Law Review* 157 (1): 1–101.

Caggiano, J. R. et al. (2011) 'Mortgage Lending Developments: A New Federal Regulator and Mortgage Reform under the Dodd–Frank Act', *Business Lawyer* 66, 457–472.

Cohen, L. (2010) 'Colston E. Warne Lecture: Is It Time for Another Round of Consumer Protection? The Lessons of Twentieth-Century U.S. History', *Journal of Consumer Affairs* 44 (1): 234–246.

Consumers Union (2008) 'An Agenda to Close Growing Gaps in Marketplace Protections', 11 December, available at consumersunion.org/pdf/Safety-of-Nation-Platform.pdf (accessed September 2016).

Consumers Union (2011) 'CU Poll: Strong Consumer Support for CFPB', 20 July, available at consumersunion.org/news/cu-poll-strong-consumer-support-for-cfpb/ (accessed September 2016).

Cooley, T. F. et al. (2011) 'Consumer Finance Protection', in V. V. Acharya et al. (eds), *Regulating Wall Street: The Dodd-Frank Act and the New Architecture of Global Finance*, Wiley Finance Series, Hoboken, NJ: John Wiley, pp. 73–84.

Department of the Treasury (2009) 'Financial Regulatory Reform. A New Foundation: Rebuilding Financial Supervision and Regulation: Rebuilding Financial Supervision and Regulation', available at www.treasury.gov/initiatives/Documents/FinalReport_web.pdf (accessed September 2016).

Durbin, D. (2009a) 'Durbin, Schumer, Kennedy Ask Treasury to Support Creation of a Financial Product Safety Commission', 24 April, available at www.durbin.senate.gov / newsroom/press-releases/durbin-schumer-kennedy-ask-treasury-to-support-creation-of-a-financial-product-safety-commission (accessed September 2016).

Durbin, D. (2009b) 'Durbin, Members of House and Senate Introduce Legislation to Protect Consumers from Unfair Credit Practices', 3 October, available at www.durbin.senate.gov/newsroom/press-releases/durbin-members-of-house-and-senate-introduce-legislation-to-protect-consumers-from-unfair-credit-practices (accessed September 2016).

Engel, K. C. and McCoy, P. (2011) *The Subprime Virus: Reckless Credit, Regulatory Failure, and Next Steps*, New York: Oxford University Press.

Gallup (2010) 'Among Recent Bills, Financial Reform a Lone Plus for Congress', Princeton, 13 September, available at www.gallup.com/poll/142967/Among-Recent-Bills-Financial-Reform-Lone-Plus-Congress.aspx (accessed September 2016).

Harney, K. (2009) 'Congress Takes a Serious Look at Reforming the Mortgage Market', *The Washington Post*, 4 April, available at www.washingtonpost.com/wp-dyn/content/article/2009/04/03/AR2009040301580.html (accessed September 2016).

Helleiner, E. and Pagliari, S. (2011) 'The End of an Era in International Financial Regulation? A Postcrisis Research Agenda', *International Organization* 65 (1): 169–200.

Johnson, S. and Kwak, J. (2011) *13 Bankers: The Wall Street Takeover and the Next Financial Meltdown*, New York: Vintage Books.

Keest, K. (2009) 'Testimony of Kathleen E. Keest before the U.S. House of Representatives Committee on Financial Services', 24 June, United States House of Representatives, Washington, DC: Center for Responsible Lending, available at www.peri.umass.edu/ fileadmin/pdf/conference_papers/SAFER/ Keest_Regulatory_Restructuring.pdf (accessed September 2016).

Kirsch, L. and Mayer, R. N. (2013) *Financial Justice: The People's Campaign to Stop Lender Abuse*, Santa Barbara: Praeger Frederick.

Liberto, J. (2010) 'Wall Street Reform: Now, It's the Law', *CNN Money*, 21 July, available at money.cnn.com/2010/07/21/news/economy/Whats_next_financial_reform/index.htm (accessed September 2016).

Limbach, J. (2009) 'Survey: Americans Want Consumer Agency for Financial Services and Products', 11 September, Consumer Affairs, available at www.consumeraffairs.com/news04/2009/09/consumer_agency.html.

MacPhee, J. D. (2009) 'Testimony of James D. MacPhee before the U.S. House of Representatives Committee on Small Business on Behalf of the Independent Community Bankers of America', 23 September, United States House of Representatives, Washington, DC, available at www.icba.org/files/ICBASites/PDFs/ test092309.pdf (accessed September 2016).

Martin, A. (2009) 'Credit Card Industry Aims to Profit From Sterling Payers', *The New York Times*, 18 May, available at www.nytimes.com/2009/05/19/business/19credit.html (accessed September 2016).

Melecky, M. and Rutledge, S. (2011) 'Financial Consumer Protection and the Global Financial Crisis', MPRA Paper, Munich Personal RePEc Archive: World Bank.

Mierzwinski, E. (2010) 'Colston E. Warne Lecture: Consumer Protection 2.0 - Protecting Consumers in the 21st Century', *Journal of Consumer Affairs* 44 (3): 578–97.

Mierzwinski, E. and Plunkett, T. (2009) Testimony of Travis Plunkett, Consumer Federation of America and Edmund Mierzwinski, U.S. PIRG, Committee on Financial Services U.S. House of Representatives, June 24, available at http://ourfinancialsecurity. org/2009/06/testimony-of-travis-plunkett-consumer-federation-of-america-and-edmund-mierzwinski-u-s-pirg/

New York Times (2010a) 'Republicans Block Bill Again, and Offer Their Plan', *Deal Book*, 27 April, available at dealbook.nytimes.com/2010/04/27/2-parties-continue-to-skirmish-over-financial-bill/ (accessed September 2016).

New York Times (2010b) 'Parties Dig in on Reform Bill for Wall Street', 27 April, available at query.nytimes.com/gst/fullpage.html?res=9C00EED81139F934A15757C0A96 69D 8B63 (accessed September 2016).

New York Times (2012) 'Deconstructing Dodd-Frank', 11 December, www.nytimes. com/ interactive/2012/12/11/business/Deconstructing-Dodd-Frank.html (accessed September 2016).

Obama, B. (2009) 'Remarks by the President on Consumer Financial Protection', The White House, available at www.whitehouse.gov/node/5187 (accessed 13 April 2015).

Palletta, D. (2010) 'Consumer Protection Agency in Doubt: Dodd Weighs Dropping Idea of Creating Independent Body in Bid to Get Financial Regulatory Revamp Passed This Year', *The Wall Street Journal*, 15 January, available at www.wsj.com/articles/ SB100 01424052748704363504575003360632239020 (accessed September 2016).

Pridgen, D. (2013) 'Sea Changes in Consumer Financial Protection: Stronger Agency and Stronger Laws', *Wyoming Law Review* 13, 1–36.

Protess, B. (2011) 'Wall Street Continues to Spend Big on Lobbying', *Deal Book*, 1 August, available at dealbook.nytimes.com/2011/08/01/wall-street-continues-to-spend-big-on-lobbying/ (accessed September 2016).

Renick Mayer, L. (2009) 'House Financial Services Committee Considers Regulating Industries That Heavily Fund Members' Campaigns', Center for Responsive Politics, Open Secrets Blog, 14 October, available at www.opensecrets.org/news/2009/10/hous e-financial-services-commi/ (accessed September 2016).

Rowley, J. and Lerer, L. (2010) 'Consumer Agency Still "Elephant" in Room in Debate', Bloomberg, 3 May, available at www.bloomberg.com/news/2010-05-03/ consumer-protection-still-elephant-in-room-for-financal-overhaul-debate.html (accessed September 2016).

The Huffington Post (2010) 'Ed Yingling: Banking Industry's Top Defender Got It Wrong Over and Over Again', 18 March, available www.huffingtonpost.com/2009/10/26/ed-yingling-banking-indus_n_333481.html (accessed September 2016).

Trumbull, G. (2012) *Strength in Numbers: The Political Power of Weak Interests*, Cambridge, MA: Harvard University Press.

US Senate (2010) 'The Restoring American Financial Stability Act of 2010', United States Senate, available at www.banking.senate.gov/public/_files/Committee_Report_S_Rept_ 111_176.pdf (accessed September 2016).

Warren, E. (2007) 'Unsafe at Any Rate', *Democracy* 7 (5), 1–19.

Warren, E. (2011) 'Elizabeth Warren Wants to Give Middle-class Families a Chance to Survive Economically with the Consumer Financial Protection Bureau', Interview. The Daily Show with Jon Stewart, 26 April, available at www.cc.com/video-clips/8330b4/ the-daily-show-with-jon-stewart-elizabeth-warren (accessed September 2016).

Warren, E. (ed.) (2014) *A Fighting Chance*, 1st edition, New York: Metropolitan Books.

Wilmarth, A. E. (2012) *The Financial Services Industry's Misguided Quest to Undermine the Consumer Financial Protection Bureau*, SSRN Scholarly Paper, Rochester, NY: Social Science Research Network, available at papers.ssrn.com/abstract=1982149 (accessed September 2016).

Wolff, S. (2012) 'The State of Lending in America & Its Impact on U.S. Households', Center for Responsible Lending, available at www.responsiblelending.org/state-of-lending/reports/5-Credit-Cards.pdf (accessed May 2015).

Woolley, J. T. and Ziegler, J. N. (2011) 'The Two-Tiered Politics of Financial Reform in the United States', Institute for Research on Labor and Employment, Working Paper, available at http://irle.berkeley.edu/files/2011/The-Two-Tiered-Politics-of-Financial-Reform-in-the-United-States.pdf

Woolley, J. T. and Ziegler, J. N. (2014) 'Who Shapes Institutional Reform: A Process-Tracing Approach to the Politics of Financial Reform in the United States, 2008–2010', Paper presented at a workshop, Sciences Po, Paris, 22–23 May.

Woolley, J. T. and Ziegler, J. N. (2016) 'After Dodd-Frank: Ideas and the Post-Enactment Politics of Financial Reform in the United States', *Politics & Society* 44 (2): 249–80.

Wyatt, E. and Lichtblau, E. (2010) 'A Finance Overhaul Fight Draws a Swarm of Lobbyists', 19 April, available at www.nytimes.com/2010/04/20/business/20derivatives.html (accessed September 2016).

Yingling, E. (2009) 'Testimony of Edward L. Yingling on Behalf of the American Bankers Association before the Committee on Banking, Housing and Urban Affairs', United States Senate, 14 July, Washington, DC: American Bankers Association, available at www.aba.com/archive/Testimony_Archive/Testimony%20Document%20Archive/July14EdYinglingSenateBankingCommitteeConsume.pdf (accessed September 2016).

Young, K. L. (2013) 'Financial Industry Groups' Adaptation to the Post-Crisis Regulatory Environment: Changing Approaches to the Policy Cycle', *Regulation & Governance* 7 (4): 460–80.

4 Policy compromise and diffuse interests in financial regulation

EU consumer finance reforms

Introduction

Although there is no overarching initiative in the EU that would be comparable to the Dodd-Frank Act, the European Commission brought forward more than forty measures to reform its financial architecture in response to the crisis that significantly altered the regulatory architecture of European financial regulation and deepened the single market in financial services (Moloney 2012, 112). Existing IPE scholarship has focused largely on explaining patterns of incrementalism of EU-level regulatory responses. Specifically, IPE scholars have attributed the incremental nature of regulatory reforms at EU level to the influence of financial sector groups and their lobbying efforts aimed at preventing regulation (Moschella and Tsingou 2013). The literature thereby echoed the popular "capture" narrative. This narrative has also been fed by media accounts of "extremely vigorous" lobbying pressure from financial service-sector lobbyists during reform debates in Brussels (Hoedeman 2009).

There is no doubt that consumer advocacy groups were largely outnumbered by financial sector lobbyists during reform debates. According to a recent study conducted by a Brussels-based NGO entitled "The fire power of the financial lobby," financial sector groups had seven times more encounters with EU institutions than NGOs, trade unions, and consumer organizations put together (Corporate Europe Observatory 2014a). More than 700 financial sector organizations lobbied for financial reforms, compared with only about 150 groups from civil society. The financial sector clearly also had much more material resources at its disposal than civil society groups. In 18 months between its foundation and December 2012, Finance Watch, a newly founded Brussels-based NGO lobbying on financial reform spent 330,000 euros on communications, meetings, and research (Finance Watch 2013b). In 2012, Deutsche Bank alone spent about 1,990,000 euros on lobbying of financial reforms at EU level.[1]

The goal of this chapter is to subject claims of regulatory capture in EU financial regulatory decision-making to more vigorous empirical scrutiny. In contrast to existing accounts of regulatory change in response to the crisis, this analysis will consider a range of regulatory policy initiatives that do not neatly confirm to capture theories. By analyzing four Directives dealing with consumer finance protection regulation in depth, I will demonstrate that the influence of private sector industry groups was more circumscribed and that non-financial interest groups saw important parts of their advocacy goals translated into policy during early reform debates (see Table 4.1). The chapter also makes a contribution to the political science literature on regulatory reform dynamics at EU level with an eye towards new consumer regulation, which is considered to be a relatively under-researched field (Moloney 2012, 117).

It is organized as follows. First, it gives an overview of regulatory change that occurred with regard to consumer finance protection at EU level, assessing the extent to which diffuse interest groups saw their preferences met in the reform outcome, based on interview material and relevant policy documents. I demonstrate that private sector groups were not successful in preventing regulatory change despite their lobbying efforts. In the next section, I describe the general post-crisis environment in which interest groups' lobbying took place. The third section traces the hypothesized causal mechanism for explaining regulatory change with a special focus on the role of non-financial interest groups in the post-crisis reform debate. In the fourth section, I conduct detailed process-analyses of four regulatory policies enacted at EU level in response to the crisis, examining the advocacy efforts of organized diffuse interest groups over the content of the proposed reform policies.

Regulatory change and group influence

After the financial crisis, Michel Barnier, then European Commissioner for Internal Market and Services, promoted an extensive reform agenda. Table 4.1 summarizes the regulatory reforms chosen for analysis and lists their content with respect to consumer relevance. At the time the field work was conducted for this project, interviewees in Brussels had identified all cases examined here as the most relevant EU-level consumer protection legislation.[2] In an effort to address failures in supervision revealed by the crisis, one of the first legislative steps of decision-makers was to reform EU-level supervisory structures. The Commission put forward a legislative proposal in September 2009, introducing major institutional innovations, including a new European Systemic Risk Board (ESRB) in charge of monitoring macro-prudential risk and three new pan-European supervisory agencies in charge of micro-prudential supervision, referred to as the European System of Financial Supervisors (ESFS). Within the new framework, consumer protection falls within the jurisdiction of the three new European Supervisory Authorities (ESAs) that work in tandem with the existing national supervisory authorities. Displeased with the legislative outcome, and after the implementation of the new regulation, consumer groups and NGOs denounced the new ESAs for placing too little importance on consumer protection in their mandate, as well as for the unbalanced composition of their stakeholder groups.[3] ALTER-EU, an NGO concerned with the asymmetry of interest representation in the EU, published a report criticizing the composition of the Supervisory Authorities for

Table 4.1 Overview of the EU's legislative initiatives (consumer finance protection)

Regulatory policy	Reform measures in line with consumer groups' demands
1 *New supervisory structure* Directives on ESRB and ESFS (September 2010), following the de Larosière report	Transformation of level-3 Lamfalussy committees into European Authorities in charge of micro-prudential oversight and limited consumer protection mandate (for example, right to ban harmful products).
2 *Retail Financial Services* Mortgage Credit Directive 2014/17/EU (February 2014)	Introduces for the first time EU-wide rules in the area of mortgage loans, harmonizing and improving consumer protection regulations across Europe.
3 Regulation for Packaged Retail Investment Products (PRIPs) (December 2014)	Improves investor protection by introducing a standardized key information document (KID) for non-vanilla products which are risky, difficult to compare, and complex to understand to increase transparency and comparability of products.
4 *Investment services* Markets in Financial Instruments Directive (MifiD) (May 2014)	Improves investor protection by introducing a partial ban on inducements, prohibiting advisors labeled "independent" from making or receiving third-party payments.

not adequately representing consumers and because banking representatives largely outweigh national consumer organizations (ALTER-EU 2011). In September 2011, BEUC submitted a complaint to the EU Ombudsman about the under-representation of consumer advocates within the stakeholder groups. Despite their continuing criticism, by securing a consumer mandate for the new authorities, consumer advocates had won a little, while financial sector groups, specifically German banks, had not expressed support for regulatory reform at EU level (Buckley and Howarth 2010, 129).

Concerning a second legislative initiative under analysis here, consumer advocates were more pleased: the Mortgage Credit Directive[4] adopted by the Commission in February 2014, which introduced for the first time EU-wide rules in the area of mortgage loans.[5] It complemented the Consumer Credit Directive of 2008, aimed at harmonizing consumer protection regulations and promoting market integration for consumer credit, by applying similar measures to mortgage loans. Prior to the crisis, no EU-wide legislation for home loans existed, except for a voluntary code of conduct, a self-regulation regime on information requirements, signed by the mortgage-lending industry and consumer groups in 2001. In the final Directive, pro-reform advocates saw important parts of their demands translated into policy. In line with their demands, a general right for consumers to repay loans early made it into the final Directive. To ensure that borrowers can meet their credit obligations, the legislation also heightens creditworthiness assessment standards. The reform also includes a general ban on tying practices where other financial products are packaged together with a credit agreement affecting consumers negatively, a provision not included in the initial Commission proposal and pushed for by consumer advocates.[6] The Directive also introduces minimum standards for advice and curbs misleading advertising of mortgage loans and creates an information requirement, in the form of a standardized information sheet (ESIS) that can be compared across borders and facilitates shopping around. Although the new regulation does not ban loans in foreign currencies, as consumer groups had demanded, it introduces additional consumer safeguards in order to protect consumers against exchange rate risk. While the initial Commission proposal only included an information requirement about implications for consumers with regard to loans in a foreign currency, the final Directive went beyond the provision and—reflecting BEUC's proposition—included a requirement for member states to set up a regulatory framework that allows consumers to convert the credit agreement into an alternative currency.[7] Accordingly, the Directive was received positively by consumer groups, which considered consumer protection strengthened (BEUC 2013b). In contrast, financial sector groups interviewed for this research project reported that their lobbying efforts to prevent the Commission from focusing more on consumer protection than on market integration had failed.[8]

A third legislative initiative under analysis here is a proposal for a Regulation for Packaged Retail Investment Products (PRIPs), introducing a new key information document (KID) for investors. The Commission introduced the proposal in July 2012 in an effort to further tighten consumer protection and rebuild investor confidence after the financial crisis. PRIPs are, simply put, investment products sold to retail customers. Since the financial crisis had shown that existing legislation did not address the growing complexity of financial products and that investment products were sold to customers that were "not right for them," the aim of the legislation was to make the risks of retail investment products easier to understand and to increase comparability of different products (European Commission 2012). As of autumn 2016, the regulation requires that investment fund managers, insurers, and banks provide consumers with a consumer-friendly information document about the investment product they intend to buy. The "KID" uses clear and plain language to allow retail customers to compare products before they make an investment decision. While industry groups complained about more paper work, Finance Watch, a leading civil society advocacy group, praised the legislation as "a win for consumer protection in Europe that could help to reduce mis-selling" (Finance Watch 2014a). Advocates saw a considerable part of their positions reflected in the final legislation, including wider scope, a warning label, enhanced disclosure of financial advisor fees and a provision for product issuers to substantiate claims about any environmental and social objectives of an investment product.

A fourth legislative initiative with an important consumer dimension was the Markets in Financial Instruments Directive ("MiFID"). In an effort to address shortcomings with regard to investor protection, the Commission introduced a review of the existing MiFID Directive in 2011, which enhanced consumer protection, by introducing structural changes to how investment advice has to be conducted.[9] Retail customers usually buy their investment products from financial advisors who are paid on sales commission or inducements, or third-party payments to investment advisors. The question of whether these inducements should be banned EU-wide became one of the most controversial issues in the legislative debate. Consumer advocates argued that this widespread commission-based practice raises conflicts of interest for advisors who sell investment products to retail investors if they receive inducements to recommend one product over another (Ford 2014). In line with the initial Commission proposal and the Council's position, the final regulation included a partial ban on inducements, despite efforts of the European Parliament to water down the provision (leaving regulation up to national discretion) and financial sector groups' initial reluctance to regulatory change.[10] For observers the new transparency-enhancing provisions were "nothing short of a revolution in consumer protection" (Johnson 2014).

Most of the new regulations have only recently entered into force (ESAs), are about to enter into force (MifiD II in January 2018), or have only very recently been transposed into national law (the KID for PRIIPs in December 2016 and the Consumer Credit Directive in March 2016). What we can see so far is that consumer protection standards have been harmonized at EU level, without going much above and beyond existing regulations in member states with high standards. But we can also see that several initiatives were undertaken at the EU level to develop useful consumer protection standards and increase transparency for consumers of financial services. There is also good evidence against the prevailing argument in the IPE literature that financial industry groups massively influenced or "captured" regulatory reform. Although overall consumer protection reforms were rather incremental and compromised solutions, they reflect certain policy alterations prompted by pro-reform advocates. How did diffuse consumer interests come to be reflected in the legislative outcome?

Contextual conditions underlying EU financial reforms

Any mechanism-based explanation of regulatory change must start with the contextual conditions that allow the hypothesized mechanism to function. The financial crisis had considerably reshaped the context in which regulatory reform was taking place. Increased salience in the post-crisis reform period was accompanied by a deep legitimacy crisis of the financial sector. There has been no shortage of media reporting of policy failure due to industry capture. ATTAC, for instance, launched a YouTube video about malpractice in the banking sector which was viewed over 100,000 times within less than a month in 2008. A number of reports were published—for example, on the one-sided composition of expert groups in favor of the financial business sector (Haar 2009) or on the political influence of Goldman Sachs.[11] In a publicly appealing event, Brussels-based NGOs under the leadership of Spinwatch, a group mainly campaigning for more lobbying transparency, awarded the "Worst Lobby Awards." In 2010 the award was given to Goldman Sachs and a derivatives lobby group for their lobbying to promote profits for the financial sector at the expense of the public interest.

The loss of legitimacy in the public eye was clearly felt by financial sector representatives. Whereas relations among policy-makers and industry groups were previously described as "cozy" or "symbiotic" (see Tsingou 2008), the legitimacy crisis changed this interaction. Relations after the crisis had come under stress, marked by policy-makers' reservations and even mistrust vis-à-vis industry groups. In the perception of many policy-makers, financial industry groups were the culprits for the crisis. According to one industry lobbyist: "The way we are perceived by parliamentarians and other policy-makers has changed dramatically since the crisis [...]. We are perceived by policy-makers as being responsible for the current crisis which puts us in a difficult position."[12] This delegitimization of the financial sector made engagements considerably more difficult in the aftermath of the crisis, as one banking lobbyist noted: "You first have to explain, you have to say, we actually did not get involved in the irresponsible activities. First you have to provide this explanation and then you can have a discussion on the content. There is always this mistrust, not only on the side of the Commission but also the European Parliament."[13] These concerns were echoed by another lobbyist: "Immediately, if you say you are representing a bank, you are dead."[14]

The crisis had drastically changed the lobbying environment in which financial sector groups had to operate. Anecdotal evidence from interviews with industry representatives in Brussels indicates divisions between decision-makers and financial sector groups, with Commission officials and MEPs giving lobbyists "a very tough time."[15] Communication levels seemed to have dropped significantly, with financial sector representatives reporting that they often found it difficult to get appointments with MEPs.[16] Financial sector groups felt that there was considerable stigma, notably among MEPs. One industry representative described the context of political debate in the European Parliament as "bashing the banks."[17] In general, industry lobbyists struggled to get access to the policy process, with changes to pre-crisis levels clearly evident, as this interviewee put it, "it is not as nice as it was 15 years ago. It has become more difficult than it was."[18]

Divisions among decision-makers and financial sector groups became increasingly visible when Commissioner Barnier asked his staff in December 2013 not to accept any more meetings with financial sector lobbyists for a certain period of time. The instructions were clearly laid out in an email from the Directorate General for Internal Market and Services (DG Markt), saying that "[i]n view of our workload and the sensitivity of our current dossier, until instructed otherwise Market DG employees should not meet with bankers, their representatives or their associations" (Corporate Europe Observatory 2014b). Policy-makers generally also started to call the industry's expertise into question. It had become increasingly difficult to convince decision-makers by making technical arguments, as one lobbyist reported: "The lobbying has been a lot tougher in the last few years, particularly [...] in the Parliament, but it has been difficult across the board, because a lot of Commission officials say, yes I understand your technical points, but my Commissioner wants something different politically."[19]

Highlighting public hostility to the banking sector in the post-crisis environment, another financial sector lobbyist confirmed the difficulties encountered by her colleagues:

> With the crisis, it is difficult to lobby [...] as a representative of the banking industry – and nobody really cares whether you are a cooperative bank, a commercial bank, an investment bank [...]. From a political point of view it is not very easy to say, yes, I support the views of the banking industry. Whether or not those views are actually reasonable or not, it is just not very popular at the moment.[20]

A Commission official confirmed that the interaction with financial industry groups had become "an adversarial relationship" after the crisis. He reported that industry groups had become "less a source of information but more of an adversary because [the Commission] want[s] to change the way they do business."[21]

With their reputation highly damaged in light of the financial meltdown, financial sector groups were put on the defensive and started changing their lobbying strategies. Some private sector participants interviewed for this project noted that they refrained from openly opposing or even vetoing legislative proposals. One lobbyist put it quite bluntly, saying that industry representatives had to "work more in the shadows" and that they could not "go outside and market position papers."[22] Another statement of the same industry representative, saying that lobbying "has become less transparent than it was," confirms the argument that the financial services industry saw itself forced to adapt to the new political environment by changing its strategies.[23] These qualitative shifts in policy-making, albeit anecdotal, indicate that financial industry groups' access to the policy-making process was curtailed after the financial crisis, thereby clearly reducing the sector's overall political influence. These changes are important, because they suggest that the financial lobby's political leverage had temporarily decreased. The next section will show that the retreat of the industry opened up new opportunities for alternative societal actors.

Advocacy for regulatory reform

Political opportunities: access and receptivity

While financial sector groups faced a difficult post-regulatory environment to promote their demands, political opportunities for pro-reform increased. Several qualitative shifts in the policy-making environment from previously relatively obscure technocratic bodies to the top of the legislative agenda of European institutions offered new access points for non-financial interest groups. After the crisis both the Commission and the European Parliament tried to address the imbalances of interest representation in advisory bodies and lobbying at EU level more generally. Starting in 2008, the statements and reports by MEPs and Commission officials reflected the emerging support of the European institutions for increased participation of civil society organizations in financial regulatory decisions (Prache 2015). In September 2008, MEP rapporteur Pervenche Berès, declared in an Opinion of the European Parliament's Committee on Economic and Monetary Affairs (ECON), "the need for funding to support consumer and SME organizations in better representing their interests by enabling them to hire experts [...] in the area of financial services" (European Parliament 2008). Regulatory decisions that had been taken by regulators in the pre-crisis context moved to legislative debates after the crisis. The greater involvement of elected politicians in the design of financial regulatory reform helped in particular non-industry stakeholders. Asked about lobbying the European Parliament, interviewees from civil society reported that they had much easier access to the Parliament after the financial crisis than financial industry groups had.[24]

Pro-reform groups also gained better access to the policy-making process when the Commission started to restructure its expert groups, which are consulted before the Commission proposes new legislation to Council and European Parliament. Pre-crisis arrangements to guarantee better representation of consumers' interests in financial regulatory decision-making had been repeatedly criticized by consumer groups as one-sided and dominated by industry experts (ALTER-EU 2009). Starting in 2008, the Commission actively promoted the development of consumer advisory groups to provide them with interlocutors in the policy-making process. EU-level expert groups that advise the Commission on financial regulation included the Forum of Financial Services Users (FIN-USE) and the Financial Services Consumer Group (FSCG). In July 2010, DG Markt established a new Financial Services User Group (FSUG), merging FIN-USE and the FSCG, in order to ensure "proportionate user representation at all stages of the development of its policy on financial services."[25] This provided consumer groups with an important source of influence in the initial drafting of Commission proposals regarding consumer finance regulations. The Commission initially funded the group, which is only rarely the case for advisory groups. Its funding also includes a small budget for independent research. The group consists of experts on consumer finance from consumer groups, small retail investors, and NGOs. Financial sector representatives are explicitly not allowed to participate in order to ensure that the users' perspective gets an adequate hearing. In January 2011, members of the FSUG came together for the first time.[26]

Because there is no reporting on which FSUG positions make it into final regulations, it is difficult to assess the advisory group's direct policy impact. The creation of a financing mechanism for the new groups, in order to make it more independent, does, however, reflect the Commission's ambition to improve consumer representation in the European decision-making process in the aftermath of the crisis. Generally, consumer advocates had a positive assessment of the new advisory group.[27] While the FSUG gives consumer associations a forum to supply the Commission with expertise on financial services from a user's perspective, it also serves as an important vehicle for consumer groups to gain timely access to information about new policy initiatives.

In November 2010, Commissioner Barnier announced that all expert groups would be restructured to end business dominance, stating that "more needs to be done to enhance the active participation of civil society organizations in Internal Market policy-making in order to fully achieve a fair balance on non-industry stakeholders' representation in our consultation process" (Phillips 2010). Although reforms promised at the time did not materialize, with advisory expert groups to DG Markt still reflecting the same composition in 2014,[28] statements of the Commissioner nevertheless signaled the opening up of a policy window in terms of access to consumer advocates. A Commission official explained the restructuring of the expert groups as an effort to avoid "negative public perceptions" about industry capture, in light of public salience.[29]

Pro-reform groups not only enjoyed greater access to the policy-making process. A Brussels-based advocate reported that after the financial crisis receptivity of DG Markt to demands coming from consumer groups had changed "as day and night."[30] Another advocate recalled about the post-crisis context that "the doors [were] always open in the Commission [...] in the financial services area."[31] The consumer lobby benefited from the importance that the Commission gave to financial services right after the economic crisis. In the words of this interviewee: "It is a lot sexier these days if you talk about consumer protection."[32]

Increased political receptivity was also displayed by the fact that Commission officials started to attend events organized by consumer groups. Whereas before the crisis it was "difficult for retail user organizations to get EU officers to participate in their rare events," the participation of EU officials at events organized by civil society groups increased in the aftermath of it (Prache 2015, 19). High-level EU bureaucrats ranging from the Head of Commissioner Barnier's Cabinet to the Deputy Director in the Directorate for Financial and Enterprise Affairs participated in events organized by Finance Watch on a regular basis. After the crisis high-level EC officials also started to attend consumer conferences organized by the Transatlantic Consumer Dialogue (TACD) in Ljubljana in May 2010 and Brussels in June 2011.[33] At the TACD financial services conference in June 2011 in Brussels, Commissioner Barnier explicitly said that he needed the input from consumer organizations and civil society.[34]

This increased political receptivity can be explained in light of public pressure in favor of reform. According to a Eurobarometer survey of the European Parliament conducted in August and September 2010, a clear majority of Europeans (70%) supported stricter financial regulations (European Parliament 2010). However, the regulatory debate about EU-level consumer protection reforms did not spark a lot of public attention, apart from some media coverage of the specialized financial or European affairs press, such as the *Financial Times* and *EurActive*. Popular interest was generally rather moderate, with Google Trends, for example, not showing any search results for the main European reforms due to the small volume of searchers by its users. But increased overall political receptivity to demands coming from pro-reform groups was accompanied by a general public in favor of regulatory change. The next section will focus on the role of these newly mobilized groups.

Mobilization of diffuse interests

Pro-reform groups at EU level clearly benefited from altered political opportunity structures. Groups that had never been involved in finance before reported that they started working on financial issues after the crisis. Other groups reported that they stepped up their activities or built new coalitions that had not existed prior to the crisis.[35] Groups such as the consumer organization BEUC, currently the only European consumer organization representing consumer interests in the field of financial services in the EU, became actively involved in the reform debates. Being the umbrella group in Brussels for 44 independent consumer organizations from 31 European countries, it channels most of the interests of the national member organizations. As of April, BEUC was reinforced by a new Brussels office of the German national consumer organization Verbraucherzentrale (VZBV), which is also actively engaged in financial regulation. Next to the European and national consumer associations lobbying on behalf of financial services users, a third group, the European Financial Inclusion Network (EFIN), was established in 2007 as a Brussels-based NGO that would build a European-wide network, including NGOs, trade unions, and consumer organizations to promote financial inclusion.

Increased funding and organizational support from the European institutions helped diffuse interest groups to overcome collective action problems and organize effectively to participate in financial reform debates. It was against the background of the crisis and in an effort to create a lobbying environment favorable to civil society input that MEP Pascal Canfin (Green Party) initiated the creation of the new NGO dubbed "Finance Watch" as a counter-lobby to the financial industry in the summer of 2010. Twenty-two MEPs from five out of seven political parties signed a petition for its creation in June 2010. MEPs called for a more balanced representation of interest groups in financial regulation: "Neither trade unions nor NGOs have developed an expertise capable of countering the banks' expertise. Therefore, there is currently no sufficient counter-power in civil society. [...] This asymmetry constitutes in our eyes a danger to democracy."[36] In the following months, more than 200 national and European politicians across party lines joined the call. In December 2010, the MEPs funded a six-month project to conduct a feasibility study for creating a new body that would represent a civil society voice in financial regulation.

Since its creation in 2011, Finance Watch has served as important organizational platform for various civil society organizations to get involved in the debate on EU-level financial reform. The new NGO provided information to its members and support for drafting position papers on highly complex financial issues in order to increase, for instance, the number of submissions to Commission consultations coming from civil society. EU funding allowed the NGO to have offices in Brussels near the political decision-making area, only a stone's throw away from

Table 4.2 Selection of members of Finance Watch

Name	Founded	Number of members	Type of organization
Bureau Européen des Unions de Consommateurs (BEUC)	1962	44 independent consumer organizations	Independent non-profit EU consumer organization
European Trade Union Confederation (ETUC)	1973	83 trade unions	Independent non-profit EU consumer organization
Oxfam	1942	17 member organizations	International organization
Solidar	1948	56 member organizations	European network of NGOs
Transparency International	1993	100 local, independent organizations	International NGO
UNI Europa	2000	320 affiliated trade union organizations	European trade union federation
ATTAC France	1998	90,000 members	French NGO
Fédération nationale de la finance et de la banque (FFB CFE-CGC)	1944	257 member organizations	French trade union federation
Institut Veblen pour les réformes économiques	-	17 member organizations	Independent think tank
VERDI (Vereinte Dienst-leistungsgesellschaft)	2001	2.2 million	German trade union
WEED (World Economy, Ecology and Development)	1990	-	German NGO

Source: Author.

the European Parliament. The NGO consists of 13 staff members in Brussels, all of whom have substantial working experience in the financial sector and 41 member organizations from civil society, including trade unions, housing groups, development NGOs, and consumer associations (Table 4.2). Its declared mission is "to strengthen the voice of society in the reform of financial regulation by conducting advocacy and presenting public interest arguments to lawmakers and the public as a counterweight to the private interest lobbying of the financial industry" (Finance Watch 2013b). Finance Watch also received wide press coverage. It appeared in 21 articles by the *Financial Times* in 2012 as well as in *Europolitics* and various national newspapers. To some, "Finance Watch has quickly become an essential and widely accepted voice in financial matters" (Mattli, quoted in Finance Watch 2014b, 46).

Diffuse interest groups also benefited from increased Commission funding in the post-crisis period (Table 4.3). In December 2011, the Commission published a call to fund a "Pilot Project" aimed at enhancing the capacity of end-users and non-industry associations "with the objective of providing policy-makers with other views than those expressed by the financial sector industry." This analysis

Table 4.3 Commission funding of European civil society organizations involved in financial regulatory policy (in €)

	2010	2012	2013	2014
European Trade Union Confederation (ETUC)	1,722,937	4,225,352	4,982,205	2,982,457
UNI Europa	1,377,329	1,477,054	1,086,262	930,637
European Consumer Organization (BEUC)	4,962,236	2,014,973	3,043,989	5,545,345
Friends of the Earth Europe	947,983	733,162	1,934,015	1,137,388
EuroFinuse*	0	225,000	287,000	396,000
Finance Watch	Not applicable	1,025,000	1,213,000	1,604,000

Source: European Commission Financial Transparency System.

*EuroFinUse created in 2012 represents about 50 European organizations of financial services users. It changed its name to Better Finance in 2014.

was based largely on an earlier assessment that "consumer bodies as well as civil society organizations do not have adequate resources to properly cover a wide range of often highly technical topics and develop the expertise to take a more pro-active role in the Union financial services policy making" (European Commission 2011c). In May 2012, two NGOs representing a users' perspective were awarded the Pilot Project grant over 1.25 million euros: Finance Watch received 1,025,000 euros[37] and EuroFinUse 225,000 euros. The call was renewed for the third year in a row for 2014. According to Prache (2015), vice chair of the FSUG, the funding is "modest compared to the lobbying power of the financial industry" and "a [historic] move" at the same time.

Governmental allies

Before the crisis, and under previous Internal Market Commissioner McCreevey who was Single Market Commissioner until 2010, the Commission's philosophy was largely non-interventionist, with its actions largely being restricted to establishing working groups and producing studies. The situation changed with the crisis and Commissioner Barnier taking office. While it is fair to say that the financial crisis spurred legislative action, the leadership of Commissioner Barnier was instrumental in bringing about policy change. One of his first acts in office in early 2010 was to tell his staff that "a consumer voice had to be taken on board."[38] In a speech at the European Financial Services Conference, Barnier (2010) called for "consideration of what needs to be done to increase consumer protection across the board." Under the banner of "restoring consumer confidence" the Commission subsequently tried to play a leading role in the promotion of financial consumer protection. Consumer advocates considered Commission Barnier to be "very consumer-friendly."[39] A leading civil society advocate testified to the good working relations with the Commissioner.[40] Throughout the reform debate systematic meetings took place between Finance Watch and Commission officials once or twice a day. A trade union representative reported that with the Commissioner taking office, regular meetings between Commission officials and labor representatives were organized to establish a permanent link of cooperation and exchange.[41]

Throughout the financial reform debates a strong pro-reform alliance between MEPs and civil society groups emerged. According to European Parliament staffers, cooperation among MEPs of the Green Party and the S&D with experts from Finance Watch was very close throughout the reform process.[42] So-called "group briefings" took place at the European Parliament where Finance Watch staff met with MEPs, their assistants and advisors to the political groups to explain technical details of regulations.[43] The European Parliament, as well as national parliaments (including the UK House of Lords, the German Bundestag, the French Assemblée Nationale, and the US Senate), invited experts from Finance Watch to testify on a regular basis on financial reform issues. In 2012, Finance Watch staff had more than a hundred meetings with policy-makers and participated in six formal parliamentary hearings in Brussels, Paris, London, and Washington (Ford 2012). In the wake of the financial crisis, consumer representatives reported that they had been able to use the European Parliament as a route to insert amendments. In interviews, European Parliament staffers confirmed that they could cooperate well with civil society groups throughout the legislative process.[44] Consumer representatives reported that European Parliament staffers would call to ask for input.[45] An European Parliament staffer interviewed for this research project used the term "reversed lobbying" to describe how he calls representatives of consumer groups in order to ask for their input about specific financial reform legislation.[46] In interviews conducted in Brussels, industry representatives also testified to the increased influence of non-financial advocacy groups. According to one financial sector lobbyist, they were "much more active, much more influential than they were before in the overall policy process" and "well connected" to the Commission, the European Parliament and the regulators.[47] This evidence suggests that pro-reform advocates on the outside had well-established working relations with sympathetic allies on the inside of the European institutions.

Diffuse interests, allies, and consumer protection reforms

How did diffuse interests come to be successfully reflected in the regulations? In what follows we describe some of the advocacy activities of diffuse interest groups surrounding each of the four policies under analysis, and document which of these were successful and which were not. The focus here is on EU-based diffuse interest groups, the way they mobilized and built pro-reform coalitions with governmental allies to induce desired changes in the content of consumer finance protection reforms. The in-depth case analyses will highlight different elements of the theoretical causal mechanism.

Legislative initiative 1: New European Supervisory Authorities (ESAs)

Following agreement by all member states in June 2010, the European Parliament voted through the new supervisory framework for financial regulation in the EU in September 2010, which came into force in January 2011. The new supervisory authorities—the European Banking Authority (EBA), the European Insurance and Occupational Pensions Authority (EIOPA), and the European Securities and Markets Authority (ESMA)—transformed and upgraded the existing supervisory structure of three so-called Lamfalussy level 3 advisory committees into "bodies with greater supervisory, rule-setting, and coordinating powers" (Eising, Rasch, and Rozbicka 2013). The ESAs have a mandate to protect consumers against abusive practices, with consultative "Stakeholder Groups" representing consumer associations in all three organizations.[48] Overall, the consumer protection mandate of the ESAs remained limited. Staffing levels are low and the ESAs have no competence to impose binding rules on national regulators in the field of consumer protection (BEUC 2013a).

A European supervisory framework was opposed by parts of the financial industry, notably the German Landesbanks, savings and cooperative banks, which reportedly influenced the German position. The Landesbanks tried to preserve their competitive advantage under national supervision, which provided a degree of protection from increased competition under a single European supervisory framework (Buckley and Howarth 2010, 128). Industry opposition to regulatory change was not unanimous, however. Consumer demands in favor of a move towards strengthened EU supervision were echoed by the European fund industry, which supported a harmonized European supervisory framework with strong authorities (EurActive 2010) as well as large German commercial banks, which expected lower compliance costs. During negotiations, neither the German nor the French government could maintain their opposition to EU-level supervision and had to soften their position (Buckley and Howarth 2010, 128).

Consumer groups, including Consumers International, FIN-USE, BEUC, the Federation of German Consumer Organizations, Which?, and trade unions such as Uni Finance, got actively engaged in the debate about reforming the EU supervisory structure.[49] The mobilization of diffuse interests and their participation in the legislative process remained limited, however, with only 12 consumer groups and trade unions participating in the public consultation, representing only about 13% of consultation submissions. Consumer groups generally argued in favor of one single European Authority in lieu of three different agencies to replace the Lamfalussy committees to ensure strong cooperation among national regulators (BEUC 2009). Consumer advocates preferred a single centralized European Financial Regulatory Authority to set prudential standards, act as coordinator-supervisor for larger EU-wide financial institutions that represent systemic risk to the financial system of the EU, and set standards for valuing financial assets (FIN-USE 2009). Modeled after the US Dodd-Frank Bill, advocates also proposed to set up a pan-EU Consumer Protection Agency alongside the new supervisory authorities. In response to the Commission consultation, FIN-USE argued in favor of the creation of a consumer regulator (a "European Financial Users Authority") with the objective of protecting consumers of financial services. The Federation of German

Consumer Organizations quoted the example of the American Consumer Agency, asking the Commission "to consider the creation of an authority of that kind" (VZBW 2009). Along the same lines, Re-Define, a Brussels-based think tank suggested a consumer regulator "with additional powers to enforce high levels of disclosure, good faith transactions and strong and robust recourse against wrongdoers" to "enforce high but minimum (national authorities are free to enforce tighter standards) standards across the EU" (Kapoor 2010). However, during the negotiations, consumer groups had to soften their position to advocate for a strong consumer mandate of the ESAs instead of an independent consumer regulator (BEUC 2010).

The debate about the new ESAs illustrates the strong cooperation among mobilized consumer advocates and MEPs as allies who supported strong investor and consumer protection rights to be granted to the authorities.[50] The European Parliament became an important "agent of change" in support of strong supervisory authorities with adequate financial and human resources (Quaglia 2013, 59). While member states had considerably weakened the legislation, MEPs tried to restore the initial Commission proposal and to further strengthen the statutory powers of the new authorities (Brunsden 2010). Member states in the Council—in particular the United Kingdom, France, and Germany—were reluctant to transfer supervisory powers to supranational authorities (Buckley and Howarth 2010, 127). The European Parliament, on the contrary, envisaged the new authorities as "watchdogs with a bite," with the ability to write regulatory standards, to temporarily ban harmful products, to make legally binding decisions for national financial institutions, and to require a review from the Commission every three years that could potentially strengthen the supervisors even more by integrating them into one supervisory body (European Parliament 2015). In plenary debate in Strasbourg in September 2010, MEPs repeatedly warned against Council efforts to water down legislation and highlighted their support for a strong consumer protection mandate for the new institutions. In particular, Green MEP Sven Giegold (German) became an important ally for consumer groups pushing consumer-friendly legislation through the ECON Committee as rapporteur for the legislation.[51] Giegold added amendments reinforcing consumer protection, notably by granting the ESAs the right to prohibit certain financial products. In line with the demands of consumer groups, the European Parliament also insisted on the presence of representatives from civil society in consultative stakeholder groups. Despite the initial reluctance of member states to transfer regulatory powers to the supranational level, the European Parliament successfully pushed for strengthened supervisory authorities in the final legislation (Quaglia 2012, 187). In line with the preferences of the member states, national regulators, however, mainly retained their regulatory functions with regard to day-to-day supervision. The final regulatory outcome was a compromise, reflecting the interests of stakeholders from both the consumer and financial sector side. Because consumer-relevant legislation has not been finalized yet (MifiD II, PRIIPS) or was only recently transposed into national law (Consumer Credit Directive in

March 2016), it remains to be seen how the new authorities will interpret their already-limited consumer protection mandate.

Legislative initiative 2: European Mortgage Credit Directive (MCD)

The MDC's objective was "to create a Union-wide mortgage credit market with a high level of consumer protection."[52] Following the co-decision procedure, the legislative process was lengthy and controversial with major disagreements arising between the European Parliament and the Council—due to the particular features of national mortgage markets—with the Commission adopting the final Directive about three years after its initial proposal. The new Directive consolidates legislation on EU level, essentially harmonizing European mortgage regulations by setting the minimum regulatory requirements in a consistent way across member states. Some provisions follow a maximum harmonization approach, leading, for instance, to more standardization of the ways customers are informed before a sale.[53]

While consumer advocates actively supported regulatory change, banks and mortgage lenders considered themselves lucky to have avoided a Directive for so long and were fairly reluctant to accept new regulations. Financial sector groups strongly opposed new EU-level mortgage regulations. Major European-level financial industry associations, including the European Banking Industry Committee (EBIC), the European Mortgage Federation (EMF), and the European Association of Cooperative Banks (EACB), as well as national associations such as the Association of German Public Sector Banks (VÖB) started lobbying the Commission on the Directive proposal before its issuance in March 2011.

Financial sector lobbyists reported that their lobbying efforts to prevent the Commission from focusing more on consumer protection than on market integration had failed and that they "certainly didn't agree with this switch."[54] From a financial sector perspective the Commission' proposal marked a "conspicuous" shift in regulatory focus "from internal market integration towards more consumer protection issues" (Ahlswede 2011). In an effort to avoid legislative action, banks and mortgage lenders tried to lay out a different narrative, arguing that irresponsible lending did not occur in the EU to the same extent as it did in the US subprime market and that "the Commission should not attempt to create EU solutions for a US problem" (European Commission 2011b). The financial sector complained about a regulatory overload, arguing that new legislation would put even more strain on lenders in times of crisis.[55] It insisted on waiting for the impact of the new Consumer Credit Directive of 2008 which had just been implemented and—by a number of member states—applied to mortgages (Dübel and Rothemund 2011, 1). However, these lobbying efforts failed to prevent the Commission from introducing new binding rules for mortgage regulations.

Throughout the reform process, actor plurality was considerably increased. About 30% of the groups that participated in the Commission's public pre-legislative consultation in June 2009 came from consumer advocacy groups, consumer and user organizations, as well as trade unions, about 20% more than participated in financial sector consultations during pre-crisis times.[56] National consumer associations served as an important information transmitter about abusive practices in relation to mortgage loans. The Commission noted that "consumer advocates, consumer and user organizations [...] provided examples of practices of unfair advertising and marketing" (European Commission 2009). A range of consumer and end user organizations, as well as trade unions got actively involved in reform debates, including EU-level associations, such as BEUC, but also national organizations, such as the Financial Inclusion Centre, a British think tank defending consumer interests in financial markets or national consumer associations, including the British consumer association Which?, the Danish Consumer Council, the Spanish ADICAE, and the German VZBV.

DG Market under Commissioner Barnier became an important ally for various interest groups in pushing for reform despite the objections of banks and mortgage lenders. The Commission had discussed reforms related to mortgage integration well before the financial crisis, but DG Markt had refrained from introducing EU-level legislation. Issues that were in the Proposal for the Directive on Mortgage Credit had already been discussed in a White Paper on the Integration of EU Mortgage Credit Markets, published in 2007 in light of the first signs of a sub-prime turmoil in the US.[57] The White Paper did, however, refrain from proposing any "hard" legislation (Reuters 2007). Under the leadership of Commissioner Barnier, the Commission came up with a new proposal for a Directive on credit agreements related to residential property, short CAARP, addressing "irresponsible lending and borrowing practices" (European Commission 2011a). The objectives of the Commission proposal, officially tabled in March 2011, were twofold. It tried to foster consumer confidence by enhancing consumer protection and drive cross-border lending by introducing a maximum harmonization approach (Tait 2011). The proposal focused on enhancing consumer protection without actually putting internal market provisions aside.[58] Consumer groups, who generally favored a broad scope for the Directive and a minimum harmonization approach in order to preserve "already existing national consumer-friendly legislation" (BEUC 2011), saw their demands largely reflected in the Commission proposal.

In April 2011 the legislative debate moved to the European Parliament, where in particular MEPs of the S&D and the Green Party became important channels through which consumer groups could articulate their policy preferences. Before the Commission issued its proposal for a Directive, officials had toured the European Parliament in order to assess whether there would be support among key MEPs across party lines for a proposal on mortgage reform and MEPs had clearly displayed their political appetite for it.[59] In July 2011 the ECON rapporteur, Spanish MEP Antolín Sánchez Presedo (S&D) issued a draft report which differed mainly in scope from the Commission proposal. The report introduced several new articles to the Commission's initial proposal.[60] Despite disagreements about details of the legislation, the socialist rapporteur relied heavily on expertise provided by consumer advocates, whom he regarded as close "allies" during reform debates.[61]

The ECON draft report was met with substantial criticism. Consumer and financial sector groups agreed that the rapporteur addressed specific deficits of the Spanish mortgage market that were hardly transferable to the European level. Financial sector groups argued that the draft included "far-fetched" ideas that had not been subject to the Commission's impact assessment.[62] In a comment to the ECON report, mortgage lenders complained that the proposal "seeks to widen the scope of proposed regulation in Europe in a range of ways that are inappropriate and unhelpful. Many of the proposals would have far-reaching and unforeseen consequences on firms, consumers, the availability of credit and even the supply of housing" (Council of Mortgage Lenders 2011). Eventually, under pressure from the ECON shadow rapporteurs, as well as financial sector groups, the rapporteur reduced the scope of the proposal and a "compromise midway" between the "big-bang approach" of the rapporteur and the "step-by-step approach" of the Commission was forged.[63] In the compromise position of the European Parliament, provisions introduced by the ECON report had either been deleted (such as the provision on portability of loans) or watered down by financial sector lobbying. Provisions that creditors should identify products that are not unsuitable for the consumer and that EBA should develop guidelines for creditworthiness assessments that were supported by the S&D and the Green Party had been deleted, in line with industry preferences and under pressure from the EPP, ALDE, and ECR groups (Giegold 2012a).

While consumer advocates found support from the Commission and rapporteurs in the European Parliament, industry groups successfully lobbied their member states in the Council, as well as national MEPs to water down reform proposals. When the legislative debate moved to the trialogue stage in June 2012, member states pushed for even greater watering down of the new articles added by the European Parliament. The final text of the Directive was largely reduced to its narrow scope with the rapporteur's added articles deleted or watered down.[64] Although industry groups managed to water down the legislation, however, they were not successful in preventing legislative action. Again, the reform outcome was a settlement among the various stakeholder groups involved. According to interviews with Commission officials, the views of consumer groups and industry associations diverged in particular on two issues: whether consumers should be able to exit credit contracts before the end of the term (the early repayment provision) and the obligation for a creditworthiness test. Both controversial issues were settled as a compromise in the final legislation.

The early repayment provision required member states to ensure that consumers have a right to repay their credit before the expiry of the credit agreement. Whereas consumer groups favored a general right to early repayment with a low level of compensation, the banking industry supported a more restricted right to early repayment with appropriate levels of compensation for creditors in the event of early repayment.[65] The final text included a compromise, with consumers being granted a general right to early repayment but lenders being entitled to a compensation fee (European Commission 2013).

The second sticking point in negotiations concerned the introduction of stricter creditworthiness tests. The initial Commission proposal introduced a legal requirement for lenders to deny the credit in the event of a negative creditworthiness assessment.[66] Consumer groups supported such a mandatory creditworthiness assessment. Financial sector groups had initially rejected a Community-wide harmonization of creditworthiness assessments, arguing that national specificities would prevent meaningful standards. In line with industry preferences, the legal requirement was finally watered down in negotiations (European Banking Industry Committee 2012). The final Directive introduced Europe-wide standards for assessing the creditworthiness of mortgage applicants, but the text of the initial proposal suggesting an obligation for lenders to deny credit was deleted. Again, both lobbying camps saw some of their preferences translated into policy.

Evidence for improvements to consumer protection remain, however, somewhat mixed. According to the British Council of Mortgage Lenders (2016), the new Directive "offers little to no specific additional benefit for consumers over and above the UK's existing regulatory framework." While consumers may benefit from some measures (such as a seven-day reflection period, when a mortgage offer is made, which is to give the consumer time to compare offers, the prohibition of misleading advertising or new harmonized rules to ensure appropriate levels of competence of staffers), the adjustment to stricter credit standards since the implementation of the Directive in March 2016 has led banks to restrict their lending to households for home purchases, with some saving banks rejecting every fourth loan application (*Süddeutsche Zeitung* 2016).

Legislative initiative 3: Retail Investment Products (PRIPS/KID)

The European institutions varied significantly in their initial negotiating positions on the key information document (KID) regulation. The scope of the regulation was one of the most controversially discussed items, with the European Parliament promoting a wider scope and the Council trying to reduce the scope, largely echoing the Commission proposal.[67] The European Parliament's compromise position was adopted in plenary in November 2013, extending the initial Commission text, thereby echoing advocacy groups' demands. In April 2014, European Parliament and Council agreed the final text, which came into force in December 2014.[68] From a consumer point of view, the Council's compromise adopted in June 2013 was less ambitious than the Commission proposal (Finance Watch 2014b, 20). The agreement in trialogue largely followed the European Parliament's consumer-friendly position, despite the opposition of segments of the financial services sector. While pension funds had successfully lobbied for an exemption, certain insurance products do fall within the scope of the KID. Reflecting these changes to the initial Commission proposal, the final regulation was named PRIIPs, including not only "packaged retail," but also "insurance-based investment products."

Opposition to the Commission proposal and subsequent European Parliament amendments came from the savings and cooperative banks, which were not eager to implement another KID and complained about an obligation to provide more paperwork when selling services. Insurance companies and pension funds lobbied member states in the Council to be excluded from the scope of the new PRIPS regulation. The Association of British Insurers (ABI), for instance, lobbied to exclude occupational pensions from the regulation "to avoid any negative disruption to pension savings" in the EU (Johnson 2013). These industry groups were clearly not in favor of the European Parliament's ambitious amendments and extension of scope for the Directive, describing the parliamentary debate as "highly political," "dangerous" and marked by "miscomprehension of what the Commission idea was." Industry was afraid that the European Parliament's amendments would "create inherent contradictions, inconsistencies, and duplicates with other legislation."[69]

The reform debate surrounding the PRIPS regulation illustrates how the policy influence of diffuse interest groups can be boosted by powerful financial sector interests when the two find themselves on the same lobbying side. Financial sector groups were not united in their opposition to new regulations. The insurance sector was split, with British and Dutch insurance companies supporting the creation of a level-playing field through new legislation and French and German companies strongly resisting the inclusion of insurance products. "Baptist-bootlegger" coalitions emerged among consumer groups and the European fund sector against parts of the insurance sector. The larger scope of the Directive was in line with the European fund sector, which lobbied for more regulation of the growing sector of retail structured products in order to address the lack of a level-playing field across retail investment products.[70] The European fund sector was also supportive of the introduction of a KID covering a wide range of investment products, including pension funds, and was largely aligned with consumer representatives in their support for the Commission's proposal to enhance investor protection.[71] A broad range of groups ranging from European investors and users of financial services, including EuroFinUse (European Federation of Financial Services Users), to financial advisers, asset managers, and life insurance companies, including Efama (the European fund industry body), and the Association of International Life Offices (AILO), was in favor of the Commission's proposal. In a joint press release of end users and the asset management sector in July 2012, groups expressed their full support. They argued in favor of a broad scope of investment products to be covered by the regulation, saying it would otherwise "miss its objective of enabling investors to easily compare one product with another" and not bring "real efficiency to the Single Market" (CFA Institute 2012).

Although the legislative proposal generated very little interest from the broader public, with a few articles in *The Financial Times* in fall 2013 reporting about the parliamentary debate, pro-reform groups probably benefited from general increased public attention to financial reform issues. Representing consumer and small investor interests, BEUC, Finance Watch, EuroFinUse, and FSUG pushed for reform. In-depth discussions had already taken place among Finance Watch and Commission officials before the Commission published its legislative proposal in July 2012.[72] In October 2012, Finance Watch published a 40-page position paper entitled "Towards suitable investment decisions? Improving information disclosure for retail investors" (Finance Watch 2012b). Pro-reform groups generally supported the Commission's proposal aimed at enhancing investor protection by making the provision of an information document about investment products mandatory. With regard to the scope of the new regulation, they advocated widening the scope, making the KID mandatory for all saving and investment products. Advocates argued that life insurance and pensions should also be within the scope of the proposal so that consumers would be able to compare products across asset classes, as well as within the same asset class.[73]

Reform advocates worked closely together and stepped up their lobbying efforts targeted at MEPs before the vote in plenary in November 2013. In May and June 2013, Finance Watch circulated mock-up KIDs showing how their reform suggestions could work in practice. Finance Watch suggested amending the Commission proposal by introducing a social usefulness dimension through disclosure among the ESG (environmental, social, and corporate governance) objectives. It also suggested the exclusion of investment with adverse societal consequences from eligible assets and introduced the idea of attaching a "complexity label" to information documents that would warn consumers when investment products are difficult to understand (Finance Watch 2013a). In November, BEUC, EuroFinUse, and Finance Watch joined forces to write a letter to members of the ECON Committee advocating wide scope for the new regulation. The letter was followed with emails of the advocacy groups to all MEPs, urging them to defend complexity labels. BEUC issued a press release, promoting wide scope for the regulation, saying that "pensions and life-insurance are top of the list of those wanting and needing to set money aside for the future" and that "it would be a huge setback if there would be no information document to compare such different products" (BEUC 2013c).

In the fall of 2012, meetings among Finance Watch staff and the shadow rapporteurs for the PRIPs dossier took place, at which advocates pushed for a warning label and wider scope. Rapporteur Pervenche Bères (S&D) became an important ally for advocacy groups promoting the consumer cause in the ECON Committee. As a result of the team-like preparation of the legislation with MEPs and advocacy groups collaborating, all of the recommendations introduced by Finance Watch were either taken up by the rapporteur's draft report published in December 2012 or were presented as amendments by MEPs. Following consumer advocates' proposals, the rapporteur's draft report included wide scope for the regulation, including stocks, bonds, and bank deposits, as well as additional product rules.[74] Echoing the suggestion by Finance Watch, the rapporteur also included a provision on information about environmental, social and governance (ESG) criteria in the KID. MEP Sharon Bowles (ALDE, UK), then chairwoman of the ECON Committee, included a complexity label (or warning label) as suggested by Finance Watch (Flood 2013b). Although the European Parliament had been deeply divided over the PRIPs regulation, and despite opposition from the EPP to extending the scope (Flood 2013a), MEPs finally adopted the new regulation, introducing a range of amendments to the initial Commission draft. Advocates also saw a considerable part of their positions reflected in the final legislation, including a wider scope (including certain insurance products), a warning label for certain investment products, enhanced disclosure of financial advisor fees, and a provision for product issuers to substantiate claims about the environmental and social objectives of an investment product.[75] All in all, the new KID can be considered an improvement for consumers.

Legislative initiative 4: Markets in Financial Instruments Directive (MifID II)

Following a public consultation among stakeholders, the Commission officially tabled the MiFID II proposal in October 2011. One year later, and after more than 2,000 amendments, the European Parliament adopted its report. After the European Parliament and the Council reached an inter-institutional agreement in January 2014, the directive was adopted in May after almost four years of legislative debate.[76] Among the most contentious issues during negotiations and a key concern to consumer groups was the question of whether inducements should be banned EU-wide. Inducements are third-party payments or sales commissions to advisors who sell investment products to retail investors. Consumer advocates argued that inducements raise conflicts of interest, providing incentives for advisors to recommend one product over another. During the legislative debate, consumer advocates found allies in DG Markt under Commissioner Barnier, parliamentarians from the S&D and the Greens, as well as member state governments. In line with the initial Commission proposal and the Council's position, the final regulation includes a partial ban on inducements, despite the efforts of the European Parliament to water down the provision (leaving regulation up to national discretion) and the financial sector group's initial reluctance to accept regulatory change.[77]

Early on, consumer groups became involved in the reform debate, promoting a general ban on commission-based investment advice. Finance Watch, BEUC, Better Finance, and Uni Europa cooperated closely with each other.[78] One day before the Commission officially introduced its legislative proposal, in October 2011, BEUC issued a press release urging policy-makers to consider the "prevention of conflicts of interest between the investment product sellers and their clients." In a position paper responding to the Directive proposal, BEUC reiterated its support for a general ban on commissions and inducements for advisors and intermediaries who recommend financial instruments (BEUC 2012). The Secretary General of Finance Watch testified at a public hearing of the European Parliament in December 2011 (European Parliament 2011). In January 2012, Finance Watch submitted a 15-page document to the EPP rapporteur detailing its technical recommendations (Finance Watch 2013b). The NGO urged the Commission to maintain a ban on inducements for the sake of independent advice (Finance Watch 2012a).

Following consumer groups' demands, the initial Commission proposal explicitly addressed conflicts of interest, thereby adopting a concern raised by consumer groups. The Commission introduced a partial ban on inducements, prohibiting advisors labeled "independent" from receiving third-party payments. The proposal ran counter to the preferences of the financial sector, which resisted regulatory change, arguing that existing MiFID requirements were adequate to regulate conflicts of interest (The British Bankers' Association 2011). The European fund sector strictly opposed a ban on inducements for advice "provided on an independent basis," as suggested by the Commission, arguing that it would reduce access to advice for retail investors (EFAMA 2012). The European Association of Public Banks argued that there is "no reason why commission-based advice should deliver less investor protection than other forms of advice investment advice" (EAPB 2011). During the subsequent legislative debate, financial sector groups had to soften their position. Instead of opposing regulatory change addressing conflicts of interest altogether, financial sector groups declared that they would favor increased disclosure to a strict ban on inducements. The EBF maintained the position that a "potential conflict of interests could be better solved by higher disclosure requirements of inducements rather than an outright ban" (European Banking Federation 2013). Despite this opposition, Commissioner Barnier defended the proposed inducement ban in plenary against efforts of the European Parliament to remove the ban, saying "mere disclosure of the commissions received by intermediaries would not make it possible [...] to ensure the proper level of investor protection."[79]

Following the Commission proposal, the legislative debate moved to the European Parliament, which followed a less consumer-friendly path than the Commission. While consumer groups found allies in the S&D and Green groups, the EPP and its rapporteur largely reflected the preferences of the (German) financial industry. The ECON draft report from March 2012 prepared by German rapporteur MEP Ferber (PPE) suggested a disclosure obligation rather than an outright ban, thereby following the industry line. This position was supported by most members of the EBF, which argued that enhanced transparency and disclosure of inducements would "enable clients to choose less costly advice" (European Banking Federation 2013). In particular the German financial sector, which defended the German commission-based model of investment advising, played an influential role in shaping the European Parliament's position to refrain from an outright ban and to support enhanced disclosure. Before the European Parliament adopted amendments proposed by the ECON Committee on October 26, 2012, industry groups had massively lobbied parliamentarians. On October 22, the European Banking Associations (EACB, EAPB, EBF, and ESBG) sent a letter to MEPs urging them to oppose an amendment that would ban inducements, arguing that such a ban would "disadvantage smaller investors who cannot afford anymore to take advice" (Giegold 2012b). The *Financial Times* reported that consumer advocates were "aggrieved about the lobbying that went on" in the run-up to the European Parliament's plenary vote in October 2012, accusing "German banks of 'browbeating' politicians to back policies that will not disrupt the profits their high-margin asset management businesses generate" (Kelleher 2012). Although consumer groups had lobbied MEPs as well, urging them to vote for an "EU-wide ban on commissions and inducements for financial advisors (not only for independent advisors)" (Giegold 2012b), the compromise position of the European Parliament eventually followed the financial sector line by refraining from an outright ban on inducements and promoting more transparency in form of enhanced disclosure instead.

The final text represents a compromise among consumer and industry groups. BEUC criticized the Directive, lamenting that "legislators failed to completely ban commissions for financial advice" (BEUC 2014). Although they left the debate somewhat displeased, objectively, consumer groups had won a little. Although the Directive does not introduce an outright ban on inducements, it includes a ban on inducements for independent advisors, which had no support from financial sector groups but was welcomed by consumer groups. In line with consumer groups' demands the regulatory framework for investor protection was generally strengthened with the updated MiFID II regulation, including increased disclosure of costs and new regulatory powers for ESMA to suspend harmful financial products. By preventing an EU-wide ban, as debated in the European Parliament, financial sector groups also won a little.

The final Directive also includes two provisions introduced by the European Parliament in line with consumer preferences. First, member states do have the discretion to go beyond the minimum standard of MiFID II, including the inducement ban (meaning that they can introduce or maintain national inducement bans), which was criticized by financial sector groups on the grounds that it would lead to a fragmentation of the single market.[80] Second, firms that classify themselves as independent will have to pass on any received commissions or fees to the retail customer.[81] The amendment by shadow rapporteur Giegold (Green Party, German) largely reflected BEUC's requests, but was strictly opposed by the German Banking Industry Committee (Tagesschau 2012). Both amendments were included in the text of the final Directive, despite financial sector opposition.

The reform debate surrounding MiFID illustrates the close working relations among individual MEPs and pro-reform advocates, mainly Finance Watch, in insider–outsider coalitions. Consumer groups found some allies in the S&D group which promoted a ban on inducements. In a plenary speech British socialist MEP Arlene McCarthy, for instance, echoed consumer groups' viewpoints that "a ban is the only way to remove this conflict of interest and give strong protection to the investor."[82] Before the plenary debate in October 2012, three conferences on MiFID II organized in close cooperation among MEPs and Finance Watch took place in Brussels. An event at the European Parliament in September brought reform-advocates together with MEPs from all political groups. The event was followed by a public conference in early October, which the EPP rapporteur, as well as high-ranking Commission officials attended. One day later, Finance Watch met with a range of MEPs from various political groups at a private event at the European Parliament. A working group was set up, which allowed MEPs and NGO staff to work together via regular conference calls throughout the legislative debate in the European Parliament (Finance Watch 2013b). In parallel, meetings also took place among national member organizations and their respective MEPs.[83] Pro-reform groups served as an important source of expertise. One lobbyist from the consumer side reported that European Parliament staffers regularly asked for input. According to interviews with pro-reform groups, the fact that the plenary debate on MiFID II in October 2012 focused on investor protection testified to their lobbying of the political groups.[84] Between June and September 2013, Finance Watch reportedly had "daily contact with relevant MEPs and their staff, Member State representatives, the Lithuanian Presidency and Commission staff, and organized weekly conference calls with Members to coordinate actions" (Finance Watch 2014b).

During Council negotiations, consumer advocates also found support from various member states, such as the United Kingdom and the Netherlands, both of which tried to use the MiFID II Directive as a vehicle to expand their existing national inducement bans to the rest of the EU.[85] In line with consumer demands and echoing the Commission proposal, the Council maintained the ban on inducements for independent advisors.

Pro-reform groups had also been able to successfully push amendments through the European Parliament and subsequent trialogue negotiations with respect to other issues related to investor protection. In line with trade union demands, the European Parliament, and notably the S&D groups, included: (i) a provision to ensure an appropriate level of knowledge among staff about products sold to clients; (ii) a provision that an employer should not set up remuneration structures in ways that could incentivize staff to recommend a particular financial product to a retail client when a different product would better meet that client's needs; and (iii) a provision on protection of employees reporting infringements within their own institution (whistle-blower protection)—none of which had been part of the initial Commission proposal (UNI Global Union 2014). All of the provisions survived trialogue negotiations and made it into the final Directive.[86]

It is worth noting that pro-reform advocates were also successful in lobbying for other key issues not specifically related to consumer protection (such as high-frequency trading and position limits on commodity derivatives), which made Finance Watch conclude on a rather positive note in January 2014: "When civil society works together, we can, step by step, make improvements in the EU's financial regulation. [...] we now have a [...] text that includes some rules that are stronger than we expected two years ago when the original Commission proposal was published" (Ford 2014). Taken together, then, the review of the MiFID Regulation was a compromise that reflected the interests of the various stakeholders involved. The final regulation considerably increases transparency for consumers of financial services. To portray the regulatory outcome as captured by industry interests would be a clear misinterpretation.

Conclusions

Political scientists studying post-crisis reforms in the EU observed little change due to financial sector lobbying aimed at blocking reforms. However, our analysis of EU-level financial reforms suggests that private sector lobbying did not always result in outright regulatory capture. Even if the financial industry was successful in weakening the regulatory standards during later stages of the policy debate, its initial attempts to block legislative actions in the early phases of the debate clearly failed. The findings suggest that MEPs were sympathetic to the preferences put forward by consumer groups, and they significantly amended the main directives according to these groups' demands when the public paid attention to the reform process. Careful empirical studies of interest group influence in the regulatory process provided a more nuanced picture of capture in the field of EU financial regulatory policy-making. Table 4.4 summarizes the findings from the reform initiatives studied above.

In the first study, diffuse interest groups had moderate success in pushing for a consumer mandate under the remit of new EU-level Supervisory Authorities, but saw their demands ignored concerning a consumer regulator modeled after the American consumer agency alongside new authorities or to integrate the authorities under a strong centralized EU-level supervisory body. Analyzing the introduction of new binding mortgage rules in the Mortgage Credit Directive as a second legislative initiative, the analysis demonstrates that private sector's lobbying efforts aimed at preventing legislative action failed. The final reform legislation was a compromise with both lobbying sides—consumer associations and financial sector groups—achieving some of their goals. In the third study on the stricter regulations of retail investment products, I showed that consumer groups were able to successfully push amendments through the European Parliament and subsequent trialogue negotiations, including warning labels for certain investment products and enhanced disclosure of fees. The fourth study of the political battles surrounding the introduction of an inducement ban in the MifiD Directive illustrated that mobilized consumer advocates saw important advocacy goals translated into policy concerning a partial ban on inducements for independent advisors. In none of these initiatives is there evidence of regulatory capture as it has been portrayed in the existing literature on financial reforms after the crisis. Although initiatives such as information documents have increased transparency for consumers of financial services, overall reform advances in the area of consumer protection must be qualified as rather limited.

The empirical evidence suggests that in the post-crisis institutional context marked by increased suspicion of policy-makers vis-à-vis the financial sector and limited access for private sector groups to the policy-making process, private sector groups' political influence was at least temporarily curtailed. In this context, political opportunities to pro-reform demands coming from diffuse interest groups increased in terms of greater access points to the policy-making process, but also via increased receptivity to consumer demands in general. The transatlantic comparison of reform processes reveals an interesting difference between group organization in the US and in the EU. While the organization of diffuse interests in the US was a strict bottom-up movement, civil society organizations in the EU benefited greatly from organizational and financial support from the European institutions. Without the impetus from the European Parliament as well as the Commission, the new NGO Finance Watch would not exist.

Table 4.4 Summary of findings

Proposition	ESAs	MCD	PRIPs	MiFID
Scope conditions present	**Yes.** Drastically changed regulatory environment; mistrust of policymakers; perception of industry groups as culprits for the crisis; atmosphere of "bashing the banks"			
1 *Favorable opportunity structures*	**Yes.** Perception of "change as from night to day" among consumer groups; easier access for diffuse groups than for industry groups to EP; Commission reaches out to consumer groups by restructuring its expert groups advising on financial regulation; public opinion generally favorable to reform			
2 *Diffuse interest coalitions*	**Yes**. i.a. BEUC, Consumers International, FIN-USE, VZBV, Which?, Uni Finance	**Yes**. i.a. BEUC, Financial Inclusion Center, Which?, Danish Consumer Council, ADICAE, VZBV	**Yes**. i.a. Finance Watch, BEUC, EuroFinUse, and FSUG; consumer groups as beneficiary of split among industry groups.	**Yes**. i.a. Finance Watch, BEUC, Better Finance, Uni Europa
3 *Policy entrepreneurs*	**No.** Due to the existence of public funding schemes of interest groups, policy entrepreneurs that are well-connected and politically savvy seem to matter less in EU policymaking.			
4 *Government allies*	**Yes.** Commission, rapporteur Giegold (Greens)	**Yes.** Commission, rapporteur Sánchez Presedo (S&D)	**Yes.** Commission, rapporteur Béres (S&D)	**Yes.** Commission, S&D and Greens, UK and Netherlands
5 *Policy outcome*	**Mixed.** Single consumer bureau did not materialize, ESAs with weak consumer protection mandate	**Mixed.** Policy came about in spite of financial sector opposition. Strengthened consumer protection, increased harmonization	**Mixed.** Policy came about. Broad scope of the KID but exemption for pension funds and certain insurers	**Mixed.** Policy came about in spite of financial sector opposition. Partial inducement ban, received commissions have to be passed on to costumer, member state discretion to go beyond EU minimal standard

Specifically, the Commission and the European Parliament allowed for consumer interests to be brought to bear on the regulatory reform agenda. The Commission, and in particular Commissioner Barnier, responsible for financial services regulation, became an important advocate for various consumer interests. For instance, concerning the MifID Regulation, the initial Commission proposal explicitly addressed conflicts of interest that arise in selling as a key issue. The proposal thereby included an issue that had been raised by consumer groups in their submissions to the public consultation preceding the legislative proposal. Also, with respect to new mortgage regulations, Barnier pushed through the legislative initiative aimed at enhanced consumer protection, despite financial sector opposition.

The European Parliament was also sympathetic to the preferences put forward by consumer groups and amended significantly the main directives according to groups' demands. MEPs were generally accessible and willing to articulate a consumer viewpoint, as highlighted during several interviews conducted for this project. In general, MEPs support for consumer protection policies can be explained by their motivation to portray the European Parliament as the institution representing citizens' interests and ally of the general public. In particular the S&D and the Green Party proved to be receptive to the preferences put forward by pro-reform groups, while MEPs of the EPP group were more industry-friendly. Findings of the case studies suggest that the success of a range of interests hinges mainly on the rapporteur in the European Parliament. Because they have to steer the legislative proposals through the ECON Committee and the plenary vote, the role of the rapporteurs proved to be instrumental in achieving consumer-friendly outcomes. Examples are the part played by Sven Giegold (Greens) in securing amendments to strengthen the new European Supervisory Authorities by granting them the right to prohibit certain financial products and the work of Pervenche Bères (S&D) in pushing through the amendments to the KID Regulation, as suggested by pro-reform advocates. With respect to the reform of mortgage credit regulations, the rapporteur Antolín Sánchez Presedo (S&D) prevented a watering-down of the Commission proposal. Consumer groups had a much harder time getting their advocacy goals translated into policy when the rapporteur came from the EPP groups, as in the case of the MifID regulation.

In the insider–outsider coalition among Commission officials or MEPs, on one hand, and advocates, on the other hand, consumer groups served as important source of expertise. Due to the lack of issue salience of the financial services dossiers, pro-reform groups acted less of a transmitter of public opinion than as an alternative source of information.

The consumer voice can also be translated into policy when it coincides with member states' concerns for leveling the playing field as in the case of the support of the UK and Dutch governments for a Community-wide ban on inducements. Both governments tried to use the MifID II Directive as a vehicle to expand their existing national inducement bans to the rest of the EU and became important governmental allies for consumer groups. In the final legislative compromise, decision-makers agreed on a partial ban on inducements. Consumer protection measures were also strengthened when the financial sector opposition split and strange-bedfellow coalitions emerged among consumer advocates and the financial services industry, as in the case of the KID Regulation, when user representatives and the European fund industry supported stricter EU regulations, against the opposition of other financial sector groups.

Interestingly, diffuse interest groups saw their preferences reflected even without the helping hand of a policy entrepreneur. One reason why EU-based diffuse interest groups do not necessarily need a policy entrepreneur to succeed at EU-level policy-making can be found in the EU-level organization of civil society access to the policy process. Contrary to AFR which was a coalition made up exclusively of civil society groups, the organization of the EU-based civil society response to the crisis was more of a top-down process, initiated by the European institutions to ensure adequate interest representation in the reform process by making new funds available for diffuse interest groups and by initiating the formation of Finance Watch as counter-lobby to the financial sector. Due to the existence of public funding schemes of interest groups, policy entrepreneurs that are well-connected and politically savvy seem to matter less in EU policy-making.

Notes

1 See European Transparency Register, available at: ec.europa.eu/transparencyregister/public/consulta-tion/displaylobbyist.do?id=271912611231-56.
2 This information is based on about 70 interviews conducted with senior officials in Brussels between July 2011 and May 2013.
3 Interview 27a with a representative of an NGO, Brussels, June 9, 2011.
4 Mortgage Credit Directive 2014/17/EU (former EU Directive on responsible lending and borrowing, also referred to as Directive on credit agreements relating to residential property, short CAARP).
5 Member States will have to transpose its provisions into their national law by March 2016.
6 Interview 27b with consumer advocate, Brussels, May 21, 2013.
7 Directive 2014/17/EU, Article 23.
8 Interview 46 with financial industry lobbyist, Brussels, May 13, 2013.
9 Including a recast Directive (MiFID II) and a new Regulation (MifiR).
10 Interview 91 with Commission official, Brussels, May 21, 2013.
11 For instance, a Brussels-based NGO released a report entitled "Doing God's work. How Goldman Sachs rigs the game," available at www.alter-eu.org/sites/default/files/documents /spinwatch_goldman_sachs _march2011.pdf, accessed June 15, 2011.
12 Interview 44, Brussels, May 22, 2013.
13 Interview 53 with a financial industry lobbyist, Brussels, June 24, 2013.
14 Interview 22 with a bank lobbyist, Brussels, May 13, 2013.
15 Interview 94 with a bank lobbyist, London, June 17, 2913.
16 Interview 95 with a consumer advocate, Brussels, June 1, 2013.
17 Interview 9 with a bank lobbyist, Brussels, May 16, 2013.
18 Interview 22 with a bank lobbyist, Brussels, May 13, 2013.
19 Interview 94 with a financial industry lobbyist, London, June 17, 2013.
20 Interview 53 with a financial industry lobbyist, Brussels, June 24, 2013.
21 Interview 45 with a Commission official, Brussels, May 22, 2013.
22 Interview 22 with a bank lobbyist, Brussels, March 13, 2013.
23 Ibid.
24 Interview 95 with a consumer advocate, Brussels, June 1, 2013.
25 Commission decision of July 20, 2010 setting up a Financial Services User Group (2010/C 199/02).
26 Interview 27b with a consumer advocate, Brussels, May 21, 2013.
27 One interviewee in Brussels criticized the merger of the consultative groups, which reduced the number of member organizations from 42 to 20 in total, as "a rationalization

of the user group representation, rather than a big change" (interview with a representative of an NGO, Brussels, June 9, 2011).

28 Corporate Europe Observatory published a report in May 2014 showing striking imbalances among stakeholder groups advising the Commission on financial regulation. The report is available at corporateeurope.org/sites/default/files/record_captive_commission.pdf.

29 Interview 75 with a Commission official, Brussels, May 22, 2013.

30 Interview 27a with an NGO representative, Brussels, June 6, 2011.

31 Interview 33 with a consumer advocate, May 23, 2013.

32 Interview 104, Brussels, May 22, 2013.

33 Interview 52a with a consumer representative, London, July 6, 2011.

34 Interview with an NGO representative, July 6, 2011.

35 Information in this paragraph is based on multiple interviews with representatives of NGOs in Brussels, conducted in June 2011.

36 See the website of Finance Watch, available at: www.finance-watch.org/about-us/why-finance-watch.

37 This Commission grant accounts for about 50% of the Finance Watch budget.

38 Interview 75 with a European Commission official, Brussels, May 22, 2013.

39 Interview 77 with a civil society representative, Paris, February 1, 2013.

40 Ibid.

41 Interview 69 with a trade union representative, January 24, 2013.

42 Interview 29, with a parliamentary staffer, Brussels, May 15, 2013.

43 Interview 71 with an NGO representative, Brussels, May 15, 2013.

44 Interviews 29 and 51 with parliamentary staffers, Brussels, May 15 and 16, 2013.

45 Interview 95 with a consumer advocate, Brussels, June 1, 2013.

46 Interview 51 with a parliamentary staffer, Brussels, May 17, 2013.

47 Interview 91 with a Commission official, Brussels, May 21, 2013.

48 Regulation (EU) No 1092/2010.

49 See public submissions to the Commission consultation on European Financial Supervision in July 2009, available at: ec.europa.eu/internal_market/consultations/2009/fin_supervision_en.htm.

50 See plenary debate in Strasbourg on July 6, 2010, available at www.europarl.europa.eu/sides/getDoc .do?type=CRE&reference=20100706&secondRef=ITE M-011&language=EN&ring=A7-2010-0170.

51 Interview 52a with an NGO representative, London, July 6, 2011.

52 See ec.europa.eu/finance/finservices-retail/credit/mortgage/index_en.htm.

53 Interview 104, Brussels, May 22, 2013.

54 Interview 46 with a financial industry lobbyist, Brussels, May 13, 2013.

55 Interview 46 with a financial industry lobbyist, Brussels, May 13, 2013.

56 In a study on the sectoral origin of groups mobilizing on financial sector consultations, Pagliari and Young (2012, 91) found that prior to the crisis less than 10% of respondents represented non-financial groups.

57 COM(2007) 807.

58 Interview 75 with a Commission official, Brussels, May 22, 2013.

59 Ibid.

60 New provisions included, among other things: (i) portability, meaning that borrowers can keep the same loan agreement when moving house; (ii) that a foreign currency loan can be converted into the currency of the Member State; (iii) transfer to another creditor if it is not to the detriment of the consumer; and (iv) transfer by the borrower to another borrower (European Association of Public Banks 2012).

61 Interview 27b, Brussels, May 21, 2013.

62 Interview 46 with a financial industry lobbyist, Brussels, May 13, 2013.

63 Interview 75 with a Commission official, Brussels, May 22, 2013.

64 Interview 46 with a financial sector lobbyist, Brussels, May 13, 2013.
65 Interview 84 with a Commission official, Brussels, June 6, 2013 and interview 53 with a financial sector lobbyist, Brussels, June 24, 2013.
66 Interview 75 with a Commission official, Brussels, May 22, 2013.
67 Interview 71 with an NGO representative, Brussels, May 15, 2013.
68 At the time of writing, the ESAs are developing draft Regulatory Technical Standards (RTS) on the content and presentation of the KIDs for PRIPs.
69 Interview 104 with an industry representative, Brussels, May 22, 2013.
70 Interview 91 with a Commission official, Brussels, May 21, 2013.
71 Interview 44 with an industry representative, Brussels, May 22, 2013.
72 Interview 71 with a civil society representative, Brussels, May 15, 2013.
73 Ibid.
74 Ibid.
75 Regulation (EU) No 1286/2014
76 At the time of writing, MiFID II is being transposed by EU governments. Since May 2014, the European Securities and Markets Authority (ESMA) has been occupied with drafting rules for implementing MiFID II, the level 2 phase of the legislation. The final legislation is expected to take effect in the member states in January 2018.
77 Interview 91 with a Commission official, Brussels, May 21, 2013.
78 Interview 71 with an NGO representative, Brussels, May 15, 2013.
79 See Barnier's statement at the plenary debate in Strasbourg on October 25, 2012, available at www.europarl.europa.eu/sides/getDoc.do?pubRef=-//EP//TEXT+CRE+20121025+ITEM-017+DOC+XML+V0//EN&language=EN.
80 Interview 44, Brussels, May 22, 2013.
81 Interview 51 with a parliamentary staffer, Brussels, May 17, 2013.
82 Available at www.europarl.europa.eu/si des/getDoc.do?pubRef=-//EP//TEXT+CRE+20121025+ITEM-017+DOC+XML+V0//EN&language=EN.
83 Interview 71 with a consumer advocate, Brussels, May 15, 2013.
84 Interview 95 with a consumer advocate, Brussels, June 1, 2013.
85 Interview 75 with a Commission official, Brussels, May 22, 2013.
86 Internal email from November 9, 2012, provided by an interviewee in Brussels.

References

Ahlswede, S. (2011) 'Consumer Protection in Financial Services', Deutsche Bank Research, 24 May, available at www.dbresearch.de/PROD/DBR_INTERNET_EN-PROD/PROD0000000000273424.pdf (accessed September 2016).
ALTER-EU (2009) 'A Captive Commission: The Role of the Financial Industry in Shaping EU Regulation', Brussels, 5 November, available at www.alter-eu.org/sites/default/files/documents/a-captive-commission-5-11-09.pdf (accessed September 2016).
ALTER-EU (2011) 'Big Business Cannot be the Non-state Interest Category Most Represented in Commission's Expert Groups!', 13 May, available at www.alter-eu.org/events/2011/05/13/alter-eu-workshop-on-expert-group (accessed June 2011).
Barnier, M. (2010) 'Forging a New Deal between Finance and Society: Restoring Trust in the Financial Sector European Financial Services Conference Brussels', SPEECH/10/178, 28 April, Brussels: European Commission, available at europa.eu/rapid/press-release_SPEECH-10-178_en.htm?locale=en (accessed September 2016).
BEUC (2009) 'Financial Supervision in the EU Report of the High-Level Group & 'Driving European Recovery' the Commission Communication—BEUC's Response', 10 April, Brussels: BEUC, available at circabc.europa.eu (accessed September 2016).

BEUC (2010) 'Financial Supervision at EU and National Levels. Consumer Interests - BEUC Position', 4 March, Brussels: BEUC, available at www.beuc.org/publications/2010-00147-01-e.pdf (accessed September 2016).

BEUC (2011) 'Credit Agreements Relating to Residential Property Proposal for a Directive. BEUC Position', 14 September, Brussels: BEUC, available at www.beuc.org/publications/2011-00395-01-e.pdf (accessed September 2016).

BEUC (2012) 'BEUC Position on MifID', 31 January, Brussels: BEUC, available at www.beuc.org/publications/2012-00064-01-e.pdf (accessed September 2016).

BEUC (2013a) 'Review of the European System of Financial Supervision–BEUC Response', 23 August, Brussels: BEUC, available at www.beuc.org/publications/2013-00558-01-e.pdf (accessed September 2016).

BEUC (2013b) 'No Home Run for Home Loans', press release, 10 September, Brussels: BEUC, available at www.beuc.org/publications/2013-00546-01-e.pdf (accessed September 2016).

BEUC (2013c) 'EU Moves to Lift Financial Investment Product Fog', press release, 19 November, Brussels: BEUC, available at www.beuc.org/publications/pr2013_025e_kid_plenary_vote.pdf (accessed September 2016).

BEUC (2014) 'Financial Advice: Conflict of Interest Rules under Attack Again', 25 July, Brussels: BEUC, available at www.beuc.eu/publications/beuc-web-2014-22_esmas_mifid_recommendations.pdf (accessed September 2016).

Brunsden, J. (2010) 'Council at Odds with MEPs over Reforms', 17 February, *European Voice*, available at www.europeanvoice.com/article/council-at-odds-with-meps-over-reforms/ (accessed September 2016).

Buckley, J. and Howarth, D. (2010) 'Internal Market: Gesture Politics? Explaining the EU's Response to the Financial Crisis', *Journal of Common Market Studies* 48 (September): 119–41.

CFA Institute (2012) 'PRIPs Regulation Must Put the Interests of Investors First, Say European Investors, Users of Financial Services, Financial Advisers, Asset Managers and Life Insurance Companies Operating Cross-Border', 3 July, Brussels, available at www.cfainstitute.org/about/press/release/Pages/07032012_68993.aspx (accessed September 2016).

Corporate Europe Observatory (2014a) 'The Fire Power of the Financial Lobby', April, Brussels: CEO, available at corporateeurope.org/sites/default/files/attachments/ financial_lobby_report.pdf (accessed September 2016).

Corporate Europe Observatory (2014b) 'Barnier's Ban on Meetings with Lobbyists', 13 January, Brussels: CEO, available at corporateeurope.org/blog/barnier-ban-meetings-lobbyists (accessed September 2016).

Council of Mortgage Lenders (2011) 'Lender Concern over Unhelpful European Report', 8 October, available at www.cml.org.uk/cml/publications/newsandviews/95/353 (accessed September 2016).

Council of Mortgage Lenders (2016) 'Mortgage Credit Directive', 9 March, available at www.cml.org.uk/policy/policy-updates/all/european-mortgage-credit-directive/ (accessed September 2016).

Dübel, H.-J. and Rothemund, M. (2011) 'A New Mortgage Credit Regime for Europe: Setting the Right Priorities', 6 July, CEPS Special Reports, Brussels: Centre for European Policy Studies (CEPS), available at www.ceps.eu/book/new-mortgage-credit-regime-europe-setting-right-priorities (accessed September 2016).

EFAMA (2012) 'EFAMA Position Paper on the Revision of MifID', 20 January, Brussels: EFAMA, available at www.efama.org/Publications/Public/MiFID-MiFIR/12-4004_

EFAMA%20position%20paper%20request%20of%20amendements%20 MIFID%20II.pdf (accessed September 2016).

Eising, R., Rasch, D. and Rozbicka, P. (2013) 'EU Financial Market Regulation and Stakeholder Consultations', Paper presented at the Institute for European Studies, Université Libre de Bruxelles, 18–19 April, available at www.intereuro.eu/public/downloads/publications/Eising_Rasch_Rozbicka_2013_EU_financial_market_regulation_and_stakeholder_consultations.pdf?phpMyAdmin=bc921356f086070c90aa893e9eb2bead (accessed September 2016).

EurActive (2010) 'EU Passes "Historic' Agreement on Bank Supervision" ', 23 September, available at www.euractiv.com/financial-services/eu-votes-historic-agreement-bank-supervision-news-498050 (accessed September 2016).

European Association of Public Banks (EAPB) (2011) 'Comments of the EAPB on the European Commission's Consultation on the Review of the MiFID', 2 February, Brussels: EAPB, available at www.eapb.eu/page? pge=index&page=position_papers&mi=6&mi=18&ssn=0&year=2011&search=position&id=2022 (accessed September 2016).

European Association of Public Banks (EAPB) (2012) 'Annual Report 2011–2012', Brussels: EAPB, available at eapb.eu/file?fle=7233 (accessed September 2016).

European Banking Federation (EBF) (2013) 'EBF Trilogue Position on MifiD2/Mifir', 13 July, Brussels: EBF, available at www.ebf-fbe.eu/uploads/EBF_003239%20-%20 EBF%20%20trilogue%20position%20on%20MiFID2.pdf (accessed September 2016).

European Banking Industry Committee (EBIC) (2012) 'EBIC Observations on the Texts of the European Commission, Council and Parliament on the Proposal for a Directive on Credit Agreement Relating to Residential Property (CARRP)', 11 July, Brussels: EBIC, available at www.ebic.org/Position%20Papers/12.7.11.EBIC%20Position%20 Paper%20on%20CARRP%20(COM).pdf (accessed September 2016).

European Commission (2009) 'Financial Services: Commission Launches Consultation on How to Ensure Responsible Lending and Borrowing in the EU', IP/09/922, 15 June, Brussels: European Commission, available at europa.eu/rapid/press-release_IP-09-922_en.htm?locale=en (accessed September 2016).

European Commission (2011a) 'Proposal for a Directive of the European Parliament and of the Council on Credit Agreements Relating to Residential Property', COM(2011) 142 final, 31 March, Brussels: European Commission, available at eur-lex. europa.eu/legal-content/EN/TXT/PDF/?uri=CELEX:52011PC0142&from=EN (accessed September 2016).

European Commission (2011b) 'New Rules for More Efficient, Resilient and Transparent Financial Markets in Europe', IP/11/383, 20 October, Brussels: European Commission, available at europa.eu/rapid/press-release_IP-11-1219_en.htm?locale=en (accessed September 2016).

European Commission (2011c) 'Pilot Project. Capacity Building of End-Users and Non-Industry Stakeholders in Union Policy Making in the Area of Financial Services', 16 December, Brussels: European Commission, available at ec.europa.eu/dgs/internal_ market/docs/grants/call-for-proposals-2011-175-h_en.pdf (accessed September 2016).

European Commission (2012) 'Commission Proposes Legislation to Improve Consumer Protection in Financial Services', 3 July, Brussels: European Commission, available at europa.eu/rapid/press-release_IP-12-736_en.htm?locale=en (accessed September 2016).

European Commission (2013) 'Statement by Commissioner Michel Barnier Following the Agreement in Trilogue on the Mortgages Directive', 22 April, Brussels: European

Commission, available at europa.eu/rapid/press-release_MEMO-13-365_en.htm (accessed September 2016).

European Parliament (2008) 'Opinion of the Committee on Economic and Monetary Affairs for the Committee on Budgets on the Draft General Budget of the European Union for the Financial Year 2009', 14 October, Brussels: European Parliament, available at www.europarl.europa.eu/sides/getDoc.do?type=REPORT&reference=A6-2008-0398&language=GA.

European Parliament (2010) 'Europeans and the Crisis. European Parliament Eurobarometer (EB Parlemètre 74.1)', 14 October, Brussels: European Parliament, available at www.europarl.europa.eu/pdf/eurobarometre/2010_10/analytical_synthesis_EN.pdf (accessed September 2016).

European Parliament (2011) 'Public Hearing MiFID Review: Objectives for MiFID/MiFIR2', 5 December, Brussels: European Parliament, available at www.europarl.europa.eu/meetdocs/2009_2014/documents/econ/dv/draftprogrammemifid_/draftprogrammemifid_en.pdf.

European Parliament (2015) 'Parliament Gives Green Light to New Financial Supervision Architecture', 22 September, Brussels: European Parliament, available at www.europarl.europa.eu/news/en/news-room/content/20100921IPR83190 (accessed September 2016).

Finance Watch (2012a) 'Investing Not Betting', 24 April, Brussels: Finance Watch, available at www.finance-watch.org/press/press-releases/328-investing-not-betting-fw-position-paper/ (accessed September 2016).

Finance Watch (2012b) 'Towards Suitable Investment Decisions?', 31 October, Brussels: Finance Watch, available at www.finance-watch.org/press/press-releases/311-towards-suitable-investment-decisions-prips (accessed September 2016).

Finance Watch (2013a) 'Discussion Paper on Product Rules for Retail Investment Products', 19 April, Brussels: Finance Watch, available at www.finance-watch.org/our-work/publications/627.

Finance Watch (2013b) 'Annual Report 2011 and 2012', 26 April, Brussels: Finance Watch, available at www.finance-watch.org/our-work/publications/599-annual-report-2011-2012 (accessed September 2016).

Finance Watch (2014a) 'PRIPs Agreement Should Help to Reduce Mis-Selling of Financial Products to Consumers, Says Finance Watch', 1 April, Brussels: Finance Watch, available at www.finance-watch.org/press/press-releases/857 (accessed September 2016).

Finance Watch (2014b) 'Annual Report 2013', 23 May, Brussels: Finance Watch, available at www.finance-watch.org/our-work/publications/876 (accessed September 2016).

FIN-USE (2009) 'The Future of Financial Services Supervision', April, Brussels: FIN-USE available at ec.europa.eu/internal_market/fin-use_forum/docs/supervision_en.pdf.

Flood, C. (2013a) Deep Divide over EU Retail Investor Protection Vote', *Financial Times*, 22 September, available at www.ft.com/intl/cms/s/0/8f90bf1e-2133-11e3-8aff-00144feab7de.html?siteedition=uk#axzz3UZVEtNZn (accessed September 2016).

Flood, C. (2013b) 'Prips: EU Parliament 'betrays' Retail Investors', *Financial Times*, 27 October, available at www.ft.com/intl/cms/s/0/cf71e2a2-3b19-11e3-87fa-00144feab7de.html#axzz3UZVEtNZn (accessed September 2016).

Ford, G. (2012) 'One Year on … What Has Finance Watch Achieved?', 14 August, Brussels: Finance Watch, available at www.finance-watch.org/hot-topics/blog/283 (accessed September 2016).

Ford, G. (2014) 'MiFID: The Counter-Lobby Makes a Difference', 27 January, Brussels: Finance Watch, available at www.finance-watch.org/hot-topics/blog/825 (accessed September 2016).

Franken, S. M. (2009) 'The Political Economy of the EC Consumer Credit Directive', in J. Niemi et al. (eds), *Consumer Credit, Debt and Bankruptcy: Comparative and International Perspectives*, Portland, OR: Hart Publishing, pp. 129–152.

Giegold, S. (2012a) 'Wohnimmobilienkredite - Was Haben Wir Erreicht, Was Verloren?' available at www.sven-giegold.de/2012/wohnimmobilienkredite-die-details/ (accessed March 2013).

Giegold, S. (2012b) 'Bankenlobby Macht Druck Vor Plenumsabstimmung Über Provisionsgetriebene Beratung', 22 Oktober, available at www.sven-giegold.de/2012/bankenlobby-macht-druck-vor-plenumsabstimmung-uber-provisionsgetriebene-beratung/ (accessed September 2016).

Hoedeman, O. (2009) 'Parliament inquiry into financial crisis should address role of lobbying', *New Europe*, Issue 855, 11 October, available at hwww.neweurope.eu/article/private-us-peacemakers-will-europes-wealthy-families-follow-lead/ (accessed September 2016).

Johnson, S. (2013) 'Consumer Body Fights Pension Lobby', *Financial Times*, 13 January, available at www.ft.com/intl/cms/s/0/27738246-5c02-11e2-bef7-00144feab49a.html#axzz3UZVEtNZn (accessed September 2016).

Johnson, S. (2014) 'Mifid II: Regulatory 'Typhoon' on Course for Europe', *Financial Times*, 26 October, available at www.ft.com/intl/cms/s/0/6eee116c-5931-11e4-a33c-00144feab7de.html?siteedition=intl#axzz3HWKkyV7h (accessed September 2016).

Kapoor, S. (2010) 'Better Consumer Protection and Tackling Systemic Risk - Two Sides of the Same Coin?', Brussels: Re-define.

Kelleher, E. (2012) 'Decision on Inducement Ban Sparks Criticism', *Financial Times*, 11 April available at www.ft.com/intl/cms/s/0/fd3dc2cc-22a7-11e2-938d-00144feabdc0.html#axzz3I6AnBRMW (accessed September 2016).

Moschella, M. and Tsingou, E. (eds) (2013) *Great Expectations, Slow Transformation: Incremental Change in Post-Crisis Regulation*, Colchester: ECPR Press.

Moloney, N. (2012) 'The Legacy Effects of the Financial Crisis on Regulatory Design in the EU', in E. Ferran et al. (eds), *The Regulatory Aftermath of the Global Financial Crisis*, Cambridge: Cambridge University Press, pp. 111–202.

Pagliari, S. and Young, K. L. (2012) 'Who Mobilizes? An Analysis of Stakeholder Responses to Financial Regulatory Policy Consultations', in S. Pagliari (ed.), *The Making of Good Financial Regulation*, London: International Center for Financial Regulation, pp. 48–56.

Phillips, L. (2010) 'Barnier to End Domination of Bank Lobby in EU Advisory Groups', *Eurobserver*, 3 November, available at euobserver.com/economic/31186 (accessed September 2016).

Prache, G. (2015) 'The Role of Civil Society in EU Financial Regulation', in P. I. Rodriguez (ed.), *Building Responsive and Responsible Financial Regulators in the Aftermath of the Financial Crisis*, Cambridge: Intersentia, pp. 185–212.

Quaglia, L. (2012) 'The Regulatory Response of the European Union to the Global Financial Crisis', in R. Mayntz (ed.), *Crisis and Control*, Frankfurt (Main): Campus Verlag, pp. 171–96.

Quaglia, L. (2013) 'Financial Services Governance in the European Union after the Global Financial Crisis: Incremental Change or Path-Breaking Reform', in M. Moschella and E. Tsingou (eds), *Great Expectations, Slow Transformation: Incremental Change in Post-Crisis Regulation*, Colchester: ECPR Press, pp. 57–72.

Reuters (2007) 'EU's McCreevy to Propose Mortgage Rules: Document', 21 November, available at www.cnbc.com/id/21913386 (accessed September 2016).

Süddeutsche Zeitung (2016) 'Ältere Erhalten Immer Schwerer Immobilien-Kredite', 12 July, available at www.sueddeutsche.de/geld/darlehen-aeltere-erhalten-immer-schwerer-immobilien-kredite-1.3073114 (accessed September 2016).

Tagesschau (2012) 'EU: Banken Sollen Provisionen Offenbar an Kunden Weitergeben', 24 September, available at www.tagesschau.de/wirtschaft/bankberatung120.html (accessed September 2016).

Tait, N. (2011) 'EU to Shake up Mortgage Rules', *Financial Times*, 31 March, available at www.ft.com/intl/cms/s/0/86401b64-5aff-11e0-a290-00144feab49a.html?siteedition=intl#axzz3Tt5eTNBR (accessed September 2016).

The British Bankers' Association (BBA) (2011) 'European Commission's Consultation on the Review of MiFID. A Response by: The British Bankers' Association', 2 February, available at circabc.europa.eu (accessed September 2016).

Tsingou, E. (2008) 'Transnational Private Governance and the Basel Process: Banking Regulation and Supervision, Private Interests and Basel II', in A. Nölke and J.-C. Graz (eds), *Transnational Private Governance and Its Limits*, London: Routledge and ECPR, pp. 58–68.

UNI Global Union (2014) 'Our Success in EU Financial Legislation', 24 April, available at www.uniglobalunion.org/news/our-success-eu-financial-legislation (accessed September 2016).

Vzbw (2009) 'European Financial Supervision Response to the Commission's Communication of 27.05.2009', 15 July, available at circabc.europa.eu (accessed September 2016).

5 Diffuse interests and the limits of lobbying

Case study of the financial transaction tax in the United States

Introduction

The 2008 financial crisis also triggered a debate about new taxes on the financial sector in the United States, including proposals for a financial transaction tax (FTT), a tax on bonuses, and taxes on financial institutions (Shackelford, Shaviro, and Slemrod 2010). This chapter will focus on the US FTT debate in the aftermath of the crisis, which shows clear signs of regulatory capture by powerful financial sector interests. The financial services industry visibly tried to exert policy influence in order to stifle the idea of taxing financial transactions in the United States at birth. A report by Public Citizen found that between January 2011 and June 2013, financial sector lobbyists opposing a US FTT outnumbered pro-tax reform lobbyists by five to one.[1] Through large contributions to election campaigns and so-called "political action committees" (PACs), lobbying by the financial services sector drew on considerable resources. In the 2012 election cycle, 40 PACs were aligned with financial sector interests, according to the report, and donated nearly $20 million to their preferred candidates. These numbers led Public Citizen to conclude that "[c]urrently, it's good to be a member of corporate America [...] industry is exploiting its advantages by deploying an overwhelming numbers of lobbyists and distributing campaign contributions that far outweigh the resources available to pro-reform advocates" (Public Citizen 2015).

A broad coalition of pro-reform advocates, including the Occupy Wall Street movement that emerged in response to the financial crisis, had initially revived the debate on a US FTT in an effort to capitalize on the post-crisis reform momentum. For these groups, a tax on financial transactions represented, among other things, an important means to raise revenues to address economic inequalities, which had been exacerbated by the financial crisis. Pro-reform campaign groups, under the leadership of National Nurses United (NNU), successfully brought the issue to the US Congress. Numerous bills containing an FTT in one form or another were introduced to Congress between 2009 and 2015. In November 2011, a press article concluded on an enthusiastic note about civil society activism: "The nurses aren't just making noise. It looks like they're changing the debate, altering the policies of the most powerful players in Washington" (Nichols 2011). This prediction did not, however, materialize. Despite considerable mobilization efforts on the part of civil society organizations—including labor unions, non-governmental organizations, and civil rights groups—lobbying efforts aimed at introducing a US FTT did not lead to legislative action. After initial signs of White House support for an FTT in 2009 (*The Huffington Post* 2011), the reform momentum soon died away. Apart from a group of progressive Democrats, none of the proposed legislation received broader political support in Congress. Although the FTT debate later regained momentum, with Senator Bernie Sanders (D-VT), proposing a broad FTT bill as part of his presidential campaign in May 2015 and Democratic presidential nominee Hillary Clinton endorsing a tax on Wall Street speculation in 2016, prospects for legislative success remain grim, against the opposition of a Republican-controlled House of Representatives.

The main question addressed in this chapter is how to explain why mobilized diffuse interests lose, even under contextual conditions conducive to their policy influence, such as the legitimation crisis caused by the financial meltdown of 2008. The question of why an FTT was not introduced in the United States, despite the mobilization of a broad pro-reform coalition in response to a major crisis, is a difficult one, because "the causes of 'non-events' are notoriously difficult to pin down" (Tannenwald 1999, 438). Studying negative cases may still be a very fruitful endeavor, however. Focusing more critical attention on cases in which diffuse interests go unrepresented despite committing efforts and funds to the legislative proposal might actually reveal other explanatory factors, beyond the diffuseness of the underlying interest.

This chapter is organized as follows. The first section gives a brief overview of the legislative proposals containing an FTT that were introduced to Congress but did not make it into law, despite considerable mobilization of pro-reform advocates and initial high-level political support. I start the analysis with a brief timeline of failed attempts to bring about regulatory change, starting in 2009, when ideas about the introduction of a fee on speculation started to float in Congressional debates. In a second step, I will carefully trace where mechanisms failed that would have allowed for diffuse interest representation in financial regulation. As noted above, there may be some value in noting the absence of necessary conditions for the success of diffuse interests in public policy. These conditions may be summarized as unforged alliances, lack of policy entrepreneurship, and weak governmental allies. Since the explanatory mechanism is set in a post-crisis context, the emphasis of the analysis will be the political debate during the years following the financial crisis, rather than the electoral campaigns from 2015 onwards.

Group influence: from forbidden topic to parliamentary agenda

Since the 1980s, each time a financial crisis hit, interest in a tax on financial transactions resurfaced in the United States and died out again shortly afterwards. Pro-reform campaigns, such as the Tobin Tax Initiative USA, a project of the Center for the Environmental Economic Development (CEED), repeatedly brought the topic to the US Congress (Patomäki 2001, 184). The idea of an FTT or "Tobin tax" was debated as a revenue-raising measure, first in 1987 with Congress debating a 0.5% tax on stock transfers. The idea gained traction again in the 1990s, with the United Nations trying to find sources of revenue for international development. In 1995, the Senate Finance Committee held various hearings on proposals containing a tax mechanism (Bartlett 2011). The numerous debates did not, however, amount to legislative action. Strict opposition usually came from financial industry lobby organizations and state bureaucracies, notably the finance ministry, which declared a tax on financial activities "a practically forbidden topic" in the United States (Patomäki 2001, 179). US governments also actively opposed any international efforts aimed at introducing a tax on financial activities. In 1996 the Helms-Dole bill, introduced intro Congress, explicitly prohibited the United Nations from endorsing any sort of global taxation (Ibid. 176). The financial crisis of 2008, once again, triggered the debate about a tax on financial transactions at national and international level. Since 2009, several legislative proposals containing a financial transaction mechanism have been introduced to the US Congress. Table 5.1 gives an overview of the most important bills containing an FTT. The proposed legislation projects differ mainly with respect to tax size, tax base, and revenue purpose. The bills in the House of Representatives introducing a small tax on financial transactions have been sponsored by Democratic Representatives including Peter DeFazio, John Conyers (HR 870), Peter Stark (HR 755), Keith Ellison (HR 6411), and others. Bills introduced in the Senate were co-sponsored by Tom Harkin (S. 2927), Bernie Sanders (S. 915), and Sheldon Whitehouse (S. 277). Most promising to reform advocates was the bill titled "Let Wall Street Pay for the Restoration of Main Street Act of 2009", first introduced by Representative DeFazio (D-OR) in December 2009, which received a number of co-sponsors in the Senate and in the House. The bill has been reintroduced several times without gaining broader political support. So far the proposed FTT bills have found only a few co-sponsors in the Senate; none of them ultimately made it into law.

In the aftermath of the crisis, the idea of a tax on Wall Street gained some support in the United States, as a revenue-raising measure (Krugman 2011), as a means to discourage risky speculative trading or as a punitive tax to make Wall Street "pay its fair share" (Public Citizen 2014). Supportive words came, for instance, from the editors of the *New York Times* (2010). A range of respected economists also expressed their backing of such a tax, including Nobel Memorial Prize-winning economists such as Joseph Stiglitz and Paul Krugman. In November 2011, Krugman (2011) reiterated his support in a column for the *New York Times*. The pro-reform camp was also joined by prominent allies including former US Vice-President Al Gore, prominent business leaders such as Warren Buffet and Microsoft founder Bill Gates, as well as a group of academics.

Proponents of an FTT also included civil society campaign groups that had come together after the financial crisis to push for financial reform. Starting with the Occupy Wall Street movement in 2009, a broad range of civil society organizations actively mobilized in support of an FTT. Under the leadership of labor groups such as NNU, one set of US advocates started the US Robin

Table 5.1 Overview of most important FTT bills introduced in Congress 2009–2015

	Sponsor	Tax imposed	Tax purpose
House bills			
HR 4191, Let Wall Street Pay for the Restoration of Main Street Act of 2009 (Dec 2009)	Rep. DeFazio	0.25% on stock transactions, 0.02% futures contracts, and 0.02% swaps	Job creation
HR 3313, Wall Street Trading and Speculators Tax Act (Nov 2011, bill reintroduced in Feb 2013, as HR 880)	Rep. DeFazio (co-sponsored by Sen. Harkin)	0.03% on financial transactions	Job creation
HR 870, 21st Century Full Employment and Training Act (Mar 2011)	Rep. Conyers	Small tax on stock and bond transactions	Full employment
H.R. 755, Investing in Our Future Act (Feb 2011)	Rep. Stark	0.005% on currency transactions	Health care, climate change i.a.
HR 676, Expand & Improve Medicare For All Act (Feb 2011)	Rep. Conyers	Small tax on stock and bond transactions	Health care
HR 6411, Inclusive Prosperity Act (Sept 2012), reintroduced in April 2013 (HR 579) and Mar 2015 (HR 1464)	Rep. Ellison	0.5% tax on stocks, a 0.1% tax on bonds, and a 0.005% tax on derivatives	Health care, climate change i.a.
Senate bills			
S 915, American Health Security Act (May 2011)	Sen. Sanders	0.25% tax on stock and 0.02% on credit default swaps	Health system
S 1787, the Wall Street Trading and Speculators Tax (Nov 2011)	Sen. Harkin	0.03% on trading transactions including stocks, bonds, treasuries, and derivatives	Infrastructure
S 2252, Rebuild America Act (Mar 2012)	Sen. Harkin	0.03% tax on stocks, bonds, treasuries, and derivatives	Infrastructure
S 3272, Comprehensive Dental Reform Act (June 2012)	Sen. Sanders	0.025% tax on stocks, bonds, and treasuries	Dental health care
S 277, Job Preservation and Economic Certainty Act (Feb 2013)	Sen. Whitehouse	0.03% FTT	Job creation
S.1373 College For All Act (May 2015)	Sen. Sanders	small tax on stocks, bonds and derivatives	Free education

Hood campaign, rallying members of Occupy Wall Street, environmental groups, faith-based organizations, and AIDS activists. The US campaign was also partly inspired by parallel developments in Europe. There, a major pro-reform network of civil society organizations had come together for a Robin Hood Tax campaign and key political leaders had expressed support for the idea. This had generated widespread public attention which did not go unnoticed in the United States.[2]

US advocates mainly supported the tax for its huge revenue potential. Labor groups such as the nurses' union and the AFL-CIO saw in the tax an important means to finance job creation programs and to fight unemployment. For health activists, revenues raised by such a transaction tax may help to stop the spread of HIV/AIDS and for environmentalists, they may contribute to combatting climate change. In mid-2009, under the umbrella of "Americans for Financial Reform" (AFR), a second set of groups started to actively promote the FTT as one of their advocacy goals for financial reform after the crisis. FTT proponents argued that "beyond the revenues to be raised, even a small FTT would have the salutary effect of discouraging the kind of high-frequency trading that has increased harmful volatility in financial markets" (AFR 2011b).

After the initial campaign goal to include the FTT in the Dodd-Frank reform law had failed, advocates started to support other legislative proposals. Out of the numerous bills containing an FTT that had been proposed in Congress since 2009, pro-reform advocates focused their lobbying efforts mainly on two bills: "The Let Wall Street Pay for the Restoration of Main Street Bill" initially introduced by Representative DeFazio in 2009, and the Inclusive Prosperity Act or "Robin Hood Tax bill" introduced by Representative Keith Ellison (D-MN) in September 2012. Both bills had been reintroduced into Congress several times, but did not find enough co-sponsors. The pro-reform group AFR actively supported a bill introduced by Representative DeFazio in December 2009. The "Let Wall Street Pay for the Restoration of Main Street Act of 2009" proposed a small tax on stock transactions, futures contracts, and swaps. Its purpose was "to fund job creation and deficit reduction." According to DeFazio's estimates, the bill would have raised $150 billion a year, with half of the annual revenue going to a job creation reserve fund. The bill was co-sponsored by twenty-five members of the House of Representatives. DeFazio's tax proposal also received backing from Nancy Pelosi, then Speaker of the House, who supported a transaction tax in cooperation with the G20 nations. Broader political support for the proposed bill failed to appear even among the Democratic Party, with other House Democrats opposing the bill in a "Dear Colleague" letter (Cover 2009). In November 2011, DeFazio introduced an updated version of the bill, this time co-sponsored by Senator Tom Harkin (D-IA), suggesting a 0.03% fee on financial transactions. In February 2013, Harkin and DeFazio reintroduced an FTT bill with the "Wall Street Trading and Speculators Tax Act" (HR 880), which would impose a tax of 0.03% on trades of stocks, bonds, and derivatives (3 cents per $100 traded). While the previous proposal set a higher tax rate, but included carve-outs for small investors and pension funds, the second proposal included a lower tax rate to release the burden on long-term investors and target traders instead (Grim 2011). According to an estimate by the bipartisan Joint Committee on Taxation, the bill would raise approximately $350 billion of revenue over 10 years.

Another bill proposing a small FTT, mainly drafted by the Robin Hood Tax campaign groups, was proposed by Democratic Representative Ellison in

September 2012. The legislation, the Inclusive Prosperity Act or "Robin Hood Tax bill" (HR 6411), was symbolically introduced on the eve of the first anniversary of the Occupy Wall Street movement. It would have levied a small tax on certain Wall Street transactions such as a 0.5% tax on stocks, a 0.1% tax on bonds, and a 0.005% tax on derivatives. The bill suggested that the collected tax revenues would go to improving health care, including the fight against AIDS, as well as to combating climate change.[3] Ellison reintroduced the Robin Hood tax bill in April 2013 and in March 2015. In early 2015, the idea was again put on the political agenda by the Democratic Party. In an Action Plan to the new Congress in January 2015, the top-ranking member of the House Budget Committee, Representative Chris Van Hollen (D-Md), proposed a small "financial market trading fee" to curb financial speculation. The plan was again backed by Democratic Minority Leader Nancy Pelosi (D-CA). The "action plan" calls for a 0.1% tax on transactions by high-volume traders generating an anticipated $800 billion in revenues over 10 years (Nichols 2015). Chances of policy success remained limited, however, with Republicans in control of both Chambers of Congress largely opposed to the idea of an FTT.

From the beginning, financial sector groups criticized the tax proposals. The Securities Industry and Financial Market Association, the Financial Services Round Table, and the US Chamber of Commerce released a statement in 2009, saying that "a day-by-day financial transaction tax is not something we are prepared to support." In an open letter to Treasury Secretary Geithner in September 2011, the groups reiterated its opposition to an FTT, arguing that "a transaction tax will cycle through the entire U.S. economy, harming both investors and businesses" (SIFMA 2011). Largely reflecting the industry's stance, the Obama administration officially opposed an FTT throughout the reform debates. Treasury Secretary Timothy Geithner strictly opposed the idea and tried to undercut international efforts to establish a global tax between 2009 and 2011 (Eisinger 2014). Jack Lew, who succeeded Geithner as Treasury Secretary in 2013, reiterated the administration's opposition to such a tax (Reuters 2013). No policy change occurred, despite considerable civil society activism. Although the idea of a tax on Wall Street speculation made it back to the national political stage in 2015 as campaign promises of Democratic presidential candidates, this chapter deals with the question of why mobilized diffuse interests lost, despite the contextual conditions conducive to their policy influence, namely a legitimation crisis caused by the financial meltdown of 2008?

Advocacy for an FTT

Context

Compared with the pre-crisis situation, the post-crisis context for regulatory reform was much less conducive to industry influence and much more permeable for diffuse interest groups agitating for change. As discussed at length beforehand, the "normal" regulatory environment characterized by low salience and little public attention had turned into a highly salient debate, with the global financial crisis constituting a crisis of meaning and legitimation. Public moral outrage was clearly visible in the spread of the Occupy Wall Street movements across major US cities. A Robin Hood Tax was also among the demands of Occupy Wall Street protesters who marched in the streets of New York, which gave the policy idea an initial "boost" (Grim 2011).

Political opportunities: access and receptivity

In this post-crisis context, political opportunities had started to open up, with the number of policy-makers receptive to reform ideas increasing in the context of somewhat heightened issue salience, not least due to the attention that the Occupy Wall Street protests had attracted. In the words of one campaigner, "before [the crisis], when we went to talk to a Congress member about an FTT, literally people would laugh. After Occupy Wall Street people started to listen to the idea. There was a sea change."[4] Under conditions of public pressure, advocates enjoyed somewhat increased access to the policy process and their calls for the introduction of a tax on Wall Street attracted attention among policy-makers. In 2011 personal meetings took place among AFL-CIO President and tax proponent Richard Trumka and key administration aides (Nichols 2011). Congressional committee hearings on financial sector reform also allowed increased policy access for pro-reform groups. In testimony before a Senate subcommittee in September 2012, Public Citizen argued in favor of a 0.03% financial speculation tax both to raise revenue and curb high-frequency trading (Hauptman 2012). Numerous meetings took place among legislators and advocates. Since 2009, advocacy groups had been continuously lobbying Congress to promote the introduction of an FTT, as one campaigner reported: "Every week, when Congress is in, a team of 2, 3 or 4 people go in, who meet with a staffer who works for a Senator or a Representative and they have a 20 minute discussion about [...] the merits of a financial transaction tax."[5] Overall, however, the access of advocates to the policy process remained somewhat limited, with numerous Senate Finance Committee hearings on tax reform between 2010 and 2015 taking place without the participation of proponents.[6]

For tax proponents, a political opportunity seemed to open up when President Obama expressed vague support for taxing the financial sector during campaign speeches in 2009 (Anderson 2009). When he testified before the House Financial Services Committee in September 2009, Paul Volcker, former US Federal Reserve Chairman and then advisor to the White House, had expressed interest in ideas for a tax on transactions between banks, while also pointing to the problem of driving transactions to other countries (Braithwaite 2009). The Harkin/DeFazio bill introduced in Congress in November 2011, suggesting a tax of 0.3% on financial transactions, reportedly generated interest in the White House. Observers commented at the time that "despite some internal opposition within the administration—most notably from Treasury Secretary Timothy Geithner and key economic advisor to the Obama administration Larry Summers—the tax may be an idea whose time has come" (*The Huffington Post* 2011). Despite official reporting of Treasury Secretary Geithner's strict opposition to a transaction fee, Minority Speaker of the House Nancy Pelosi reported after a personal conversation with Geithner that "he was more open to some such fee than had been reported" (Rogers 2009). Based on interviews with key players within the administration as well as internal documents, Ron Suskind reported in his detailed journalistic account of the first two years of the Obama administration that the White House strongly supported an FTT in 2009 (Suskind 2011), with budget director Peter Orszag being in favor and the President himself even saying at one meeting, "we are going to do this!" (Suskind 2011, cited in *The Huffington Post* 2011). In January 2010, the Obama administration eventually proposed a Financial Crisis Responsibility Fee or bank fee, characterized as a way to make the financial sector pay for the benefits received through the TARP bailout. The fee would only apply to firms that received the TARP subsidies and with more than $50 billion in consolidated assets (The White House 2010). But neither a bank fee nor a transactions tax gained political traction.

Overall, political receptivity remained rather restrained. One advocate described political receptivity in Congress as "polite rejection."[7] The *New York Times* called the Obama administration's support of the FTT by the end of 2011 "lukewarm," "expressing sympathy but saying it would be hard to execute, could drive trading overseas and would hurt pension funds and individual investors in addition to banks" (*New York Times* 2011). Pleas coming from the AFR pro-reform coalition in November 2011, requesting that President Obama and Treasury Secretary Geithner "urge the Joint Select Committee on Deficit Reduction to examine a small levy on financial speculation as a revenue-raising measure," went unheard (AFR 2011b).

In February 2013, a new opportunity seemingly opened up, with Timothy Geithner and Larry Summers, two main FTT opponents leaving the White House after a staff turnover. Despite the official opposing stance of the government towards a FTT, Senator Harkin reported that the new Treasury secretary, Jack Lew, had been much more open to the idea (Zornick 2013). A pro-reform advocate interviewed in fall 2013 confirmed the increased political receptivity of Treasury officials after the leadership change, saying that "whenever we met with Treasury, they had good questions, which shows that they are interested. But recently they are becoming more open to the idea. Last time we met, they said, we are not saying no."[8]

On the whole, the lack of political enthusiasm might be explained by a closer look at public salience generated by the proposed FTT. A closer analysis of the media coverage of the FTT across the Atlantic reveals a clear disparity (Figure 5.1). By tracing the use of the word "financial transaction tax" in newspapers, the increase in issue salience becomes evident in Germany, France, and the United Kingdom. Unlike in Europe, where the FTT received substantial media attention, even in countries where it was not enacted, the FTT never turned into a high salience issue in the US. Although it is noteworthy that salience somewhat increased in 2011, with the FTT coming onto the political agenda of the G20 meeting in Cannes in November that year, media attention in the United States remained at a relatively low level.

Given the severity of the social repercussions caused by the financial crisis, one might expect that the public would rally round the general idea of regulatory reform and the more specific notion of a Wall Street tax dedicated to raising revenue for deficit reduction. A closer look at opinion polls in the United States reveals that public opinion was generally sympathetic to the idea of an FTT, but that it remained relatively unknown to a wider audience. An opinion poll conducted by the International Trade Union Confederation (ITUC) in June 2012 offers further evidence of the low salience of the issue in the United States. The polling numbers show that public opinion was generally sympathetic to the idea of a Robin Hood Tax, but that general awareness among US citizens was relatively low. Only 17% of respondents in the United States indicated that they had heard of a tax on financial transactions. After the concept of taxing financial transactions had been explained to respondents, a large majority of Americans (63%) indicted that they would support such a tax. In comparison, familiarity with the Robin Hood Tax was much higher in European countries, with 88%of respondents in France, 67%of respondents in Germany, and 37%of respondents in the United Kingdom indicating that they had heard about the tax before. France had the strongest support with 88% in favor of the tax, followed by 82% in Germany and 76% in the United Kingdom (International Trade Union Confederation 2012).

Measuring public salience based on the google search data confirms that the American public was rather unaware of a financial transaction or "Robin

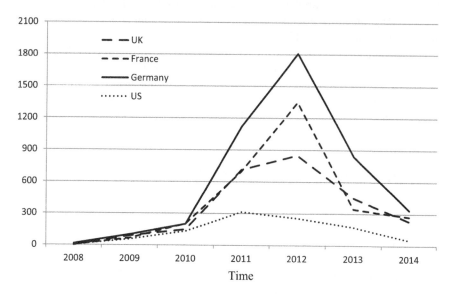

Figure 5.1 News coverage of the financial transaction tax.
Source: Factiva[9]

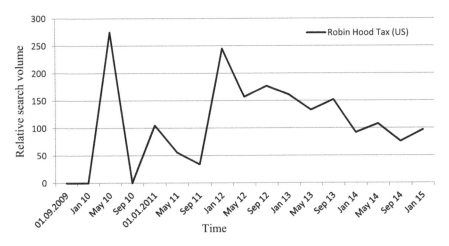

Figure 5.2 Internet search for "Robin Hood Tax."

Source: Google trends, available at www.google.com/trends/, accessed April 29, 2015.

Hood" tax. Figure 5.2 relies on Google search data to show the relative importance of the topic in internet searches. The term "Robin Hood Tax" was almost non-existent as a Google search term in 2009. Public attention only slightly increased when legislation was introduced in Congress in spring 2010 with the first FTT bill, introduced by Representative DeFazio. Another smaller spike in public interest followed in fall 2011 with the second introduction of the Harkin/DeFazio tax bill. It then fell again, until a brief period of attention in the summer of 2012, coinciding with the introduction of an FTT in France.

To sum up, political receptivity to an FTT in the aftermath of the crisis had somewhat increased, but remained "lukewarm." Public salience of the issue remained rather low, with Americans being largely unaware of the idea. Nevertheless, the policy proposal of a Robin Hood Tax floated in Congress and was debated in the White House. Pro-reform advocates discussed their reform ideas with Congress, as well as with Treasury officials.

Mobilization of diffuse interests and coalitions not forged

Based on the perception of the opening of a policy window, albeit a small one, pro-reform advocates started to build coalitions among themselves. The financial crisis had spurred a reform momentum with "more and more groups joining in," as one organizer remembered.[10] The introduction of a national FTT found strong grassroots support in the United States. The FTT became a rallying point for a broad range of civil society organizations, including labor unions and nongovernmental organizations. As one advocate put it, "unique about this is, we have meetings of the endorsing organizations, typically people who haven't even met each other before."[11] Starting in the spring of 2009, the broad-based civil society coalition "Americans for Financial Reform"—including more than 250 organizations ranging from labor and consumer groups, to civil rights organizations and small businesses—started to mobilize for the inclusion of an FTT in the Dodd-Frank reform law. Initially created in May 2009, the tax became one of several advocacy goals for AFR. Public Citizen, a Washington-based public interest group, officially took over the FTT taskforce within the coalition. When it became clear that the FTT would not be part of the Dodd-Frank Act, advocates started to give priority to other issues (such as a new consumer regulator). But the idea of a tax on Wall Street nevertheless "built up speed [...] and increased peoples' interest in it," as one organizer reported.[12]

A second group, the US Robin Hood Tax Campaign, joined the pledge for reform. Modeled after the existing European campaign, the US coalition was formally launched in June 2012, with 174 member organizations, including labor unions, consumer groups, environmental groups, faith-based organizations, housing activists, AIDS activists, and small businesses. First meetings among groups were convened in Washington, D.C. in 2009. As part of a steering committee, the nurses' union NNU and two Washington-based NGOs—Health GAP and National Peoples' Action—took over an initial leadership role. Prominent consumer advocacy groups, such as Public Citizen, and the largest US trade unions, such as the AFL-CIO, joined the meeting and became part of the broad coalition.[13] The idea mainly gained support because of its huge revenue-raising potential for easing global problems. Advocates mobilized in support of a tax on Wall Street as a mechanism to explicitly raise revenue "to protect American schools, housing, local governments and hospitals, to pay for lifesaving AIDS medicines, to support people and communities around the world, and to deal with the climate challenges."[14] According to the campaign, the tax would impose a small sales tax of 0.5%t (or 50 cents per $100) on Wall Street transactions, generating $300 billion, according to the campaign. Initially branded "the nurses campaign to heal America," the campaign was officially rebranded in June 2012, into the "Robin Hood Tax" campaign and close working relations were established with the UK-led European tax campaign to support the US campaign.[15] While the FTT was one lobbying priority among many for AFR, the Robin Hood Tax group focused on the FTT in a single-issue campaign.

In late 2011 and early 2012 pro-reform groups engaged in an outside lobbying campaign, using demonstrations, information events, press releases, and petitions to spread their message to the broader public. In a transnationally coordinated campaign, staffers of the European campaign spent several months in Washington, D.C. to set up the American campaign and Facebook website to align it with the European advocacy goals. Common campaign meetings started to take place in the United Kingdom and the United States.[16] Their campaign website (Robinhoodtax) presented the main arguments in favor of an FTT featuring all member organizations and supporters of the pro-reform campaign.

Although AFR and the Robin Hood Tax campaign had several member organizations in common, the two pro-reform coalitions stayed separate, instead of building a strong alliance. Early on, tensions among organizers had emerged, with the groups deciding to split into two different campaigns. Despite loose working relations, cooperation among the two US advocacy groups remained limited, and divisions among campaign groups became visible, as one advocate reported: "At global meetings there are often weird moments, why are US people fighting with each other?"[17] The two campaign groups were divided over the size of the tax and the question whether tax revenues should be specified in the reform proposal or not. While the international NGOs of the Robin Hood Tax campaign focused on a high tax rate and the purpose of the tax revenue, such as the fight for global climate change, the AFR campaign aimed for the introduction of a small tax rate to curb speculation in general, without specifying the revenue purpose. In the words of one AFR advocate: "We felt we should not even discuss how the money is going to be spent, because you divide over how it is going to be spent and we don't have the money yet."[18] Disagreement among the two coalitions also emerged about how to brand the campaign. Eventually, AFR refrained from adopting the populist term "Robin Hood Tax" and decided to lobby for a more neutral "Wall Street Speculation Tax" instead.[19]

Both campaign groups targeted their lobbying efforts at Congress. Numerous meetings took place among legislators and both campaign groups. Reflecting the divide between them, the campaign groups focused on two different bills, the "Let Wall Street Pay for the Restoration of Main Street Act" introduced by Representative DeFazio and later co-sponsored by Senator Harkin of 2009 and the Inclusive Prosperity Act or "Robin Hood Tax bill" introduced by Representative Keith Ellison in September 2012. What mattered most to campaigners was that both bills were stand-alone bills, "explicitly speaking about introducing a FTT mechanism, not attached to anything else."[20] While the Robin Hood Tax coalition mainly supported the Ellison bill with its higher tax rate and explicit revenue purposes, the AFR coalition was more supportive of the lower tax rate in the Harkin/DeFazio bill. One advocate of the Robin Hood Tax campaign reported about the divisions among the two groups: "We want them to be more supportive of higher rate, the 0.5 per cent rate that is in the Allison bill that we are pushing. They would like us to be more supportive of the DeFazio/Harkin. [...] We had never been happy with Harkin/DeFazio bill, the rate is too low, it doesn't generate enough money, no commitment to where the money will go".[21]

While AFR focused on legislative lobbying, the Robin Hood Tax campaign tried to generate more grassroots support aimed at raising public attention. The first public stunts were organized in the US by NNU under the campaign heading of "Heal America, Tax Wall Street." Numerous public demonstrations in close cooperation with the Occupy Wall Street Movement's "Tax Wall Street" campaign followed, with activists demanding "that the 1% pay the 99% back for taking our homes, jobs and money" (Robin Hood Tax Campaign 2010). In June 2011, the nurses' union organized the first public demonstrations, bringing 1,500 nurses together with labor and health activists to campaign for the FTT and against austerity. Protests took place outside the New York Stock Exchange and in front of the US Chamber of Commerce in Washington, D.C. In October 2011, members of Occupy Wall Street, together with members of the Robin Hood Tax

Campaign, organized another "Wall Street March," rallying thousands of activists to march from Zuccotti Park to Wall Street, pressuring policy-makers for a tax on financial transactions (Greenhouse and Bowley 2011). Organizers were trying to exploit the fact that nurses as care-givers with no self-interest were effective messengers, generally perceived as a very trustworthy source of information.[22] When the US Robin Hood campaign was officially launched on June 22, 2012, protesters demonstrated in front of JPMorgan Chase branches in 16 cities, including Boston, Chicago, Los Angeles, and Washington (Cohn 2012).

In an effort to circumvent domestic opposition, US pro-reform groups also targeted the international political process, advocating a global FTT. Both US groups also became actively involved in a growing international coalition. Both groups joined an existing network of international campaigners. The Institute for Policy Studies, a Washington-based think tank, started to host one-hour conference calls every three weeks and weekly telephone calls to coordinate the actions of international FTT campaigners around the globe.[23] In November 2011, NNU, in cooperation with the Robin Hood Tax campaign, organized a press event at the G20 summit in Cannes bringing in the celebrity endorsement of UK Oxfam spokesman and actor Bill Nighy. At a staged event, nurses from Australia, Ireland, France, South Korea, and the United States symbolically injected an FTT as an emergency measure to resuscitate the "sick" global economy (National Nurses United 2011). As one organizer remembered: "We were big in the street theater, [showing] how the globe is sick. So the nurses' campaign to heal America became the nurses' campaign to heal the world."[24] The event in Cannes was followed by another protest on May 18, 2012, aimed at the G8 leaders summit at Camp David. NNU organized a protest in Chicago with an estimated 1,000 people, including nurses, community groups, health activists, and members of the Occupy movement participating. Protesters wore green Robin Hood hats, demanding a "Robin Hood tax" (The Guardian 2012). Other international meetings took place among groups. NNU, national and international trade unions federations, including ITUC and Public Services International (PSI), together with international NGOs including Stamp Out Poverty and Oxfam, organized a first international meeting in London in January 2012 that brought together more than 40 activists from all over the world to discuss joint actions and decide on a common long-term agenda. A series of follow-up meetings at the international level were convened in Chicago and at the World Social Forum in Tunis in 2013.[25]

To sum up, the financial crisis seemingly opened a policy window for progressive reform demands and led to the mobilization of pro-reform advocates demanding the introduction of an FTT to raise revenue for pressing social problems. Although newly mobilized interest groups formed a broad-based pro-reform coalition, they could hardly act as transmitter of public opinion. Interest in an FTT remained relatively low among the broader US population and pro-reform groups were not successful in rallying the public behind the Robin Hood Tax. On top of that, the two US campaign groups failed to adequately cooperate with each other and organize their lobbying efforts in concert. The fact that there was no real partnership among the two pro-reform coalitions and that pro-reform advocates were divided among themselves about the appropriate tax proposal might partly explain the ineffectiveness of the campaigns to rally broader public and political support.

Weak governmental allies

Advocacy groups reached out to Congress starting in mid-2009 to identify supportive political actors. Albeit only a few, pro-reform advocates were able to recruit policy-makers to become active proponents of an FTT among the members of the Congressional Progressive Caucus, a group including 1 Senator and 75 members of the House of Representatives. In April 2011, the Congressional Progressive Caucus proposed a "People's Budget" for the fiscal year 2012, suggesting a "Wall Street gaming tax" on certain financial transactions (US House of Representatives 2012). The main legislative proposals including a tax were subsequently introduced by members of the Progressive Caucus, including the proposed bills by Peter DeFazio, Grijalva, Conyers, Ellison, and Sanders. Advocates successfully recruited legislators to join their cause, as one interviewee reported:

> In essence we know the people in Congress, who are placed well and will take up progressive ideas, but aren't too radical, so it is not like, 'oh no that guy again'. AFL-CIO and Public Citizen reached out to progressive Democrats such as Representatives DeFazio and Harkin, both on committees related to tax policy. [...] Ellison [...] is a progressive champion and that is how people identified those offices.[26]

Subsequently, alliances among insiders and outsiders emerged that pushed for the introduction of an FTT in numerous bills introduced into Congress. The main legislative initiatives developed in close cooperation among progressive Congressmen and pro-reform advocates. Tight links existed, for instance, among AFR, Senator Harkin, and Representative DeFazio, who have introduced several bills containing an FTT since 2009. One advocate remembered a meeting convened by the Representatives a few months after Dodd-Frank had passed in July 2010 with more than 50 pro-reform advocates present and at least 30 different organizations who worked on the FTT.[27] Insiders also worked hand in hand with groups on the outside, with respect to an Inclusive Prosperity Act or as the Robin Hood Tax introduced by Democratic Representative Keith Ellison in September 2012. In accordance with the Robin Hood Tax campaigners, the bill suggested that collected tax revenues would go to improving health care, including the fight against AIDS, as well as to combating climate change.[28] At 0.5%, the bill also suggested a slightly higher tax rate than the Harkin/Defazio bill. One of the pro-reform advocates explained the degree of cooperation in terms of legislation: "We helped write the Ellison bill. [...] We wanted someone to champion it and Ellison was willing to do so. NNU met with Ellison, they had the relationship; National People's Action backed up a little bit. The [Robin Hood Tax] coalition [...] helped draft legislation."[29]

The AFR coalition was more supportive of the bill introduced by Representative DeFazio and Senator Harkin. The two Congressmen worked hand in hand with advocates of the AFR coalition to develop legislation. A member of the AFR coalition discussed not only his key allies, but also how those allies helped to mobilize support within Congress: "Both offices [Harkin, Defazio] had been leading advocates on FTT for a while and so we have been working with them very closely. We have a track record with them, they are champions of the legislation, it helps that they are also talking to colleagues, getting the word out."[30] The AFR coalition also organized meetings among the Congressional offices and external financial experts, as one advocate recalled about their cooperation in early 2013:

> We put them in touch with other experts. They are interested in people with financial industry backgrounds to hear some criticism and want to know what Wall Street thinks. They love to hear when people on Wall Street have good things to say about the FTT. We helped coordinate the meeting. We put them in touch with Avinash Persaud, Wallace Turbeville and John Fullerton—all former JP Morgan.[31]

Although legislation stalled, pro-reform advocates and their governmental allies successfully put the FTT on the agenda of Congress, as one advocate put it, "just having someone to introduce legislation on FTT is huge domestically."[32] After legislation had been introduced, advocates tried to rally support among members of Congress to co-sponsor the bills. When Ellison reintroduced the Inclusive Prosperity Act (H.R. 6411) in Congress in September 2012, campaign groups launched a campaign asking supporters to urge other members of Congress to co-sponsor the bill (Nichols 2012). In April 2014, a print ad of the Robin Hood Tax Campaign appeared in the *New York Times* featuring a casino floor table urging voters to call their members in Congress to support the Inclusive Prosperity Act (HR 1579) to "stop Wall Street's high-speed gamblers."[33] Similarly, the AFR coalition threw its weight behind the bill proposed by DeFazio and Harkin in November 2011, with a letter urging the Joint Select Committee on Deficit Reduction to support a small levy on financial speculation (AFR 2011a). Overall lobbying success remained, however, limited, with pro-reform advocates being able to recruit only a handful of policy-makers, mainly from the Congressional Progressive Caucus leaders.

More prominent officials decided not to become advocates for an FTT. None of the sponsors of the various bills introduced in Congress had a comparable standing to the chairmen of the committees, Representative Frank and Senator Dodd, who pushed the consumer agency through Congress. Despite his general support for the idea of an FTT, the influential House Financial Services Committee Chairman Barney Frank considered the FTT in 2009 as a deal breaker for the Dodd-Frank legislation.[34] One advocate described how the FTT debate in Congress following the passage of Dodd-Frank came to nothing between 2011 and 2013, because, to the displeasure of advocates, they could not count the chairman of the House Financial Services Committee, Republican Representative

Bacchus among their allies: "This bill is going nowhere until a chairman says, he likes it, and Bacchus is not going to say that." The lack of support of a chairman meant that the bandwagon effect of other policy-makers joining the pro-reform coalition failed to appear. In the words of one advocate, the motivation of political actors in Congress to support the FTT bill without the chairman's backing was diminished: "It is not appropriate for me to sponsor a bill and tell people on the finance committee what to do; or I am on the finance committee and I am holding my fire; I don't want to do something the chairman isn't already doing and this isn't one of those things. So this is why we got pretty much no co-sponsors for Harkin/DeFazio."[35]

Despite the shock of the financial crisis and considerable mobilization of civil society groups in favor of taxing Wall Street, the FTT did not become a politically viable idea in the United States. The likelihood of success in the policy process of bills containing an FTT was considered to be so low that various banking associations did not even start to actively lobby against it. One industry lobbyist interviewed for this project reported that his association refrained from explicit counter-lobbying to proposed legislation by Harkin and DeFazio, saying "there is no real support behind it" and that proposed bills in Congress "just don't go anywhere." He also reported that the association was preparing arguments in case the bill did go somewhere.[36] Commenting on the likelihood of policy success, another industry representative confirmed that from the industry's point of view, "reality is, it is not going anywhere," saying that his organization only "lobbied for a while."[37] For banking lobbyists the momentum of the proposed bills was so low that there was simply no need to actively oppose it.

To sum up, although advocates found a few members in Congress with enough interest in the FTT to raise it on the political agenda, the pro-reform side could not rally enough co-sponsors for the proposed bills. With no prominent government ally leading the way on the FTT—neither the leadership of a powerful chairman, nor presidential support—and therefore diminished likelihood of policy success; outside lobbying could not rally Congressional support for a FTT. Despite close cooperation in insider–outsider coalitions among pro-reform advocates and individual policy-makers on numerous bills introducing an FTT, there was no bandwagon to join for other members of Congress. As a result, this reform wagon never left the station.

Conclusions

This chapter suggests that the advocacy function of mobilized diffuse interests in the realm of finance is tightly constrained. In the case of the transaction tax in the United States, activists—although organized in pro-reform campaign groups—had only limited success in altering government preferences during the post-crisis reform debate. None of the numerous bills that floated in Congress between 2009 and 2015 received sufficient political support, despite changes in the post-crisis institutional context in which financial regulation policies were developed with signs of increased political receptivity, as well as access of pro-reform groups to the policy-making process. What, then, explains the failure of diffuse interests' advocacy efforts in the immediate aftermath of the crisis?

Table 5.2 summarizes the main findings. Findings suggest that elements contributing to the shortcomings of the campaign by labor unions, consumer groups, environmental groups, and health activists on a transaction tax included a lack of efficient mobilization among pro-reform groups. Despite the extensive lobbying resources mobilized by outside groups as broad-based pro-reform coalitions, political support for a US FTT remained weak in the face of strict financial industry opposition and in the absence of prominent government allies in defense of diffuse interest groups. Neither were advocates able to forge coalitions with well-positioned policy entrepreneurs, nor with potent governmental allies who would push their cause through Congress.

Although a number of academic and private sector economists, such as Paul Krugman, Joseph Stiglitz, and Avinash Persaud, and development economists, such as Jose Ocampo and Stephanie Griffith-Jones, made important contributions to support a tax, including reports detailing technical feasibility, economic utility, and social desirability, none of the prominent voices could rally enough public and political support. Despite attempts, policy entrepreneurship defending diffuse interests largely failed on the national political stage.

Table 5.2 Summary of findings

Propositions	Findings
Scope conditions present:	**Yes.** Boost of idea for FTT through Occupy Wall Street marches.
1 **Favorable opportunity structures:** politicians under public salience and electoral constraints become more receptive and grant new access points to diffuse interest groups.	**Mixed.** "Sea change" in political receptivity in the perception of advocates; initial signs of support from the White House; and low public attention.
2 **Diffuse interest coalitions:** the organization as advocacy coalition spurred by the perception of a window of opportunity allows diffuse interest groups to promote reform goals.	**Mixed.** Broad-based advocacy efforts, i.e. Robin Hood Tax Campaign, Americans for Financial Reform, but little success in mobilizing public.
3 **Policy entrepreneurs:** activism of entrepreneurs as source of innovation, expertise, institutional resources, etc., thereby leveraging advocacy groups' influence.	**No.** Failed entrepreneurship of experts such as Columbia professor Griffith-Jones or financial expert Persaud to make viable political connections.
4 **Government allies:** Joining the bandwagon public officials actively side with mobilized diffuse interests to promote same policy solution.	**Mixed.** Insider–outsider coalitions only with low-level allies, such as progressive Members of Congress introduced bills, but no support from high-level allies (such as committee leaders or the President).
5 **Outcome:** Policymakers enact financial reforms reflecting diffuse interests.	**No.** FTT on Congressional agenda (several bills introduced), but no legislative success.

Findings also suggest that much of the success of diffuse interests in Congress hinges on the support of the President or party leaders in Congress who have an incentive to respond to broad interests as political leaders with "collective responsibility" (Derthick and Quirk 1985, 142). In the case of the FTT, political leaders did not endorse the reform policy between 2009 and 2014. Prominent political actors failed to actively promote the FTT in Congress as governmental allies. While the influential chairmen of the committees responsible for financial reform, Barney Frank and Chris Dodd actively backed the consumer agency as key governmental allies, lobbying efforts of diffuse interest groups failed to recruit prominent officials as governmental allies in the case of the US FTT. Pro-reform advocates found only a handful of relatively weak governmental allies in progressive legislators who were willing to take up the reform cause and actively promote a US FTT. Given the lack of presidential support for the introduction of a FTT, as well as the lack of support of prominent political actors such as the influential chairmen of the committees dealing with financial reform, a bandwagon effect for reform failed to appear.

The reform issue was also of moderate salience among the broader public and so incentives to act in the public interest remained relatively low. The pro-reform campaigns were not successful in their mobilization efforts to make a transaction tax salient and appealing for broader audiences. Other issues regarding a transactions tax also constrained and complicated reform advocacy. In the context of the crisis, conventional mechanisms that account for its lobbying influence, such as revolving doors between members of the industry and the regulatory agencies traditionally granting industry lobbyists privileged access, were at least temporarily undermined. One possible explanation for why financial industry dominance persisted even in a situation of severe financial crisis is thus the structural power of financial sector groups. Research revolving around the concept of "financialization" has identified the growing centrality of the financial industry in the US economy as a major trend in socioeconomic developments (Aalbers 2008; Krippner 2011; van der Zwan 2014). Due to the central position of finance in capitalist systems, policy-makers "are wary of introducing policies that may disrupt the 'golden goose' of financial sector accumulation and they are more likely to listen to the concerns of financial industry groups [...]" (Pagliari and Young 2013). The structural importance of finance might therefore explain why an FTT with potential distorting effects on "market efficiency" and capital flows has not gained widespread political support and has been met with reluctance by a majority of policy-makers, even in the face of a major financial crisis.

It was only in the context of the 2016 US presidential elections that the idea of a FTT made it back onto the national stage. The Robin Hood campaign culminated in May 2015, when long-time FTT advocate and presidential candidate Senator Sanders announced the College for All Act, including an FTT to allow for tuition-free public education, at a common press conference in Washington, D.C. Hillary Clinton's presidential campaign later took up the proposal and endorsed a narrow tax on Wall Street speculation. In July 2016, then, the Democratic Party Platform endorsed "a financial transactions tax on Wall Street to curb excessive speculation and high-frequency trading, which has threatened financial markets." While this seemed encouraging to pro-reform advocates, it is noteworthy that the party platform is non-binding for members in case of a legislative decision. The Democratic platform and the resolution passed by the Democratic National Committee in September that year also remained unclear on tax rate and revenue purpose, leaving a lot of leeway for further debate. Given the strong opposition of the financial industry, as well as of the Republican Party which has been in power since the 2016 presidential election, these political endorsements of a US FTT turned out to be empty election promises.

Notes

1 Lobbying concerned the Wall Street Trading and Speculators Tax Act (FTT) first introduced as S. 1787; H.R. 3313 in the 112th Congress and re-introduced as S. 410; H.R. 880 in the 113th Congress.
2 Information in this paragraph is based on interviews conducted with advocates in Washington, D.C. in fall 2013 and spring 2014.
3 The full text of the bill is available at www.govtrack.us/congress/bills/112/hr6411/text.
4 Interview 28 with a civil society representative, Washington, D.C., September 12, 2013.
5 Interview 40 with a civil society representative, Washington, D.C., September 11, 2013.
6 A full list of hearings conducted by the Senate Finance Committee can be accessed at: www.finance. senate.gov/hearings/?maxrows=all.
7 Interview 72 with a civil society representative, Washington, D.C., September 6, 2013.
8 Interview 40 with a civil society representative, Washington, D.C., September 11, 2013.
9 Articles containing the search term 'financial transaction tax' in British newspapers, "taxe sur les transactions financières" in the French language press and "Finanztransaktionssteuer" in the German language press, which refer to the relevant groupings of major publications proposed by Factiva (incl. *The Financial Times, The Guardian, The Economist, CNN, New York Times, Washington Post, Le Monde, Le Figaro, Agence France Presse, Frankfurter Allgemeine Zeitung, Süddeutsche Zeitung, Reuters, Spiegel Online*).
10 Interview 10 with a civil society representative, Washington, D.C., September 28, 2013.
11 Interview 116 with a civil society representative, Washington, D.C., September 4, 2013.
12 Interview 10 with a civil society representative, Washington, D.C., September 28, 2013.
13 Interview 28 with a civil society representative, Washington, D.C., September 12, 2013.
14 Further information about the campaign can be retrieved from: www.robinhoodtax.org.
15 Interview 116 with a civil society representative, Washington, D.C., September 4, 2013.
16 Interview 28 with a civil society representative, Washington, D.C., September 12, 2013.
17 Interview 81 with a civil society representative, Washington, D.C., September 11, 2013.
18 Interview 10 with a civil society representative, Washington, D.C., September 28, 2013.
19 Ibid.
20 Interview 81 with a civil society representative, Washington, D.C., September 11, 2013.
21 Interview 28 with a civil society representative, Washington, D.C., September 12, 2013.
22 Interview 116 with a civil society representative, Washington, D.C., September 4, 2013.
23 Ibid.
24 Ibid.
25 Ibid.
26 Interview 81 with a civil society representative, Washington, D.C., September 11, 2013.
27 Interview 10 with a civil society representative, Washington, D.C., September 28, 2013.
28 The full text of the bill is available at: www.govtrack.us/congress/bills/112/hr6411/text.
29 Interview 28 with a civil society representative, Washington, D.C., September 12, 2013.
30 Interview 40 with a civil society representative, Washington, D.C., September 11, 2013.

31 Ibid.
32 Interview 81 with a civil society representative, Washington, D.C., September 11, 2013.
33 The full text of the ad is available at: http://nurses.3cdn.net/16e1bdbd6705192175_
x8m6vqhh8.pdf.
34 Interview 114 with a Congressional staffer, Washington, D.C., March 17, 2014.
35 Interview 72 with a civil society representative, Washington, D.C., September 6, 2013.
36 Interview 1 with a financial services lobbyist, Washington, D.C., September 20, 2013.
37 Interview 100 with a financial services lobbyist, Washington, D.C., September 16, 2013.

References

Aalbers, M. B. (2008) 'The Financialization of Home and the Mortgage Market Crisis', *Competition & Change* 12 (2): 148–66.

Americans for Financial Reform (AFR) (2011a) 'Financial Speculation Tax', 21 October, available at big.assets.huffingtonpost.com/wallstreettax.pdf (accessed September 2016).

Americans for Financial Reform (AFR) (2011b) 'AFR Letter: Urge the Super Committee to Support FTT', 28 October, available at ourfinancialsecurity.org/2011/10/afr-letter-urge-the-super-committee-to-support-ftt/ (accessed September 2016).

Anderson, S. (2009) 'U.S. Government and Business Leaders on the Financial Transactions Tax', *Ethical Markets*, available at www.ethicalmarkets.com/2009/12/16/u-s-government-and-business-leaders-on-the-financial-transactions-tax/ (accessed September 2016).

Bartlett, B. (2011) 'Taxing Financial Transactions Is a Bad Idea', *Policy Perspectives: Tax Notes*, 19 December, available at www.academia.edu/3465424/Taxing_Financial_T ransactions_Is_a_Bad_Idea (accessed September 2016.)

Braithwaite, T. (2009) 'Volcker Backs New Bank Taxes', *Financial Times*, 24 September, available at www.ft.com/intl/cms/s/0/e5d0231a-a905-11de-b8bd-00144feabdc0.html#i xzz2OeUM3fFz (accessed September 2016).

Cohn, M. (2012) 'Campaign for Robin Hood Tax on Wall Street Rebooted', *Accounting Today*, 22 June, available at www.accountingtoday.com/blogs/debits-credits/robin-hood-tax-wall-street-jpmorgan-chase-63092-1.html (accessed September 2016).

Cover, M. (2009) 'Pelosi Endorses 'Global' Tax on Stocks, Bonds, and Other Financial Transactions', *CNS News*, 4 December, available at www.cnsnews.com/news/article/ pelosi-endorses-global-tax-stocks-bonds-and-other-financial-transactions (accessed September 2016).

Eisinger, J. (2014) 'Geithner Book Reveals Consensus, Not Vision, During Financial Crisis', *New York Times*, 21 May, available at dealbook.nytimes.com/2014/05/21/geithner-book-reveals-consensus-not-vision-during-financial-crisis/ (accessed September 2016).

Greenhouse, S. and Bowley, G. (2011) 'Tiny Tax on Financial Trades Gains Advocates', *New York Times*, 6 December, available at www.nytimes.com/2011/12/07/business/ global/micro-tax-on-financial-trades-gains-advocates.html (accessed September 2016).

Grim, R. (2011) 'Key Financial Reform Gets Boost from Occupy Wall Street', *The Huffington Post*, 26 October, available at social.huffingtonpost.com/2011/10/26/ transaction-tax-financial-speculation-occupy-wall-street_n_1024692.html (accessed September 2016).

Hauptman, M. (2012) ''Computerized Trading: What Should the Rules of the Road Be?'', Written Testimony of Micah Hauptman before the Committee on Banking, Housing and Urban Affairs', United States Senate, 20 September, Washington, DC: Public Citizen, available at www.citizen.org/documents/hauptman-testimony-on-compute rized-trading.pdf (accessed September 2016.)

International Trade Union Confederation (2012) 'ITUC Global Poll 2012–How Banks Can Contribute to Society: Very Strong Popular Support for Financial Transactions Tax', 18 June, available at www.ituc-csi.org/ituc-global-poll-2012-how-banks (accessed September 2016).

Krippner, G. R. (2011) *Capitalizing on Crisis the Political Origins of the Rise of Finance*, London: Harvard University Press.

Krugman, P. (2011) 'Things to Tax', *New York Times*, 27 November, available at www.nytimes.com/2011/11/28/opinion/krugman-things-to-tax.html (accessed September 2016).

National Nurses United (2011) 'U.S. Nurses to Join RNs from Across Globe at G-20 Summit to Press for Financial Transaction Tax', 13 October, available at www.nationalnurses united.org/press/entry/u.s.-nurses-to-join-rns-from-across-globe-at-g-20-summit-to-press/ (accessed September 2016).

New York Times (2010) 'The Tax-Cut Deal', 18 December, available at www.nytimes.com/2010/12/19/opinion/19sun1.html (accessed September 2016).

New York Times (2011) 'Tiny Tax on Financial Trades Gains Advocates', 6 December 6, available at www.nytimes.com/2011/12/07/business/global/micro-tax-on-financial-trades-gains-advocates.html

Nichols, J. (2011) 'Nurses Prescribe a White House Rethink on Financial Transactions Tax', *The Nation*, 3 November, available at www.thenation.com/blog/164378/nurses-prescribe-white-house-rethink-financial-transactions-tax (accessed September 2016).

Nichols, J. (2012) 'We're Not Broke, We Just a Need Robin Hood Tax', *Madison*, 19 September, host.madison.com/news/opinion/column/john_nichols/john-nichols-we-re-not-broke-we-just-a-need/article_b21573c6-019b-11e2-9a2a-001a4bcf887a.html (accessed September 2016).

Nichols, J. (2015) 'As Top Democrats Embrace a Robin Hood Tax, It's Time for Activists to Go Big', *The Nation*, 12 January, available at www.thenation.com/blog/194673/top-democrats-embrace-robin-hood-tax-its-time-activists-go-big (accessed September 2016).

Pagliari, S. and Young, K. L. (2013) 'Leveraged Interests: Financial Industry Power and the Role of Private Sector Coalitions', *Review of International Political Economy* 21 (3): 575–610.

Patomäki, H. (2001) *Democratising Globalisation: The Leverage of the Tobin Tax*, London: Zed Books.

Public Citizen (2014) 'Cost of a Financial Transaction Tax to Average Investor Would Be Microscopic Compared to Existing Fees, Public Citizen Report Shows', 12 March, available at www.citizen.org/pressroom/pressroomredirect.cfm?ID=4109 (accessed September 2016).

Public Citizen (2015) 'Lax Taxes—Corporate Tax Lobbying Report', 6 June, available at www.citizen.org/documents/corporate-tax-lobbying-report.pdf (accessed 27 April 2015).

Reuters (2013) 'Lew Says U.S. Still Opposed to Financial Transaction Tax', 11 April, available at www.reuters.com/article/2013/04/11/us-usa-tax-lew-idUSBRE93A0NR20 130411 (accessed September 2016).

Robin Hood Tax Campaign (2010) 'Robin Hood on Wall Street', 28 October, available at www.robinhoodtax.org/blog-entry/robin-hood-wall-street (accessed September 2016).

Rogers, D. (2009) 'Nancy Pelosi Pushes Global Financial Fee', *Politico*, 3 December, available at www.politico.com/news/stories/1209/30200.html (accessed September 2016).

Shackelford, D. A., Shaviro, D. N. and Slemrod, J. (2010) 'Taxation and the Financial Sector', *National Tax Journal* 63 (4): 781–806.

SIFMA (2011) 'SIFMA and Other Associations Submit Comments to the Secretary of the US Department of Treasury Opposing a Financial Transaction Tax in the US', 22

September, available at www.sifma.org/issues/item.aspx?id=8589935595 (accessed September 2016).

Suskind, R. (2011). *Confidence Men. Wall Street, Washington, and the Education of a President*, New York: Harper Collins.

Tannenwald, N. (1999) 'The Nuclear Taboo: The United States and the Normative Basis of Nuclear Non-Use', *International Organization* 53 (3): 433–468.

The Guardian (2012) 'G8 Summit at Camp David and Nato Protests in Chicago', 18 May, available at www.theguardian.com/world/us-news-blog/2012/may/18/nato-chicago-summit-g8-camp-d.

The Huffington Post (2011) 'Financial Transaction Tax Sparks Hopes That Obama Will Play Robin Hood In 2012', December 12, available at www.huffingtonpost.com/2011/12/16/financial-transaction-tax-obama-2012_n_1153841.html (accessed September 2016).

The White House (2010) 'President Obama Proposes Financial Crisis Responsibility Fee to Recoup Every Last Penny for American Taxpayers', Washington, D.C., 14 January, available at www.whitehouse.gov/node/7736 (accessed September 2016).

US House of Representatives (2012) 'The People's Budget. Budget of the Cogressional Progressive Causus. Fiscal Year 2012', available at grijalva.house.gov/uploads/The%20CPC%20FY2012%20Budget.pdf (accessed September 2016).

Zornick, G. (2013) 'Financial Transactions Tax Introduced Again—Can It Pass This Time?', *The Nation*, 28 February, available at www.thenation.com/blog/173134/financial-transactions-tax-introduced-again-can-it-pass-time (accessed September 2016).

van der Zwan, N. (2014) 'Making Sense of Financialization', *Socio-Economic Review* 12 (1): 99–129.

6 Diffuse interests and the limits of capture

Case study of the EU FTT

Introduction

In January 2013, 11 euro-zone states—including France, Germany, and Italy—decided to introduce a financial transaction tax (FTT) with the goal of making the financial sector contribute to the cost of economic recovery after the 2008 financial crisis, as well as creating disincentives for transactions in certain kinds of financial instruments considered to have contributed to the crisis.[1]

The case of the EU FTT shows all the signs of far-reaching industry capture. The political debate about an EU FTT was the subject of vocal and widespread campaigns by civil society activists who have put such a tax at the center of reform demands in response to the crisis. Pro-tax campaigns, promoting a small tax on the financial sector, the revenue from which would go to boost public finances, as well as global development assistance, were mobilized to pressure policy-makers. The initial European Commission proposal of September 2011 included a broad-based FTT, with very few exemptions; very much in line with demands from pro-reform advocates. However, as a consequence of massive industry lobbying, exacerbating differences among member states during subsequent negotiations, the Commission proposal was considerably watered down (Zimmermann 2014; Schulmeister 2014). The initial start date for an FTT of January 2014 had to be repeatedly postponed. Despite continued statements of support for such a tax by heads of state and government, as well as finance ministers of participating member states renewing their political commitment to an FTT—such as a commitment to such a tax by Germany's Chancellor Angela Merkel and French President Francois Hollande at a summit in April 2016—the start date of January 2017 has passed again. There is widespread agreement among experts that the final version of the FTT would differ substantially from the initial proposal, likely to be a narrow tax with many exemptions for various financial instruments (KPMG UK 2015; PWC 2013; *Financial Times* 2014a).

From the beginning, the financial sector rallied its troops against the proposed reform. Ahead of a G20 Summit in Cannes in November 2011, the Global Financial Market Association (GFMA), which speaks for the leading financial firms, sent an open letter to policy-makers, urging them "to reject any FTT proposal that might be raised and discussed at the upcoming G20 Finance Ministers and Leaders meetings" (GFMA 2011). Financial industry groups were unified in their opposition with "nobody in the industry in favor of a FTT."[2] Surprisingly, despite their unified opposition to an FTT, financial sector groups' initial attempts to block legislative action in the early phases of agenda-setting clearly failed. Financial sector efforts to water down legislation, as well as its advocacy for exemption, were much more successful during later stages of the policy process, once legislation introducing a broad-based FTT had been officially proposed. For pro-reform groups, the proposed Directive was "nevertheless a great success," as Peter Wahl (2014), the German pro-tax campaign leader, concluded. Given unified financial sector opposition, "it is a real surprise," as another pro-tax advocate put it, "that the idea of a general FTT made it up to an official proposal of the European Commission" (Schulmeister 2014, 28).

At the time of writing, the Commission's draft proposal is still being discussed at Council level. Although no policy change has occurred yet, I argue that dismissing the pro-tax campaigns organized by European civil society as marginal would miss important contributions to policy formation made by these non-financial groups during the early agenda-setting phase. Focusing on lobbying success during the agenda-setting phase of the policy process instead of actual policy change at EU level is interesting because the likelihood of eventual passage and implementation is relatively high. Notably, Mahoney (2008, 64) finds that policy initiatives at EU level have a passage rate of more than 80%, in comparison with only 11% in the United States (US). EU interest groups that see their advocacy goal reflected on the EU agenda have therefore already won more than half the battle. Moreover, to see a policy proposal on the EU's agenda that has been bitterly opposed by the financial sector is puzzling itself. Especially due to the structural power of finance, scholars have usually assumed that industry interests dominate the policy process in its early stages, able to block policy change even before the agenda is set (Young 2014, 372).

Hence, this raises questions about constraints on regulatory capture by concentrated financial sector interests. If the financial sector lobby was able to massively water down the proposed FTT during negotiations, why was it not more successful in preventing the political decision to introduce an FTT among eleven member states during the agenda-setting stage? Conversely, why were newly mobilized interest groups successful in pushing for substantial reform in the initial agenda-setting phase but not beyond? It is these questions that this chapter attempts to address.

The chapter offers one of the first scholarly analyses of broad-based Robin Hood Tax campaigns that emerged in Europe in response to the 2008 financial crisis. It will present empirical evidence for the conjectures set out in the theoretical framework in Chapter 2, based on interviews with financial lobbyists, policy-makers, and leading advocates of the Robin Hood Tax campaigns at EU level and in five different European countries (Austria, France, Germany, Italy, and the United Kingdom). Providing such an analysis is an important aim, given that this political episode is of high interest: not only was it highly publicly salient but also the debate on taxing the financial sector remains an important issue on the political agenda.

The chapter is structured as follows. We will first outline the main characteristics of the proposed legislation as presented by the European Commission in two different draft Directives (September 2011 and February 2013). After a brief description of the chronological order of events in the policy debate, the first section of the chapter attempts to trace the causal mechanism whereby concerted advocacy campaigns of diffuse interest groups were able to push for regulatory reform in tandem with active government allies at very early and highly salient stages of the policy-making process. The ability of financial sector groups to forge broad-based coalitions with other business groups and to refocus their lobbying strategy on the more "quiet" policy formulation stage will serve as an explanation of why the success of diffuse interests was largely restricted to the agenda-setting phase of the legislative process. The final section briefly summarizes the main findings and concludes.

Regulatory change and group influence

In September 2011, the Commission adopted a proposal for a Council directive on a common FTT system to be implemented by January 1, 2014 across the then 27 member states.[3] The objectives of this initial proposal were: (i) to avoid fragmentation of the internal market due to uncoordinated national financial taxes; (ii) to ensure that the financial sector makes a fair contribution to recover the costs of the financial crisis, as well as to compensate for the "under-taxation" of the financial sector due to the value added tax (VAT) exemption and acquire new resources for the EU; (iii) to create disincentives for transactions that do not enhance the efficiency of financial markets, such as high-frequency trading (HFT); and (4) to enable the development of an FTT at global level. With its intention to deter short-term trading "to dis-incentivize excessively risky activities by financial institutions," the EU proposal follows in spirit the tax proposal as it was originally presented by James Tobin, an American Nobel Memorial Prize-winning macroeconomist, with the objective to "throw sand in the wheels of our excessively efficient international money markets" (Tobin 1978). The proposed tax essentially aimed at "limiting undesirable market behavior" by rendering transactions considered risky to market stability much more costly. Unlike the tax on inter-currency transactions to stabilize financial markets as envisioned by Tobin, the EU FTT would, however, exclude spot currency transactions from its scope.

After an EU-wide introduction of an FTT as advocated for by civil society groups and proposed by the Commission in its initial draft Directive in September 2011 was rejected by a majority of member states—including the United Kingdom, Sweden and Luxembourg—a sub-group of 11 member states, spearheaded by France and Germany, decided to go ahead by introducing the FTT on a smaller geographical scale. In February 2013 the Commission adopted a second proposal for a Council Directive to implement an FTT through the enhanced co-operation procedure (ECP) which allows a group of member states to proceed with the implementation of the tax. After the European Parliament had given its consent, the Council adopted a decision in January 2013, authorizing 11 member states (Belgium, Germany, Estonia, Greece, Spain, France, Italy, Austria, Portugal, Slovenia, and Slovakia) to go ahead with enhanced cooperation.

Table 6.1 summarizes the main legislative characteristics of the proposed FTT. The Commission's comprehensive tax proposals following an "all institutions, all markets, all instruments" approach (Schulmeister 2014) reflected important advocacy demands of pro-tax activists. Largely in line with activists' preferences, the proposed tax had a wide scope, including derivatives and pension funds.[4] The tax would be levied on all financial transactions between financial institutions when at least one party to the transaction is located in the EU ("residence principle"). The proposal included a harmonized minimum of 0.1% tax rate on shares and bonds and of 0.01% on derivatives with revenues generated being shared between the EU and member states. The Commission estimated that the tax would raise around 57 billion euros every year (European Commission 2011b). The Commission's second proposal for eleven countries mirrored the scope and objectives of its original FTT proposal. After lobbying of pro-tax activists for an anti-avoidance measure to prevent relocation of financial activities, the second Commission proposal complemented the residence principle with an "issuance principle," whereby the tax would also be levied on financial institutions based in non-FTT jurisdictions when they trade in financial instruments that are issued in FTT jurisdictions (Grahl and Lysandrou 2013). Although pro-tax group' demands for an even higher tax rate of 0.5%, as well as for using revenues generated by the FTT to fund international development, were not reflected in the Commission proposal, the draft Directives were very close to their advocacy goals (Wahl 2014).

After the initial victory of civil society groups, member states made little progress towards implementation. Negotiations on the FTT in the Commission's formal indirect taxation working party among the then EU27, as well as in informal meetings among the participating eleven member states were subject to massive lobbying by the financial services sector, which led to political gridlock and made the introduction of a broad-based FTT increasingly unlikely (Zimmermann 2014, 3). Disagreement about key elements of the tax emerged among participating member states, including whether the residence or issuance principle should be adopted; the scope of any exemptions; maximum and minimum tax rates; and revenue allocation; as well as collection mechanisms. The German government was known to advocate a broad scope with few exemptions, while France and Italy advocated for a smaller scope with an exemption for bonds, certain types of derivatives, and repos.[5] Having introduced their national FTTs in 2012 and 2013, respectively, France and Italy started to promote their versions of the tax at EU level.

In June 2013, the Commission considered the implementation of a more limited tax on shares, expanded to bonds and derivatives in a step-by-step approach.[6] In May 2014, then, ten participating euro-zone countries (except Slovenia) announced in a joint declaration the progressive introduction of a scaled back version of the original FTT proposal that would "first focus on the taxation of shares and some derivatives" (*Financial Times* 2014b). In the eyes of MEP Sven Giegold, pro-reform advocate and co-founder of ATTAC Germany, the new

Table 6.1 The Commission's proposed FTT for enhanced co-operation (as of February 2013)

Policy	Measures in line with civil society groups' demands
Financial instruments subject to tax	Range covers all instruments which are negotiable on the capital market, money market instruments including repurchase agreements (repos), units or shares in collective investment undertakings (including undertakings for collective investment in transferable securities [UCITS] and alternative investment funds), and derivatives contracts.
Financial institutions subject to tax	Banks, markets, credit institutions, insurers and reinsurers, collective investment funds and their managers, pension funds and their managers, leasing companies, and special purpose companies.
Residence principle	The FTT would apply to financial transactions where at least one of the parties is established in an EU Member State and either that party or another party is a financial institution.
Issuance principle	The FTT would also apply to financial institutions based in non-FTT jurisdictions when they trade in financial instruments that are issued in FTT jurisdictions.
	Compromises/losses for civil society groups
Tax rate	Minimum rate of 0.1% for securities and minimum rate of 0.01% for derivatives.
Use of revenue	Use of tax revenue for international development not included.
Participants	Participating member states restricted to 11, via enhanced co-operation procedure.

Source: Adapted from Grahl and Lysandrou (2013).

proposal was "false labelling" and "window dressing" (Giegold 2014). Despite the official rhetoric of the participating member states in January 2015 "that the tax should be based on the principle of the widest possible base and low rates" (ECOFIN Council 2015), it seems likely that the draft Directive will be significantly less ambitious than the original Commission proposal and end up as a narrow-based FTT, similar to the 0.5% UK stamp duty reserve tax on a limited number of transactions. The FTT has largely been emptied of its critical elements and is now likely to miss the mark of effectively tackling speculative trading (Schulmeister 2014; Zimmerman 2014). After an ECOFIN meeting in December 2015 which revealed significant differences among the ten remaining participants (with Estonia having dropped out), the implementation of an FTT any time soon becomes even more questionable.

The policy debate

The crisis generated a debate about various proposals for imposing new taxes on the financial sector to contribute to economic recovery. Starting in 2009, the IMF, G20, and European Commission explored alternative forms that a contribution of the financial sector could take, including a resolution fund which would pay for future bank bailouts, a value-added tax on financial services, a financial activities tax (FAT) on the profits and wages in the financial sector, and an FTT.

The first official statements of support for an FTT were voiced by the German Chancellor Angela Merkel and the French President Nicolas Sarkozy in 2009. Both political leaders called for a debate on the FTT at the G20 Pittsburgh summit in September 2009 in order to recoup some of the costs incurred by the crisis. In the final communiqué, political leaders at the G20 called on the IMF to review "the range of options countries have adopted or are considering as to how the financial sector could make a fair and substantial contribution toward paying for any burdens associated with government interventions to repair the banking system." In a Resolution of June 2010 the European Council stated that

> the EU should lead efforts to set a global approach for introducing systems for levies and taxes on financial institutions with a view to maintaining a world-wide level playing field and will strongly defend this position with its G20 partners. The introduction of a global financial transaction tax should be explored and developed further in that context.[7]

After it had become clear at the subsequent G20 meeting in Toronto in June 2010 that there would be no consensus in favor of a global FTT, Germany and France pushed for an EU-wide FTT on the agenda of the European Council.

The Commission initially took a critical stance, favoring a financial activities tax (FAT) levied on profits and wages in the financial sector. Algirdas Šemeta, at the time Commissioner for Taxation and Customs Union, stated in October 2010 that he supported the idea of an FTT at global level, but that a FAT would be the preferable option at the EU level (European Commission 2010). Strong political pressure came from member state governments, mainly driven by France and Germany, in favor of an FTT. An EU-FTT also received broad political support in the European Parliament. In March 2011, MEPs voted in favor of an EU-wide tax on financial transactions by an overwhelming majority (with 529 votes in favor, 127 against, and 19 abstentions). Although the European Parliament has only consultation rights on the issue of an FTT, the political weight of a large cross-party majority among MEPs in favor of the tax sent a clear signal of broad political support for policy change to the Council and the Commission.[8] The European Parliament reiterated its support in subsequent resolutions.

In light of the political pressure from key member states, strong public support for an FTT, as well as civil society advocacy, the Commission changed its position. The first person to succumb to the pressure of the Franco-German alliance was Commission President Barroso, who "pushed the Commission services to draw up an FTT proposal" (Van Vooren 2012). By June 2011, the Commission announced its proposal for an EU-wide FTT for financing the EU budget in the context of the Multiannual Financial Framework. The proposal identifies such a tax as basis for a new own-resource system giving extra room for maneuver to national governments and contributing to general budgetary consolidation efforts.[9] In September 2011, then, the Commission presented a first draft Directive for an EU-wide FTT. After the Commission proposal met with resistance from some member states, notably the United Kingdom, the

Netherlands, and Sweden, a sub-group of 11 member states, led by France and Germany, decided to proceed with the implementation of a transaction tax via "enhanced co-operation," binding only participating member states to introduce the tax. Following requests from member states, the Commission adopted a new proposal for a Council Directive in February 2013 implementing enhanced co-operation in the area of an FTT. An attempt by the United Kingdom to challenge the legality of the FTT on the basis that it is extra-territorial and thereby undermines the European free market was rejected by the European Court of Justice in April 2014.

From the beginning, individual public interest groups supported an FTT. A network of development NGOs had been campaigning for a "Tobin tax" on currency trading for decades, since the idea first gained political traction as part of the anti-globalization movement in the 1990s to raise money for developing countries (Brassett 2013; Patomäki 2001). In September 2009, a group of NGOs sent a letter to the G20 urging heads of state and government to implement an international financial transactions tax "to pay for the cost of the crisis in the North," "to assist countries in the South to meet their development objectives," and to "contribute to a reduction in speculation" (WEED 2009). By late 2009 to early 2010 groups, supporting an FTT became more organized. Several national campaigns in support of such a tax—dubbed a "Robin Hood Tax," spanning not only currency transactions, but all sorts of financial instruments—were initiated by civil society groups, which were successful in gathering widespread political support in Germany, Italy, and the United Kingdom. Campaign groups promoted a tax with 50% of the revenue to be spent domestically and 50% internationally.[10] When prospects for the introduction of a global or EU-wide tax faded, groups mobilized for an FTT via enhanced co-operation, with revenues to be shared between international development, member states, and the EU institutions. The political decision to introduce an FTT among a sub-group of EU member states, with the support of the European Commission and the European Parliament, was a major success for the mobilized civil society coalition.

Conversely, and unsurprisingly, tremendous opposition to the proposal came from the banking industry. From the very beginning, financial industry groups were unified in their opposition to an FTT. In the words of one interviewee: "All [...] financial institutions agreed that we completely disagree."[11] The day the Commission presented its proposal for the introduction of an EU-wide FTT in September 2011, the *Financial Times* headline read: "Business attacks transaction tax plan." According to the article, "the proposal has been fiercely resisted by financial and business interests in Europe, pointing to a fierce political battle that lies ahead" (*Financial Times* 2011). After it had become clear that 11 member states were going ahead with its implementation and the likelihood of legislative success increased, industry groups intensified their lobbying against the legislative proposal to implement an FTT.[12] The proposal was substantially watered down during subsequent negotiations among the participating member states, which started in February 2013. Nevertheless, the decision to introduce a policy directed at punishing the financial sector speaks to the inability of financial sector groups to influence the policy agenda in line with their preferences. At the same time, the civil society campaigns in favor of an FTT were successful in channeling public support and influence the initial agenda-setting phase.

How can we explain the initial victory of diffuse interest groups who saw their preferences largely reflected on the policy agenda? Reversely, how can we explain the initial failure of financial sector groups to derail an EU FTT, despite their unified opposition, as well as their success in watering down proposed legislation once legislative debate had moved to the policy formulation stage? In what follows I will trace the advocacy activities of concerted advocacy campaigns by civil society groups, their ability to capitalize on the crisis and to forge coalitions with important government allies pushing for the same policy solution, leading to the decision among eleven European countries to introduce an FTT in January 2013. Subsequently, I will also explore reasons for failures of advocacy and shed light on the strength of the banking lobby during the policy-formulation phase.

Advocacy for an FTT

Contextual conditions: post-crisis financial regulatory environment

In the midst of a crisis of legitimation caused by the financial crisis, the dialogue among policy-makers and private sector groups was generally more adversarial than during pre-crisis times. Increased issue salience of financial reform also made the regulatory dialogue less conducive to private sector influence. Expressing frustration about heightened public attention regarding the proposed tax on financial transactions, one industry lobbyist complained that it was "difficult to have reasonable discussions if it becomes so much politicized."[13] The context for regulatory debate had noticeably changed for private sector groups and the mood swing in public opinion was clearly felt by industry lobbyists. This industry representative complained: "If there are behaviors which should be prohibited, let's prohibit them. But pretending to introduce a tax to regulate is an argument which uses the fact that there is a political opinion shared by citizens that banks are bad."[14] Public outrage and delegitimization of the industry were clearly felt by financial sector lobbyists who perceived the FTT as retribution for wrongdoings that led to the crisis. In the words of one interviewee: "We are the ones to be punished."[15]

The increase in issue salience in the regulatory reform context was accompanied by divisions among policy-makers and the private sector. One important way in which the regulatory environment has changed is that policy-makers started to call financial sector groups' expertise into question. The salience of financial debates had clearly weakened incentives for elected officials and politicians to openly heed demands coming from the financial sector. Wolfgang Schäuble, the German finance minister, for example, dismissed arguments from the opposing camp in November 2011: "The objections made by some who claim it would mean a substantial drop in employment and in the economy generally seem to rest on exaggerated and sharply challenged projections – and, more important, ignore the potential of such a tax to stabilize currency markets in a way to boost rather than damage the real economy" (*The Telegraph* 2011).

Interviews conducted with industry groups in Brussels and London corroborate the story that their influence on the particular content of the proposed FTT prior to the publication of the Commission's first draft Directive in September 2011 was rather limited. Before the financial crisis, industry groups were used to exchanging information with Commission officials at early stages of the legislative process, even before the publication of draft Directives. In the post-crisis regulatory environment, the financial sector had temporarily lost its privileged access to the policy-making process. One industry representative complained that there had been no pre-legislative discussion among financial sector groups and Commission officials before the first FTT draft proposal was published in September 2011, apart from the Commission's public consultation in early 2011.[16] In the perception of one financial sector representative, the Commission worked on the draft Directive "in complete isolation, not with the industry."[17] Another lobbyist reported that information exchange was difficult, with the Commission "shying away" from working with financial sector groups.[18] Other commentaries from financial lobbyists confirm that it was "difficult to have constructive discussions" with the European Commission and the European Parliament on the FTT.[19] This interviewee stated that his association was "having a very tough time" when trying to engage in discussions with policy-makers about the FTT.[20] Financial sector participants were generally frustrated by the policy process and their inability to exert influence.[21]

In the post-crisis context, industry groups realized that their arguments seemed to matter less to policy-makers. For financial sector lobbyists who reported having meetings with the responsible Commissioner Šemeta, as well as with Commission officials, discussions "did not have a significant impact." Disgruntled lobbyists reported that Commission officials were generally "dismissive" about financial sector concerns,[22] that the financial sector perspective was "irrelevant to them" and that the draft proposals did not reflect any interaction with the financial sector.[23] This explains why industry representatives were irritated when they read the first Commission draft. Private sector lobbyists reported that they thought the Commission draft, once proposed, was "that bad, you have to restart from scratch," that "not a single measure [was] acceptable," that it did not "accurately reflect how the financial markets work," and that the design of the tax was "fundamentally flawed."[24] Taken together, then, there is good evidence that the financial industry was not able to exercise effective influence over the agenda-setting phase of the regulatory policy process.

Changes to the post-crisis financial regulatory environment also forced financial industry groups to adapt their advocacy strategies. From the beginning, groups saw their advocacy efforts directed at blocking or vetoing any legislative proposal regarding an FTT largely curtailed. This financial sector representative complained that in the context of the crisis industry groups "were not in a position to take action" to affect policy decisions.[25] Aware of the potentially negative consequences for their reputation, financial sector groups did, for example, employ only limited outside lobbying strategies to oppose an FTT. In the context of huge bailout costs using public money, the financial services industry was facing serious reputational problems and saw itself deprived of the usual lobbying repertoire, as one financial lobbyist reported: "It is very difficult for the banking sector for example to go all out and oppose an FTT when they are beneficiaries of government bailouts [...] The financial sector has found it very difficult to publicly articulate their opposition to the FTT without seeming to be just serving their own interest. [...] the financial services sector has such a bad reputation."[26] Private sector groups also refrained from publishing position papers opposed to the FTT.[27] These findings suggest that the direct leverage of financial industry groups over the agenda-setting phase of the policy-making process was more constrained than in the past.

Political opportunities: access and receptivity

In the context of "noisy" politics, with financial reform decisions under public scrutiny, policy-makers' reservations towards industry lobbying were accompanied by new political opportunities for diffuse interest groups, in terms of access to the policy-making process and increased receptivity to pro-reform demands. First, new access points opened up for groups representing diffuse interests to actively participate in the policy process via the "national route." In the wake of the crisis, access to policy-makers at national level who were sympathetic to the reform cause allowed advocates to press governments to champion the FTT in the Council of Ministers or the European Council. In particular, the support of the French and German governments, two key member states responsive to reform demands, created pressures to adopt EU-level reform. High-level contacts with national governments were key to campaigners, as one leading advocate reported: "In the German campaign, they have some informal but high level relations with people in ministries. [...] Because we are small we don't have the capacity to take blunt action, we have to make the action pinpoint and that depends on good intel and contacts. We have good high-level contacts, especially in Germany and France."[28] German pro-tax activists, and their organizer Jörg Alt, a Jesuit priest, gained particular access to the Christian Democratic Party (Schulmeister 2014, 15).

Simultaneously, diffuse interest groups had access to EU-level decision-making via the "Brussels route" by lobbying the European institutions. Concerning access to the European Commission, one advocate reported that the responsible directorate-general, the Directorate General for Taxation and Customs Union (DG Taxud), was "one of the most accessible units."[29] The involvement of the European Parliament in the consultation procedure also opened up new opportunities for influence for civil society groups. The European Parliament, which had already demonstrated considerable sympathy to the idea of a transactions tax in 2000 following the Asian financial crisis (see Patomäki 2001, 178), provided diffuse interest groups with points of access which they used effectively to secure the adoption of a pro-reform stance. MEPs demonstrated considerable sympathy with the demands of diffuse interests, especially within the relevant parliamentary committees, such as the Special Committee on the Financial, Economic and Social Crisis (CRIS) established in October 2009, which led to the first European Parliament resolution indicating support for an FTT. Civil society groups had also been consulted by the rapporteur, Social Democrat MEP Anni Podimata, in the preparation of an "own initiative report" on innovative financing, including a proposal for an EU-wide FTT. In March 2011 the European Parliament adopted the Podimata report favoring the introduction of an EU-wide FTT.

The move to the G20 as agenda-setter for global financial reform offered another access point for diffuse interest groups. In parallel to the G20 meetings, Labour 20 and Civil 20 meetings were set up in 2010, representing the interests of workers as well as civil society at G20 level, an unprecedented move in global financial governance. At the London G20 in April 2009, a civil society delegation, including environmental groups, labor unions, and NGOs, which would later mobilize as the Robin Hood Tax Campaign, met with finance ministers and Treasury officials, urging them to propose a global FTT. One advocate reported about regular meetings with G20 leaders at the various summits dealing with financial market reform: "For the first time there was an L20 and the leaders of the trade union movements do what they call speed dating, groups will talk to heads of state. They were pushing the FTT in those meetings."[30]

Increased access of non-financial groups to the decision-making process was also accompanied by increased political receptivity of policy-makers to pro-reform demands. Civil society groups advocating for a Tobin tax to curb speculation had existed for over a decade, with little or no political receptivity to their demands. Despite the considerable mobilization of pro-reform groups after the Asian financial crisis in 1997/98, interests groups were unable to gain traction. According to one organizer who had been involved in the policy debate since the 1990s, the campaign for a global Tobin tax following the Asian financial crisis hit a "brick wall." He reported that "a lot of momentum built up, a sense that maybe something could happen here."[31] After the 2008 crisis, "high-level people in different countries were interested in what we were saying."[32] In the post-crisis context, political receptivity to pro-reform demands had clearly increased "compared to 2007 when we were those obscure socialist groups in Europe and people would have laughed at our prospects," as one advocate put it.[33] With MEPs concerned about re-election, it is little surprising that political receptivity was particularly high in the European Parliament. In the context of the crisis it was not popular for any political group to be against the FTT or to defend the financial services industry.

Most importantly, governments displayed a clear pro-reform orientation. France and Germany were publicly supportive of an FTT. French President Nicholas Sarkozy and German Chancellor Angela Merkel called for a debate on the FTT at the G20 Pittsburgh summit in September 2009. After it had become clear at the G20 meeting in Toronto in June 2010 that there would be no consensus in favor of a global FTT, France and Germany pushed even harder for an EU-wide tax. In a joint letter to the Belgian EU Presidency in July 2010, France and Germany's finance ministers, Christine Lagarde and Wolfgang Schäuble, stated their support for an EU-wide FTT, saying that the EU "shall pursue its efforts towards the setting up of such a tax that is both feasible and necessary" (EurActive 2010). With national elections looming in April 2012, the FTT presumably became "a pet project to woo voters" for French President Sarkozy (Van Vooren 2012). In Germany, the Social Democratic Party (SPD) pushed for the inclusion of the FTT in the coalition agreement with the Christian Democrats (CDU) in exchange for its support for the euro zone's fiscal compact, the new budget discipline treaty in early 2012 intended to tackle the euro crisis (*Financial Times* 2012).

Political receptivity towards pro-reform demands can be explained in light of increased issue salience and public pressure in favor of reform. Figure 6.1 provides empirical evidence for increased issue salience across different member states. By tracing the use of the word "financial transaction tax" in newspapers the increase in issue salience is clearly visible in Germany, France, and the United Kingdom. The FTT received substantial media attention, even in the United Kingdom, a country that opted out of the coalition of 11 countries proceeding with the introduction of a FTT. Media attention notably increased in 2011 with the FTT rising to the political agenda of the G20 meeting in Cannes in November that year. This was followed by a spike in attention in 2012, with the European Parliament voting in favor of an EU-wide FTT in May 2012 and 11 member states announcing their commitment to introduce a FTT via enhanced cooperation in June 2012, after failed Council negotiations for an EU-wide solution.

A public opinion poll carried out by ITUC in June 2012 offers further evidence of the high salience of the FTT debate in Europe. Only 12% of respondents in

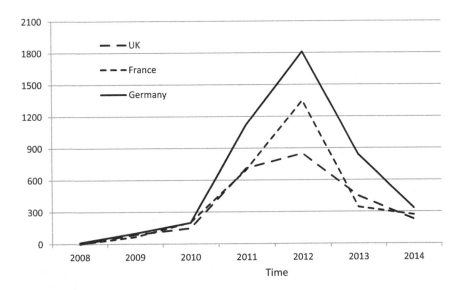

Figure 6.1 News coverage of the financial transaction tax.

Source: Factiva.[34]

France indicated that they had never heard of a tax on financial transactions. About 30% of respondents in Belgium, Greece, and Germany, and 37% of respondents in the United Kingdom answered that they were not familiar with the idea (International Trade Union Confederation 2012). The vast majority of respondents in EU countries, therefore, were able to take a position on a rather opaque financial regulatory issue. Early on, polling data found indications of widespread public support. In October 2010, a European Parliament Eurobarometer survey with 1,000 respondents found that 47% of Europeans supported a banking tax or a tax on financial transactions. Only 32% were opposed and another 21% answered "don't know" to the question whether they support a banking tax or a tax on financial transactions (European Parliament 2010). Remarks by Commissioner Šemeta in a speech in October 2010 also testify to the increased issue salience of the topic: "In recent months, there has been very wide public debate on this issue. Many different opinions have been voiced on whether and how to introduce a new bank tax, and indeed it is a subject that attracts a lot of popular attention" (Šemeta 2010). In a second Eurobarometer poll from 2011, when asked whether they were in favor of the principle of a taxation tax, a majority 61% of the respondents (with some variation among member states) answered that they supported the principle of an FTT. A staggering 81% of the respondents supported the idea of introducing such a tax in the EU, if international agreement could not be reached (European Parliament 2011). With the FTT becoming a high-profile issue in regulatory reform debates, and media coverage increasing, voters started to pay attention to the issue and electoral considerations became important to policy-makers. We shall now discuss how these opened-up political opportunity structures incentivized the development of collective action among pro-reform interest groups.

Mobilization of diffuse interests

The context of the financial crisis and notably the political opportunity structures it opened up was an important trigger for interest group mobilization beyond financial industry groups. As one advocate put it, "the FTT is a brilliant case of trade unions and civil society coming together and pushing for the same thing."[35] In the perception of another advocate, "cooperation [among NGOs and trade unions] has rarely been as smooth as in this case."[36] As such, the crisis turned out to be a major catalyst for the mobilization of diffuse interest groups and the formation of new transnational alliances among trade unions, NGOs, and grass-roots groups pushing for an FTT.

The mobilization of diffuse interest groups into an efficient network of closely coordinated national and European-level campaign groups was facilitated by pre-existing campaigns. Core ideas related to a Tobin tax had been developed before the 2008 crisis by a number of economists and campaign groups, who then played an important role as advocates for reform when the crisis hit. The crisis spurred renewed collective action among pre-existing advocacy groups and brought the FTT back to the top of the agenda for those groups who had made the FTT one advocacy goal among others. European civil society groups "revitalised and expanded the old network" (Wahl 2014, 4). The idea of a Tobin tax had first been put on the international agenda by the United Nations Development Programme (UNDP) in 1996 as an instrument for innovative financing for development. A first transnational political movement taking up the idea of a Tobin tax as part of a new global financial architecture emerged after the Asian financial crisis in 1997/98, notably with the creation of ATTAC, the Association pour une Taxe sure les Transactions financières pour l'Aide aux Citoyens (Association for the Taxation of Financial Transactions for the Benefit of Citizens) in Paris (Patomäki 2001; Wahl 2014). Dozens of other organizations have since included the Tobin tax into their reform demands, including development NGOs, such as the UK-based War on Want campaign against poverty, which in 2002 turned into the Tobin Tax Network and in 2005 into Stamp Out Poverty. In subsequent years, the institutional framework of the "Leading Group on Innovating Financing for Development," which brings civil society representatives and international organizations together, provided a platform to continue discussions on FTTs.[37]

What is important here is that when the financial crisis hit in 2008 European groups lobbying for a "Tobin tax" had a long history of campaigning that they could build on, as one advocate put it, "[...] because we had done a lot of the work, we weren't starting from scratch. We actually knew how to take advantage of that particular situation."[38] By the end of 2009, beginning of 2010, proponents of the FTT had their common position and arguments in favor of a tax, as well as counter-arguments to industry objections clearly laid out in a paper produced by NGOs that had been involved in discussions surrounding a Tobin tax for more than a decade, including the Halifax Initiative, a Canadian coalition of NGOs, ATTAC, and the faith-based network CIDSE.[39]

According to interviews with advocates, renewed broad pro-reform coalitions were made possible by a widespread perception among interest groups of a policy window for pro-reform demands. In the words of one NGO representative: "Since the end of 2008 and the financial crisis, a political space had opened up that was questioning the role of the banks and how they had been operating and looking both at reregulation of the sector and potentially greater taxation of the sector."[40] Another advocate reported that "with the crisis, the tide had turned and all of a sudden the FTT was part of political debates."[41] Pro-reform groups were keen to take advantage of the policy window the crisis had opened, as this interviewee put it, "when the campaign started, it was pure political opportunity; there was political space to exploit and that is what NGOs did."[42] Pulling together common organizational resources, groups established a loose European-level network to coordinate campaign strategies. In January 2009, several NGOs—including the European ATTAC groups, Friends of the Earth and the Seattle to Brussels Network—organized a first "network meeting" among European civil society actors in Paris to organize a campaign for comprehensive financial reform and decreasing the influence of financial institutions. A network of sub-groups emerged that decided to start campaigning for the introduction of a FTT at EU level. As a first common action, groups set up the campaign website "Make Finance Work." Table 6.2 gives an overview of the main national- and EU-level civil society coalitions advocating for an FTT.

Table 6.2 Main national- and EU-level civil society coalitions advocating for an FTT

Name	Founded	Number of members	Leading member organizations
Steuer gegen Armut (Germany)	2009	98 organizations	WEED and DGB
Steuer gegen Armut (Austria)	2009	—	ATTAC Austria
ZeroZeroCinque (Italy)	2009	50 organizations	ATTAC Italy and Action Aid
La Tasa Robin Hood (Spain)	2009	—	Oxfam
Make Finance Work (EU)	2009	—	ATTAC Austria
Robin Hood Tax Campaign (UK)	2010	125 organizations	Stamp Out Poverty, Oxfam, TUC, and Comic Relief
Don't Let the Big Fortunes Escape (Belgium)	2010	30 organizations	Le Réseau pour la Justice Fiscale (RJF) and ATTAC Wallonie-Bruxelles
Robin Hood Tax Campaign (Netherlands)	2011	—	Oxfam and Novid
FTT campaign (France)	2011	21 organizations	ATTAC France, Oxfam, Coalition Plus, and CGT

Following the creation of the European network, groups started to organize national-level campaigns, launching their own campaign websites by the end of 2009, such as the Italian "ZeroZeroCinque" campaign comprising 50 different civil society organizations or the German "Steuer gegen Armut" ("Tax against poverty") campaign, including 98 labor groups, NGOs, and faith-based organizations. In France, the "Taxe sur les transactions financières" campaign led by ATTAC also stepped up its advocacy efforts. In the United Kingdom, the "Robin Hood Tax Campaign" was officially launched in February 2010, bringing together about 125 organizations, including labor unions, development NGOs, faith-based organizations, and AIDS advocates. First meetings among key organizations forging the coalition including Stamp Out Poverty and Oxfam, two UK-based development NGOs, and the Trades Union Congress (TUC) started to take place in November 2009.[43] Follow-up meetings among NGOs took place to further coordinate national campaign actions at European level.[44] Weekly steering group meetings and videoconferences started to take place to coordinate national and European campaign efforts.[45] The conferences bringing together the European groups were also echoed at the international level, with regular calls organized by the Washington-based Institute for Policy Studies, bringing organizations worldwide together to push for a global FTT at the G20 summits.[46] International meetings were convened twice a year. The campaign groups also prepared briefings for journalists, especially at important meetings such as French-German summits.[47]

Pro-reform groups played an important role in transmitting public opinion to decision-makers, adopting campaigning methods designed to demonstrate that their policy demands have broad popular support. Groups launched, for example, an online petition targeting the European Commission. In response to the Commission's public consultation on taxation of the financial sector launched by the Commission in February 2011, citizens could sign up for an online petition supporting an FTT, which was send directly as a citizen response to the Commission. According to organizers, 400,000 emails had been sent to Commissioner Šemeta, Commission President Barroso, and the national Commissioner requesting the introduction of an FTT.[48] In its summary report of the consultation, the Commission noted that they had received "a very large number of petitions," with citizens being "generally in favor of a broad-based FTT" (European Commission 2011a). The pro-reform coalition organized another successful online petition targeting MEPs, urging them to vote in favor of a report on a common FTT system, including an FTT, prepared by rapporteur socialist MEP Podimata. A proposal for an EU-level FTT had been deleted from the report following a close ECON committee vote on the report with opposition to the proposed FTT coming from liberal and conservative MEPs. Following the ECON vote, the petition launched by pro-reform groups gathered several hundred thousand signatures within a week. In plenary in March 2011, although Liberals and Conservatives were much less enthusiastic about the proposed FTT than Greens and Social Democrats, a large majority of MEPs across national and party lines voted in favor of the Podimata report, including an EU-wide tax on financial transactions. Finally, advocates launched a third online petition targeted at member state governments, ahead of a European Council meeting in June 2011. Again, hundreds of thousands of petitions were sent to decision-makers sending a clear signal for reform. Action at European level was also complemented by actions at national level. In November 2009 the German campaign, for example, gave a petition that gathered 66,000 signatures within six weeks to MPs in the German Bundestag, which was followed by a hearing in the petition committee.[49] Between 2010 and 2012, members of the campaign were invited to give testimony on the FTT in front of four different expert hearings of the Bundestag. The role as transmitter of public pressure was also strategically employed by pro-reform groups in the lobbying efforts. After meeting Commissioner Šemeta in April 2012, a statement by the Robin Hood Tax Campaign reads: "This week EC Tax Commissioner, Algirdas Šemeta, received a civil society delegation representing FTT campaigns from France, Germany, Italy, Spain, Austria, Belgium, Denmark and the UK, as well as representation from the trade unions and green groups. […] The delegation sent him a clear message that many millions of European citizens are now behind a Robin Hood Tax" (Stamp Out Poverty Campaign 2012). Industry representatives testified in interviews that civil society efforts to mobilize public support were quite successful in the policy debate. According to one industry lobbyist, pro-reform advocates "substantially influenced" the positions of the MEPs and the final report on innovative financing at a global and European level.[50]

Public opinion clearly mattered in the regulatory process. Campaign websites set up by pro-reform groups aimed at mobilizing a broader public by providing comprehensible summaries of transaction tax debate and catchy slogans, such as, on the website of the UK campaign: "*In a nutshell, the big idea behind the Robin Hood Tax is to generate billions of pounds – hopefully even hundreds of billions of pounds. That money will fight poverty in the UK and overseas. It will tackle climate change. And it will come from fairer taxation of the financial sector.*" Groups also referred to public opinion in their submissions to the Commission's public consultation on taxation in February 2011. Oxfam wrote:

> Taxing the financial sector is highly popular. A You Gov poll commissioned by Oxfam and carried out in six European Countries found that the majority of people in the UK, Germany, France, Spain and Italy support a financial transaction tax. And on average more than 80% of citizens in the Netherlands, UK, Germany, France, Spain and Italy believe banks, hedge funds and other financial institutions have a responsibility to repair the damage caused by the economic crisis they helped to cause.[51]

Decision-makers explicitly referred to public pressure when explaining their decision to implement an FTT. Commissioner Šemeta, for example, referred to overwhelming public support for the legislative proposal in a speech in front of the plenary of the European Parliament:

> Europe needs to reconnect with its citizens. And the FTT is a prime example of a project which can help to achieve this. 64 per cent of EU citizens support the FTT, according to the latest Eurobarometer survey. This is a highly popular initiative, which Europeans believe in […]. The broad-based FTT is the one that […] many stakeholders and citizens want.
>
> (Šemeta 2014)

Interviewees supporting the tax linked the success of the campaign to widespread public support, saying that campaign actions mattered most when they reflected favorable public opinion.[52] Pro-reform advocates reported that policy-makers "value when we do involve European citizens […]. Anything that shows the popularity of the idea strengthens their case."[53] Proponents of the tax also explained the political success of the idea in the European Parliament with reference to public support: "MEPs reacted pretty quickly to the ground swell of support in their constituencies. Citizens across Europe are in favor of an FTT, it is popular with the voters."[54] Another campaigner made the same argument, explaining Commissioner Šemeta's support of the tax as "partly due to public pressure."[55] This proponent of the tax simply said: "We have public opinion."[56]

Similarly, interviewees from the financial services industry opposed to the introduction of the tax explained their inability to prevent regulatory reform by referring to "the weight of public opinion." One industry attributed pro-reform campaigns "significant impact," because "they have been very effective in engaging public support."[57] In the eyes of one interviewee, "NGOs and the mobilization of citizens [were] far better placed than any industry body" in the political debate.[58] Another financial industry lobbyist clearly linked political reform efforts to public opinion, saying that "pretending to introduce a tax to regulate is an argument which uses the fact that there is a political opinion shared by citizens that banks are bad and not managing rightly."[59] Private sector groups felt that adverse public opinion put them at a disadvantage in reform discussions; as one interviewee put it, "quite a lot of the public debate hasn't happened in the way I think it would have been useful to happen [...] because the financial services sector [...] is so tainted by the financial crisis."[60]

As predicted, diffuse interest groups acted as a transmitter of public opinion, putting increasing pressure on policy-makers to actively pursue regulatory change, even counter to the interests of the more powerful financial lobby. In the next section we will focus on the role of legislators in bringing about actual reform change.

Government allies

In light of the electoral popularity of the FTT, it is scarcely surprising that the European Parliament acted as a real champion of reform, voicing the concerns of European citizens. Although the Parliament's role regarding the FTT was merely consultative, it was clear to pro-reform advocates that a large cross-party majority among MEPs in favor of a transaction tax would send a clear signal of political support for policy change to the Council and the Commission.[61] The case of the FTT is characterized by an insider–outsider coalition. Early on, members of the Party of European Socialists and the European Green Party became active government allies, defending diffuse interests on the political stage. Although close ties among groups and parties, notably between the European ATTAC movement and the Green Party, existed, group–legislator relationships were formalized after the financial crisis. Under the official framework of a pro-reform coalition dubbed "Europeans for Financial Reform" (EFFR), interest groups on the outside worked together with policy-makers on the inside pushing for the same policy solution. In early 2009, the European Socialist Party together with the Green Party organized a coalition of pro-reform groups, mainly in tandem with trade unions. The coalition, bringing together the socialist and green parties in the European Parliament with trade unions and development NGOs, was organized by the President of the Party of European Socialists, Poul Nyrup Rasmussen, modeling the coalition after the "Americans for Financial Reform" initiative. By setting up the EFFR coalition, the Party of European Socialists had actively pursued the objective of "working and networking with partners from civil society" in order to empower civil society lobbying in the field of financial regulation usually dominated by financial sector groups. According to participants, the existing cooperation among the S&D group and labor unions was formalized, so that for the first time an insider–outsider coalition emerged.[62] Within the formalized EFFR coalition, 23 groups, including the trade union movement, represented by the European Trade Union Confederation (ETUC), as well as national-level unions, such as the German DGB and the British Trades Union Congress (TUC), were able to take part in monthly meetings with MEPs. Table 6.3 gives an overview of the main interest groups involved in the EFFR coalition.

Overall, the campaign run by pro-reform advocates and MEPs pushing for the same policy objective was closely coordinated. For EFFR a new position of

Table 6.3 Participants in the "Europeans For Financial Reform" coalition

Name	Founded	Number of members	Type of organization
Party of European Socialists	1973	32 member parties	European political party
The Greens	2004	16 member parties	European political party
Global Progressive Forum (GPF)	2001	5 partners	NGO
Foundation for European Progressive Studies (FEPS)	2004	50 foundations and think tanks	Social democratic think tank
European Trade Union Confederation (ETUC)	1973	83 trade unions	Independent non-profit EU consumer organization
Solidar	1948	56 member organizations	European network of NGOs
Austrian Trade Union Federation (ÖGB)	1945	1,333,421	Trade union
Confederation of German Trade Unions (DGB)	1949	6 million	Trade union
IG Metall	1891	2.4 million members	Metalworkers' union
TUC	1868	6.5 million	Trade union
UNI global union	2000	20 million	Global union federation

a "Project Officer for Financial Reform" in Brussels to coordinate the meetings was created. With preferences largely aligned, for advocates, the cooperation with MEPs across party lines was "positive, without any reservations."[63] According to one trade union representative, the European Parliament was a "good ally" and pro-reform advocates "were in safe hands in the EP."[64] Individual MEPs also became important allies to pro-reform groups, such as Social Democrat MEP Anni Podimata, who prepared a report on a common FTT system as the rapporteur for the S&D group. This provided another important access point for the diffuse interest groups. In March 2011, the European Parliament adopted the Podimata report favoring the introduction of an EU-wide tax on financial transactions. Sven Giegold, a German MEP and spokesperson of the Green Party on finance and the economy, was another ally, actively promoting pro-reform demands in the ECON Committee of the European Parliament. As co-founder of the German ATTAC, as well as a member of the Tax Justice Network, the Green MEP has been supportive of a Tobin tax for over a decade.[65]

In early 2010, the EFFR coalition officially launched its campaign "A Financial Transactions Tax, Now." A campaign website was set up, summarizing the main arguments in favor of an FTT. The pro-reform groups framed the case for introducing an FTT not only in terms of curbing high-risk speculative activities but also as a means of enhancing fairness by increasing government revenue to support long-term public investment. For pro-reform advocates, the FTT was one answer to the financial crisis and for the banking sector to make a useful contribution.[66] In January 2011, grassroots groups advocating for an FTT—including the UK Robin Hood Tax Campaign, the German Tax against Poverty and ATTAC—entered into an informal alliance with the EFFR coalition.[67] Meetings as well as monthly teleconferences started to take place among national grassroots campaigns and the EFFR coalition to synchronize reform tactics, coordinate campaigns, and agree on common advocacy strategies.[68] One example of successful cooperation among the advocacy coalition was the coordinated response by civil society organizations to the Commission's public consultation on taxation of the financial sector, launched in February 2011. The Make Finance Work network, the Robin Hood Tax Campaign, and the EFFR coalition closely coordinated their replies to the Commission's consultation, providing all member organizations with a common template. Answers to the consultation questionnaire were drafted in cooperation with leading academics (e.g., economist Stephan Schulmeister at the Austrian Institute of Economic Research) sending a clear message to the Commission that an FTT should be introduced at EU level.[69] Non-financial groups had significantly increased their mobilization in the regulatory debate with NGOs, trade unions, and research institutes submitting even more replies to the Commission's public consultation than financial sector groups (European Commission 2011a).

After mounting political support for an FTT from 11 member states, including Germany and France, as well as overwhelming majority in the European Parliament, the European Commission jumped on the reform bandwagon and became an important political ally for diffuse interest groups starting to actively promote a FTT in 2011. In June 2011, Commission President Barroso publicly supported an EU-wide FTT (*Politico* 2011). Lobbying activity was focused mainly on DG Taxud. Civil society representatives reported that they had meetings on a regular basis with the cabinet, or the team of personal advisors to the Commissioner, discussing questions of the technical feasibility of the tax, the tax rate, the tax base as well as the principle of residence and ownership.[70] Numerous meetings among cabinet-level Commission officials of DG Taxud and pro-reform advocates, including TUC, Oxfam, and Stamp out Poverty took place "with very frank discussions and exchange of technical details of the proposal," in the perception of one of the participating interest group representatives.[71] Before and after the Commission issued its draft Directives, formal as well as informal meetings took place among advocacy groups and the Commissioner for Taxation and Customs Union, Algirdas Šemeta, personally.[72]

Several comments from pro-reform advocates and Commission officials illustrate the coordination among interest groups and DG Taxud, regarding the proposed FTT. One advocate gave the following explanation of the degree of cooperation and teamwork among pro-reform interest groups and Commission officials:

> Basically we have a common objective here. It is about understanding where they think the problems are and for us as civil society to be able to make interventions either through some degree of high level contact or through grassroots [...]. It is our intention with the campaign to strengthen this relationship [...].We need the intel from them and they can sometimes value our expertise.[73]

One advocate active on the FTT noted the degree of agreement among Commission officials and campaigners, working hand in hand to promote their shared policy goal: "We worked quite close with them [Commission officials] in terms of edging the Robin Hood Tax argument. There was a good working relationship among NGOs and the Commission. [...] Some speeches by Šemeta we could have written ourselves."[74] In April 2012, Stamp Out Poverty, one of the leading advocacy groups, published the following statement on its website about a meeting with the Commissioner to display the degree of support the civil society campaign received from the Commission: "The meeting was informative about next steps and it was held in a good spirit. We gave the Commissioner a Robin Hood Tax badge as we were leaving, which he was happy to wear for a photograph" (Stamp Out Poverty Campaign 2012).

Pro-reform groups in turn were eager to gain the Commission's recognition by deploying technical advice to become an accepted interlocutor. One campaign leader reported:

By talking to us [Commission officials] realized that we were not ignorant on the subject because we spent a lot of time researching it and developing 'myth-busting' briefings, countering every single argument from the financial lobby and we called upon our own experts to get into the 'nitty-gritty' of the proposal. So [Commission officials] would see, they are not dealing with immature [people] campaigning for a good idea, very naively.[75]

On the other side, one Commission official confirmed how helpful the cooperation with interest group allies was during the legislative process in framing technical arguments to counter the opposition from financial services groups:

Some of those [nonfinancial groups] had gone one step further, not only requesting the introduction of a Tobin Tax to fight poverty in the world but also investigating technical feasibility, how such a tax could be designed. How can you best respond to critiques from the banking lobby? Interest groups tried to provide assistance to the Commission [...] which was sometimes quite helpful.[76]

Pro-reform advocates were important partners in providing necessary technical expertise to counter arguments against economically harmful effects of the proposed FTT to both the European Parliament and the European Commission. While exchanges with the Commissioner were highly political, technical policy debates took place among advocates and Commission officials at officer level.[77] This gave pro-reform groups opportunities to press for their policy demands to be considered in the impact assessments and draft Directives. To acquire the necessary technical know-how, campaign groups closely cooperated with development economists, such as Columbia professor Stephanie Griffith-Jones and Stephan Schulmeister at the Austrian Institute for Economic Research. Also former financial industry employees or "City insiders" such as Avinash Persaud of Intelligence Capital and Sony Kapoor of Re-Define became part of the civil society network.[78]

One example of a technical input from campaign groups included in the Commission's impact assessment concerns the potential effects of the FTT on economic growth. A first impact assessment presented by the Commission in September 2011 estimated that a FTT would lead to negative effects on GDP (European Commission 2011c). The impact assessment's conclusion was then repeatedly cited in position papers by financial industry associations opposing the measure (*Financial Times* 2012; Alternative Investment Management Association 2012). In cooperation with experts, civil society activists provided the necessary technical expertise to the European Parliament and the Commission to make an important counter-argument casting doubt on the initial calculations. In a report prepared for the Robin Hood Tax campaign, two experts—Griffith-Jones and Persaud—were able to show that the model used by the Commission to measure effects of a FTT on the level of GDP had been recently updated and would lead to a far more positive estimate in its updated version (Griffith-Jones and Persaud 2012). In February 2012, the two experts gave testimony in front of the European Parliament's ECON Committee hearing, opposing the calculations in the impact assessment. Echoing their report, they argued that the overall impact of a FTT would be positive, leading to a 0.25% increase in GDP and not, as argued by the Commission's impact assessment, to a long-run loss of GDP of -0.53% (Economic and Monetary Affairs Committee 2012). Advocacy groups also arranged meetings among Commission officials and tax experts, who laid out economic arguments in favor of a transactions tax, as well as technical details of its feasibility.[79] In a second impact assessment presented in February 2013, the Commission eventually changed its calculations and rephrased its conclusions, saying that depending on the simulation, if an FTT was used for productive public investment, it might show a positive impact on GDP (European Commission 2013).

A second example concerning the debate on the issuance principle illustrates how pro-reform groups successfully included technical amendments in the Commission's second draft Directive by lobbying member states and the European Parliament. According to one Commission official, the Commission adopted the issuance principle in its second draft Directive in February 2013 after the European Parliament had included an amendment in its opinion in May 2012, suggesting complementing the residence principle with the issuance principle. He clearly linked the Parliament's adoption to civil society input.[80] Campaign leaders reported that a range of face-to-face meetings with Commission officials and MEPs took place between May and December 2012, with groups pushing for the inclusion of the issuance principle. In parallel with their lobbying efforts at EU level, pro-reform advocates also addressed the member state governments and national-level tax officials, notably in France and Germany.[81]

To sum up: policy-makers in tandem with newly mobilized non-financial interest groups formed a broad-based pro-reform coalition as a countervailing force to financial sector interests. The European Commission and the European Parliament became important government allies to diffuse interest groups, pushing for the same policy solution. Advocates favoring a broad-based FTT closely cooperated with MEPs, as well as with Commission officials, in "insider–outsider" coalitions, trying to find arguments against industry objections referring to technical feasibility, as well as economic desirability. Advocates found strong government allies in MEPs, notably in the S&D and Green Party who promoted the proposal of an FTT in the ECON Committee and before plenary votes. Although the European Parliament's opinion has no legally binding character regarding the FTT, its support sent a clear political signal to the Commission and the Council. In addition, pro-reform advocates had well-established working relations with Commission officials and the Commissioner responsible for taxation. The coalition of pro-reform advocates was an important partner in deploying necessary technical expertise to decision-makers at an early stage of the policy formation process.

While this causal explanation has tried to answer the question of why financial sector groups, despite their unified position against regulatory change, could not prevent the decision to introduce an FTT by 11 member states, in the next section we will try to shed some light on changing reform dynamics during the policy formulation phase, which led to a considerable watering down of the proposed legislation.

Changed contextual conditions: low-salience politics

When the legislative debate moved to the policy formulation stage, salience slowly faded away and the FTT made the headlines less and less often. The decline in issue salience is again visible in Figure 6.1. An upsurge in interest in the issue in 2012, when 11 member states signaled their willingness to proceed with the introduction of an FTT by enhanced co-operation, was followed by a steady decline in press coverage throughout 2013, until mid-2014 when it registered the lowest level of attention since the start of reform debates in 2009. The drop in public attention parallels the move of legislative debates from the top of policy agendas to working group meetings. Shortly after the Commission had presented a second draft Directive for enhanced co-operation in February 2013, negotiations moved to the Commission's indirect taxation working party. These working party meetings (among all the then 27 member states) were characterized by a noticeable "quietening" of regulatory debates, with much less public scrutiny. Negotiations started to take place in unofficial meetings among participating member states prior to the formal working party meetings. Discussions about proposed legislation were thereby narrowed down from a broader public debate to a limited circle of participants and non-official working party papers. It is also indicative of the fading salience of the policy issue that in June 2013 the FTT was not included on the agenda of the ECOFIN Council, nor that of the EU's Summit. Reform discussions in informal meetings resulted in a perceived lack of transparency in the decision-making process. Non-participating member states criticized the negotiations as "closed process," "a political deal negotiated largely in secret" (*Financial Times* 2014b). In June 2012, Green MEP and supporter of the FTT Lamberts expressed his frustration about the policy process:

> [I]t has become clear that the proposal for the tax, presented by the European Commission in February, is being torn apart by governments with close relationships to the financial lobbies. Since they [governments] are acting behind closed doors, in ambassadors' meetings, in central bankers' gatherings, beyond public pressure and democratic accountability, they feel free to destroy the Commission's ambitious proposals.
>
> (Lamberts 2013)

When debates moved from high issue salience to lower issue salience and from broad democratic debate toward special interest bargaining, new possibilities opened up for exemption, delay, and modification, beneficial to industry interests. It is therefore hardly surprising that financial industry groups started to step up their lobbying efforts directed at member states' negotiations in the Council. According to one financial sector representative: "We haven't even tried to contact the Commission on this. Parliament is an area where we might be lobbying more but we haven't done anything. We believe that it is really the governments that are going to decide and primarily the French and German governments."[82] Up until the decision to proceed via enhanced cooperation at the beginning of 2013, the likelihood of legislative success of an EU-wide FTT seemed too remote to financial sector groups to actively engage in counter-lobbying. Such groups had therefore limited their lobbying efforts to stating their opposition to a FTT in the public consultation without investing resources into organizing concerted advocacy campaigns trying to block legislation. One interviewee reported that industry lobbyists conceded that they did not take the proposed FTT seriously, thinking that "anything in the European context could always be blocked by the UK" without realizing "that in fact, [enhanced cooperation] was a way around it."[83] Similarly, industry lobbyists interviewed for this project reported that they did not actively lobby against proposed legislation in the early phases of the legislative process, when the Commission presented a draft Directive for an EU-wide FTT in September 2011.[84] For banking lobbyists the possibility that the EU would agree on a FTT seemed far from imaginable. With the second Commission proposal in February 2013, 11 member states signaled their willingness to proceed with an FTT and the chances of legislative success of such a tax improved greatly. Industry groups subsequently changed their lobbying strategy and started to actively push back, launching "a concerted and broad attack" against the FTT from March to June 2013 (Persaud 2013).

Financial sector groups employed four different lobbying strategies, mainly addressed at the participating member states. First, they started a massive outside lobbying campaign. One effect of increased salience and actor plurality was that opponents of an FTT had been rather reticent in making a public case outright opposing such a tax in the early phases of the policy process and the memory of the financial crisis still fresh. After the second Commission proposal and under conditions of more quiet politics, financial industry groups changed their lobbying strategy. In early 2013, banks (Goldman Sachs, Deutsche Bank, Citigroup, and Morgan Stanley) and their lobbying associations (International Banking

Federation [IBF] and European Fund and Asset Management Association [EFAMA]) published a range of research reports presenting empirical evidence against an FTT. In its research report "Financial Transaction Tax: how severe?" Goldman Sachs claimed the proposed FTT would lead to a massive tax burden for the banking sector, amounting to 170 billion euros. The report further claimed that "the burden of the FTT would fall on retail investors" (Goldman Sachs 2013). In a research report from March 2013, Deutsche Bank stated its opposition to the proposed tax more explicitly, saying that "this is a bad law and should be scrapped" (Deutsche Bank Research 2013). Several more studies, press releases, and commentaries in major newspapers brought arguments forward against the FTT (Bloomberg Business 2013; *Financial Times* 2013a, 2013b).

A second advocacy strategy employed by financial sector groups was to advocate for exemptions from the scope of the tax. German MEP Giegold remarked in July 2013: "Many opponents of the tax in the financial industry and in politics have changed their strategy in the last couple of months: Instead of fighting the tax directly, they are now demanding all sorts of exemptions from different sides" (Giegold 2013). EU financial sector groups lobbied over a wide variety of these exemptions, typically arguing that the inclusion of the respective financial instruments within the scope of the tax would lead to liquidity problems. Third, financial sector groups focused on timing and actively lobbied for delaying implementation of the proposed FTT. Financial industry lobbying added up to what *Der Spiegel*, a German weekly news magazine, called a "revolt" aimed at delaying implementation (Hesse and Pauly 2012). As a fourth advocacy strategy, in an effort to leverage their political influence, financial sector groups tried to tie their interests with those of other private sector groups, which were indirectly affected by the introduction of an FTT. With their expertise and credibility discredited by the crisis, financial sector groups had to choose their coalition partners wisely, in order to be able to make convincing counter-arguments to proposed policy reforms. In fact, financial sector groups in the euro zone deliberately chose not to organize joint campaigns with US- and UK-based financial firms because there was a perception that arguments coming from them were counterproductive in efforts to convince policy-makers to oppose an FTT. As this financial sector representative reported: "There is a risk that lobbying [...] is not very helpful because it is all a bit the Anglo-Saxon conspiracy to preserve its financial markets [...]. We share information but we are not involved in any joint initiatives."[85] Although they refrained from joining campaigns, financial groups could take advantage of the counter-mobilization of non-financial groups within the business community. Policy-makers were not eager to publicly support banking industry arguments opposed to regulatory reform, but they were equally shying away from supporting regulatory reform that would have negatively affected corporate activity and economic growth. A significant number of corporate actors actively mobilized against the introduction of an FTT. In May 2013, German companies including Bayer and Siemens voiced their opposition to the proposed FTT, highlighting its damaging effects for companies and the export-oriented German economy (*Financial Times* 2013c). One financial industry representative explained the lobbying strategy as follows: "The better way for the financial sector to address this topic is to get other parties on board. When Deutsche Bank complains, people say it must be good but if Siemens says it is detrimental to clients, you make a strong argument."[86] Although business actors were not the actual target of the regulation, they feared downstream costs of the tax by raising the cost of corporate debt. Rather than stressing the potential effects of the tax on financial markets, business associations emphasized the damaging consequences for growth and corporate activity. Accordingly, the American Chamber of Commerce argued in letters sent to participating member states that the tax "will have serious implications not just for the financial institutions but for the 'real economy' – on businesses in every sector who legitimately use financial instruments in the normal course of their business."[87] Similarly, in its research report from March 2013, Deutsche Bank found that "most importantly, the FTT will hurt the real economy" (Deutsche Bank Research 2013).

Next to business groups, financial industry groups found another important ally in the community of central bankers. Financial sector groups repeatedly criticized the proposed FTT at advisory groups meetings with ECB staff in spring 2013 (Corporate Europe Observatory 2013). In April and May 2013, the heads of the German, French, and British central banks publicly expressed their reservations towards an FTT (*Financial Times* 2013d). After reports and lobbying by the financial industry had shed considerable doubt on the desirability of the tax, political support clearly faded. In May 2014, German finance minister Schäuble declared that the options, interests, and situation of the various participants were so divergent that states should start by introducing a limited taxation of shares and some derivatives (*Wall Street Journal* 2013).

With member states in the Council having the final say, the national route, where interest groups try to persuade their governments at national level or the national officials in the permanent representation in Brussels, was the key means for industry groups trying to exert influence. While financial sector groups did not fare very well given the high salience and public pressure in the early stages of the policy cycle, they were able to bounce back and influence public policy as soon as the contextual conditions provided by the financial crisis started to fade away. The latest reform proposals of a scaled-down version of the tax indicate that financial industry lobbying was highly successful. A united lobbying front among industry groups, as well as lobbying coalitions with business, provided the financial sector with important leverage over the negotiations in Council working groups.

Conclusions

This chapter has examined the role of organized civil society in the policy process leading to the decision to introduce an FTT among 11 EU member states. Detailed process-tracing made it possible to test for a causal relationship in the advocacy process between political opportunities, organized diffuse interest groups, their involvement in close insider–outsider coalitions with legislators and the (preliminary) reform decision. Although financial sector groups proved highly successful in watering down initial reform proposals, the EU FTT cannot be read as a case of unmediated industry influence on public policy. The findings of the case study suggest that scholarly work on financial regulatory politics would benefit from a more nuanced understanding of the traditional capture narrative.

Table 6.4 summarizes the main findings. The causal mechanism was hypothesized to function in a post-crisis regulatory context. Interview material with financial sector lobbyists presented in the case study provided confirmatory evidence that the direct leverage of financial sector groups over the agenda-setting phase of the policy-making process was more constrained than in the past with regard to the FTT. The financial sector complained about a lack of consultation and subsequently perceived proposed regulatory reform extremely negatively. The analysis then moved to the organized advocacy efforts of European civil society groups, examining a variety of detailed policy changes that these groups sought during reform debates. In an effort to capitalize on the crisis and increased salience which opened a policy window for reform, diffuse interest groups actively mobilized in coalitions promoting a "Robin Hood Tax." A pro-reform campaign saw insider–outsider coalitions emerge among non-financial groups and legislators acting as a countervailing force to industry interests, spurred by public pressure. By deploying specific expertise in crafting legislation to Commission officials, pro-reform groups managed to see some of their major preferences reflected in initial draft proposals. Although the European Parliament had only a consultative role, the close cooperation among MEPs and groups had important political consequences, sending a clear signal of broad-based political support to member states and Commission. Although experts played an important role in the policy process, giving testimony to the Commission and parliamentary committees, none made any viable political connections to become a policy entrepreneur for pro-reform groups at EU level. Despite this lack of entrepreneurship, diffuse interest groups did fare quite well during the early stages of the policy process. This supports the proposition that policy entrepreneurs that are well-connected and politically savvy matter less in EU policy-making due to the existence of public funding schemes that lead to a more balanced representation of diffuse interest groups in the policy process.

Pro-reform groups also effectively channeled and transmitted public opinion to decision-makers. In the context of heightened salience, policy-makers in turn had strong incentives to react to public pressure and to become active allies defending diffuse interests in the policy process, even against financial sector preferences. This response to public opinion explains the initial success of campaign groups in support of a broad-based FTT. In the post-crisis context, heads of states and governments became interested in the FTT as a populist policy measure to appease public opinion. In those early phases of the reform, financial industry groups, faced with adverse public opinion, were not successful in vetoing policy change. Industry groups saw themselves deprived of their full lobbying repertoire and largely refrained from outside strategies. Taken together, then, there is substantial evidence that EU financial industry groups were largely unsuccessful in their attempts to block regulatory change during the agenda-setting phase, although they had bitterly opposed a FTT from the beginning.

The chapter also highlighted the limitations of diffuse interests' lobbying capacity to influence regulatory change. The impact of NGO campaigns was largely restricted to the agenda-setting phase of the reform process. By contrast, the crisis-shaken private financial sector was back on its feet not long after the financial meltdown, increasing lobbying efforts and slowly trimming back reform advances, watering down financial reforms during the policy formulation phase. This corresponds to Culpepper's (2011) argument about the rise of "quiet politics" in financial regulation. Where public salience is high, business power is low. Under conditions of high public salience, elected officials have an incentive to respond to public opinion. Interest groups matter, because they can serve as an important transmitter of public opinion to decision-makers. As soon as the interest of the public and the media starts to fade away, highly organized business interests "bounce back" much more quickly and capture the policy process through their lobbying capacity and under much less public scrutiny. Pro-reform groups, so it seems, have only been able to delay financial industry capture, not to prevent it.

Contextual conditions that allowed the causal mechanism to function in the first phase of reform negotiations changed dramatically when regulatory

Table 6.4 Summary of findings

Propositions	Findings
Scope conditions present:	**Yes.** Little to no pre-legislative discussion among financial industry groups and Commission officials before the first FTT proposal was published.
1 **Favorable opportunity structures:** politicians under public salience and electoral constraints become more receptive and grant new access points to diffuse interest groups.	**Yes.** Easy access of civil society groups to the European Parliament, European Parliament committees, and DG Taxud.
2 **Diffuse interest coalitions:** the organization as an advocacy coalition spurred by the perception of a window of opportunity allows diffuse interest groups to promote reform goals.	**Yes.** European network among civil society groups as well as national-level campaigns (i.e., Robin Hood Tax Campaign and Steuer gegen Armut).
3 **Policy entrepreneurs:** activism of entrepreneurs as source of innovation, expertise, institutional resources, etc. thereby leveraging advocacy groups' influence.	**No.** No signs of entrepreneurship on the part of experts to make viable political connections.
4 **Governmental allies:** joining the bandwagon, public officials actively side with mobilized diffuse interests to promote same policy solutions.	**Yes.** Insider–outsider coalition among groups and MEPs (S&D and Greens), Taxud Commissioner Šemeta, and key governments (France and Germany).
5 **Outcome:** policymakers enact financial reforms reflecting diffuse interests.	**Mixed.** Decision to introduce tax taken by 11 EU member states, but successful industry attempts to water down legislative proposal.

debate moved to the actual policy formulation stage. Findings of the case study correspond to Young's (2014) argument that financial sector groups reacted to the new regulatory environment by shifting the focus of their advocacy efforts to different stages of the policy-making cycle. First, under much less public scrutiny, negotiations among the 11 participating member states were much more conducive to private sector lobbying than the previous debate. Working group meetings received, for example, considerably less press coverage than previous FTT debates. While diffuse interest groups were able to capitalize on the regulatory environment and the political opportunities provided by the shock of the financial crisis, initial advocacy success turned out to be only temporary.

The massive mobilization of the financial industry as a unified front in opposition to the proposed FTT was a second factor that considerably restrained the policy influence of diffuse interests. Adapting to the new regulatory environment, financial industry groups changed their lobbying strategies with emphasis on delaying implementation and aimed at forging lobbying alliances with the broader business community to dilute proposed legislation. Financial groups could also take advantage of increased mobilization of non-financial corporate actors opposing an FTT. By linking their arguments against the proposed tax to harmful effects on the business community or end-users, rather than solely on financial institutions, financial sector groups successfully lobbied for a reduction of the tax's scope, exempting, for instance, pension funds.

The case study of the EU FTT clearly reveals that industry capture exists. The active lobbying of EU financial industry groups was, however, more circumscribed than commonly assumed. Indeed, policy-makers largely ignored industry attempts to veto regulatory change during the agenda-setting phase. The EU FTT case thus also evokes the extent to which regulatory capture by concentrated industry interests is constrained, both by increased interest group plurality in the policy debate, and by the active involvement of government allies in the defense of diffuse interests. During the early phases of the policy process the advocacy efforts of financial sector groups aimed at blocking regulatory change were largely frustrated. It was only during the subsequent policy formulation phase, when debates moved from a more political debate on redistributive possibilities to a more technical debate on feasibility, that new opportunities for financial sector lobbying opened up, making possible the increasing influence of concentrated interests. It remains to be seen how much the proposal will be watered down in Council negotiations or if an FTT will ever see the light of day.

Notes

1 Council decision taken on January 22, 2013 authorizing enhanced co-operation in the area of a financial transaction tax (2013/52/EU).
2 Interview 16 with a financial industry representative, London, June 18, 2013.
3 Proposal for a Council Directive on a common system of financial transaction tax and amending Directive 2008/7/EC, Brussels, September 28, 2011.
4 Interview 68 with an NGO representative, September 13, 2013.
5 Internal and non-official paper provided by financial lobbyist, June 2013.
6 Ibid.

7 European Council, Resolution of June 17, 2010.
8 Interview 21 with a Commission official, Brussels, May 12, 2013.
9 Communication from the European Commission, A Budget for Europe 2020.
10 Interview 43 with an NGO representative, London, June 12, 2013.
11 Interview 104 with an industry representative, Brussels, May 22, 2013.
12 Interview 21 with a Commission official, Brussels, May 12, 2013.
13 Interview 104 with an industry representative, Brussels, May 22, 2013.
14 Interview 47 with an industry representative, Brussels, May 14, 2013.
15 Interview 104 with an industry representative, Brussels, May 22, 2013.
16 Interview 57 with an industry representative, London, June 20, 2013.
17 Interview 16 with a financial industry representative, London, June 18, 2013.
18 Interview 57 with an industry representative, London, June 20, 2013.
19 Interviews 47 and 70 with industry representatives, Brussels, May 14, 2013; London, June 20, 2013.
20 Interview 94 with an industry lobbyists, London, June 24, 2013.
21 Interview 70 with an industry representative, London, June 20, 2013.
22 Interview 57 with an industry representative, London, June 20, 2013.
23 Interview 70 with an industry representative, London, June 20, 2013.
24 Interviews 47, 57, and 70 with industry representatives, Brussels May 14, 2013; London, June 20, 2013.
25 Ibid.
26 Interview 70 with an industry representative, London, June 20, 2013.
27 Interview 47 with an industry representative, Brussels, May 14, 2013.
28 Interview 43 with an NGO representative, London, June 12, 2013.
29 Interview 17 with a trade union representative, Brussels, May 24, 2013.
30 Interview 103 with a trade union representative, London, June 18, 2013.
31 Ibid.
32 Interview 43 with an NGO representative, London, June 12, 2013.
33 Interview 15 with an NGO representative, London, June 17, 2013.
34 Articles containing the search term "financial transaction tax" in British as well as US newspapers, "taxe sur les transactions financières" in the French language press and "Finanztransaktionssteuer" in the German language press, which refer to the relevant groupings of major publications proposed by Factiva (including *The Financial Times, The Guardian, The Economist, CNN, The New York Times, Washington Post, Le Monde, Le Figaro, Agence France Presse, Frankfurter Allgemeine Zeitung, Süddeutsche Zeitung, Reuters, Spiegel Online*).
34 Interview 17 with a trade union representative, Brussels, May 24, 2013.
35 Interview 11 with a trade union representative, Brussels, April 10, 2013.
36 Interview 43 with an NGO representative, London, June 12, 2013.
37 Ibid.
38 Unofficial, non-public document provided by interviewee, Brussels.
39 Interview 43 with an NGO representative, London, June 12, 2013.
40 Interview 99 with an NGO representative, February 29, 2013.
41 Interview 73 with an NGO representative, Paris, November 14, 2012.
42 Interviews 43 and 103 with civil society representatives, London, June 12 and 18, 2013.
43 Interview 99 with an NGO representative, February 29, 2013.
44 Interview 43 with an NGO representative, London, June 12, 2013.
45 Interview 99 with an NGO representative, February 29, 2013.
46 Interview 73 with an NGO representative, Paris, November 14, 2012.
47 The petition could be accessed online at Europeansforfinancialreform.org
48 Interview 99 with an NGO representative, February 29, 2013.
49 Interview 109 with an industry representative, May 14, 2013.
50 Oxfam submission to the Commission public consultation on taxation of the financial sector, European Commission, DG Taxud, February 2011.

51 Interview 17 with a trade union representative, Brussels, May 24, 2013.
52 Interview 43 with an NGO representative, London, June 12, 2013.
53 Interview 17 with a trade union representative, Brussels, May 24, 2013.
54 Interview 103 with a trade union representative, London, June 18, 2013.
55 Interview 32 with an NGO representative, Brussels, June 1, 2011.
56 Interview 70 with an industry representative, London, June 20, 2013.
57 Interview 94 with an industry lobbyists, London, June 24, 2013.
58 Interview 47 with an industry representative, Brussels, May 14, 2013.
59 Interview 70 with an industry representative, London, June 20, 2013.
60 Interview 21 with a Commission official, Brussels, May 12, 2013.
61 Interview 32 with an NGO representative, Brussels, June 1, 2011.
62 Interview 11 with a trade union representative, Brussels, April 10, 2013.
63 Interview 17 with a trade union representative, Brussels, May 24, 2013.
64 Interview 88 with an NGO representative, Brussels, May 26, 2013.
65 Interview 17 with a trade union representative, Brussels, May 24, 2013.
66 Interview 99 with an NGO representative, February 29, 2013.
67 Interview 18 with an NGO representative 18, Paris, July 11, 2011.
68 Interviews 32 and 88 with NGO representatives, Brussels, June 1, 2011 and May 16, 2013.
69 Interview 68 with an NGO representative, Washington, D.C., September 13, 2013.
70 Interview 17 with a trade union representative, Brussels, May 24, 2013.
71 Interviews 43 and 68 with NGO representatives, London, June 12, 2013; Washington, D.C., September 12, 2013.
72 Interview 43 with an NGO representative, London, June 12, 2013.
73 Interview 68 with an NGO representative, Washington, D.C., September 13, 2013.
74 Interview 17 with a trade union representative, Brussels, May 24, 2013.
75 Interview 21 with a Commission official, Brussels, May 12, 2013.
76 Interview 88 with an NGO representative, Brussels, May 26, 2013.
77 Interview 43 with an NGO representative, London, June 12, 2013.
78 Interviews 43 and 99 with NGO representatives, London June 12, 2013; February 19, 2013.
79 Interview 21 with a Commission official, May 24, 2013.
80 Interviews 103 and 58 with civil society representatives, London, June 18, 2013 and interview with national-level campaigner conducted via Skype, April 22, 2013.
81 Interview 70 with an industry representative, London, June 20, 2013.
82 Interview 43 with an NGO representative, London, June 12, 2013.
83 Interview 47 with a financial industry representative, Brussels, May 14, 2013.
84 Ibid.
85 Interview 9 with a financial industry lobbyist, May 16, 2013.
86 Unofficial, non-public paper on the FTT, April 2013, provided by bank lobbyist, London, May 2013.

References

Alternative Investment Management Association (2012) 'Financial Transaction Tax. An Assessment of the European Commission's Proposed Financial Transaction Tax', AIMA research note, January 2012.

Bloomberg Business (2013) 'EU Aides Say Transaction Tax Design Hurts Sovereign Debt', 22 May, available at www.bloomberg.com/news/articles/2013-05-21/eu-aides-say-transaction-tax-design-hurts-sovereign-debt (accessed 19 September 2016).

Brassett, J. (2013) *Cosmopolitanism and Global Financial Reform: A Pragmatic Approach to the Tobin Tax*, New York: Routledge.

Corporate Europe Observatory (2013) 'Robbing the Robin Hood Tax: The European Central Bank Weighs In', July 17, available at http://corporateeurope.org/financial-lobby/2013/07/robbing-robin-hood-tax-european-central-bank-weighs, accessed September 14, 2015.

Culpepper, P.D. (2011) *Quiet Politics and Business Power: Corporate Control in Europe and Japan*, Cambridge: Cambridge University Press.

Deutsche Bank Research (2013) 'Financial Transaction Tax. Counterproductive', available at www.goldmansachs.com/s/GMeT_othermailings_attachments/635004849176172500 89163.PDF (accessed September 14, 2015).

ECOFIN Council (2015) 'Joint Statement by Ministers of Member States Participating in Enhanced Cooperation in the Area of Financial Transaction Tax', January 27, available at https://home.kpmg.com/content/dam/kpmg/pdf/2015/08/Joint%20Statement%20by%20finance%20ministers%20of%20EU%20Member%20States%20to%20kickstart%20the%20FTT%20(PDF%2087%20KB).pdf

Economic and Monetary Affairs Committee (2012) 'Getting the Best Out of a Financial Transaction Tax', February 7, available at www.europarl.europa.eu/news/en/pressroom/20120206IPR37347/getting-the-best-out-of-a-financial-transaction-tax

EurActive (2010) 'Germany, France Push for Financial Transactions Tax', 12 July, available at www.euractiv.com/euro-finance/germany-france-push-financial-tr-news-496236 (accessed September 2016).

European Commission (2010) 'Press Release – Commission Outlines Vision for Taxing the Financial Sector', IP/10/1298, 7 October, Brussels: European Commission, available at europa.eu/rapid/press-release_IP-10-1298_en.htm (accessed September 2016).

European Commission (2011a) 'Summary Report' Brussels: European Commission, available at ec.europa.eu/taxation_customs/resources/documents/common/consultations/tax/financial_sector/summary_results_en.pdf (accessed September 2016).

European Commission (2011b) 'Press Release – Financial Transaction Tax: Making the Financial Sector Pay Its Fair Share', 28 September, Brussels: European Commission, available at europa.eu/rapid/press-release_IP-11-1085_en.htm?locale=en (accessed September 2016).

European Commission (2011c) 'Impact Assessment Accompanying the Document Proposal for a Council Directive on a Common System of Financial Transaction Tax and Amending Directive 2008/7/EC', working paper, Brussels: European Commission, available at ec.europa.eu/smart-regulation/impact/ia_carried_out/docs/ia_2011/sec_2011_1102_en.pdf (accessed September 2016).

European Commission (2013) 'Impact Assessment Accompanying the Document: Proposal for a Council Directive Implementing Enhanced Cooperation in the Area of Financial Transaction Tax. Analysis of Policy Options and Impacts', Brussels: European Commission, available at ec.europa.eu/taxation_customs/resources/documents/taxation/swd_2013_28_en.pdf (accessed September 2016).

European Parliament (2010) 'Europeans and the Crisis. European Parliament Eurobarometer (EB Parlemètre 74.1)', 14 October, Brussels: European Parliament, available at www.europarl.europa.eu/pdf/eurobarometre/2010_10/analytical_synthesis_EN.pdf (accessed September 2016).

European Parliament (2011) 'Europeans and the Crisis. European Parliament Eurobarometer. Summary', 22 June, Brussels: European Parliament, available at www.europarl.europa.eu/pdf/eurobarometre/2011/juin/22062011/eb752_financial_crisis_analytical_synthesis_en.pdf (accessed September 2016).

Financial Times (2011) 'Business Attacks Transaction Tax Plan', 28 September, available at hwww.ft.com/intl/cms/s/0/f9d2188a-e9ec-11e0-a149-00144feab49a.html#axzz2Nns kvMIJ (accessed September 2016).

Financial Times (2012) 'Fear Transaction Levy Will Cut Tax Revenues', 10 January, available at www.ft.com/intl/cms/s/0/079dc598-3891-11e1-9ae1-00144feabdc0.html# axzz2Nns kvMIJ (accessed September 2016).

Financial Times (2013a) 'Funds Hit at Planned European Transactions Tax', 30 April, available at www.ft.com/intl/cms/s/0/411cb28c-b1aa-11e2-b324-00144feabdc0.html# axzz2RpNXyGSM (accessed September 2016).

Financial Times (2013b) 'Banks Call on BoE to Oppose Financial Transaction Tax', 5 May, available at www.ft.com/intl/cms/s/0/948b16a6-b589-11e2-850d-00144feabdc0. html #axzz2Sa5SdDEN (accessed September 2016).

Financial Times (2013c) 'German Companies Weigh in against Tobin Tax', 8 May, available at www.ft.com/intl/cms/s/0/5cb60a60-b7d2-11e2-bd62-00144feabdc0.html#axzz 2Sa5 SdDEN (accessed September 2016).

Financial Times (2013d) 'ECB Offers to Help Rethink Robin Hood Tax', 26 May, available at www.ft.com/content/c3121802-c480-11e2-9ac0-00144feab7de (accessed September 2016).

Financial Times (2014a) 'Robin Hood Tax Has Roots in 17th Century', 30 April available at www.ft.com/intl/cms/s/0/ad56782e-d06d-11e3-af2b-00144feabdc0.html?siteedition= intl#axzz3ZpxAa7BT (accessed September 2016).

Financial Times (2014b) 'Eurozone Divided over Financial Transaction Tax Deal', 6 May, available at www.ft.com/intl/cms/s/0/d8a5d630-d529-11e3-9187-00144feabdc0.html# axzz3aTjJISHn (accessed September 2016).

GFMA (2011) 'GFMA Submits Letter to G20 Finance Ministers in Opposition to the Financial Transaction Tax', available at www.gfma.org/correspondence/item.aspx?id= 49 (accessed September 2016).

Giegold, S. (2013) 'Hinter Den Kulissen: Wechselbad Der Gefühle in Strasbourg. Von Verratenem Investorenschutz & Erfolg Bei Der Finanztransaktionssteuer', July 31, available at www.sven-giegold.de/2013/strasburg-wechselbad-der-gefuhle/ (accessed September 2016).

Giegold, S. (2014) 'Das Ist Keine Finanztransaktionssteuer', May 6, available at www. sven-giegold.de/2014/das-ist-keine-finanztransaktionssteuer/ (accessed September 2016).

Goldman Sachs (2013) 'Financial Transaction Tax: How Severe?', Goldman Sachs Global Investment Research, available at www.steuer-gegen-armut.org/fileadmin/Dateien/ Kapagnen-Seite/Unterstuetzung_Ausland/EU/2013/201 3.05._GS_on_Fin_1_Trans action_ tax__FTT__-_Bottom_Up_Analysis_Europe.pdf (accessed September 2016).

Grahl, J. and Lysandrou, P. (2013) 'The European Commission's Proposal for a Financial Transactions Tax: A Critical Assessment', *Journal of Common Market Studies* 52 (2): 234–249.

Griffith-Jones, S. and Persaud, A. (2012) 'Financial Transaction Taxes', working paper, available at www.europarl.europa.eu/document/activities/cont/201202/20120208ATT 37596/20120208ATT37596EN.pdf (accessed September 2016).

Hesse, M. and Pauly, C. (2012) 'Financial Lobby in Revolt: How Much Longer Can Transaction Tax Be Delayed?' *Spiegel Online International*, 20 March, available at www.spiegel.de/international/europe/financial-industry-lobbyists-delay-financial-transaction-tax-a-822186.html (accessed November 2015).

International Trade Union Confederation (ITUC) (2012) 'ITUC Global Poll 2012 – How Banks Can Contribute to Society: Very Strong Popular Support for Financial Transactions Tax', available at www.ituc-csi.org/ituc-global-poll-2012-how-banks (accessed September 2016).

KPMG UK (2015) 'European Financial Transaction Tax', 17 December, available at home. kpmg.com/uk/en/home/services/tax/corporate-tax/european-financial-transaction-tax. html (accessed 19 September 2016).

Lamberts, P. (2013) 'The Robin Hood Tax Is under Attack', *The Guardian*, 7 June, available at www.theguardian.com/commentisfree/2013/jun/07/robin-hood-tax-under-attack (accessed November 2015).

Mahoney, C. (2008) *Brussels versus the Beltway. Advocacy in the United States and in the European Union*, Washington, DC: Georgetown University Press.

Patomäki, H. (2001) *Democratising Globalisation: The Leverage of the Tobin Tax*, London: Zed Books.

Persaud, A. (2013) 'Europe Should Embrace a Financial Transaction Tax', *Financial Times*, 28 May, available at www.ft.com/intl/cms/s/0/ba8e4232-c79b-11e2-9c52-00144feab7de.html?siteedition=intl#axzz2UYOZaMQz (accessed September 2016).

Politico (2011) 'Barroso to Push for Financial Transaction Tax', 21 June, available at www.politico.eu/article/barroso-to-push-for-financial-transaction-tax/ (accessed September 2016).

PWC (2013) 'EU Financial Transaction Tax: Will the Commission's Proposal Survive?', Financial Services Tax News, July 2013, available at www.pwc.com/jp/en/taxnews-financial-services/assets/eu-ftt-201307-e.pdf (accessed September 2016).

Schulmeister, S. (2014) 'The Struggle Over the Financial Transactions Tax–A Politico-Economic Farce', WIFO Working Paper, 25 June, available at www.wifo.ac.at/publika tionen?detail-view=yes&publikation_id=47272 (accessed September 2016).

Šemeta, A. (2010) 'Taxing the Financial Sector', SPEECH/10/530, 7 October, Brussels: European Commission, available at europa.eu/rapid/press-release_SPEECH-10-530_ en.htm?locale=en (accessed September 2016).

Šemeta, A. (2014) 'Financial Transaction Tax: Time to Engage, Compromise and Deliver', 4 February, Brussels: European Commission, available at europa.eu/rapid/ press-release_SPEECH-14-92_en.htm?locale=en (accessed September 2016).

Stamp Out Poverty (2012) 'Stamp Out Poverty Campaign: Cameron and Osborne Become More Isolated Opposing the FTT Whilst Europe Marches on', available at www. stampoutpoverty.org/wf_library_post /lid11552/ (accessed September 2016).

The Telegraph (2011) 'Archbishop of Canterbury Rowan Williams Calls for New Tax on Bankers', 1 November, available at www.telegraph.co.uk/news/religion/8863794/Arch bishop-of-Canterbury-Rowan-Williams-calls-for-new-tax-on-bankers.html (accessed September 2016).

Tobin, J. (1978) 'A Proposal for International Monetary Reform', *Eastern Economic Journal* 3–4 (October): 153–59.

Van Vooren, B. (2012) 'The Global Reach of the Proposed EU Financial Transaction Tax Directive: Creating Momentum through Internal Legislation', *EUI Working Papers, Robert Schuman Center for Advanced Studies*, no. 2012/28: 1–23.

Wahl, P. (2014) 'The European Civil Society Campaign on the Financial Transaction Tax', Working Paper, No. 20, Global Labour University project 'Combating Inequality', Geneva, February, available at www.global-labour-university.org/fileadmin/GLU_ Working_Papers/GLU_WP_No.20.pdf (accessed September 2016).

Wall Street Journal (2013) 'EU Tax Should Start with Derivatives, Shares Says German Finance Minister', 5 May, available at www.wsj.com/news/articles/SB100014240527 02303417104579543533755401604?mod=dist_smartbrief (accessed September 2016).

WEED (2009) 'International Financial Transaction Tax on the Pittsburgh Agenda', available at www.globaleverantwortung.at/images/doku/g20_pittsburgh_financialtransaction tax_sept09.pdf (accessed September 2016).

Young, K. (2014) 'Losing Abroad But Winning at Home: European Financial Industry Groups in Global Financial Governance since the Crisis', *Journal of European Public Policy* 21(3): 367–88.

Zimmermann, H. (2014) 'EU-11 Als Globale Avantgarde? Die Verhandlungen Um Eine Finanztransaktionssteuer', Global Governance Spotlight 2: Stiftung für Entwicklung und Frieden (SEF).

7　Conclusion

The explanation of success

For reforms to occur after the crisis, a diffuse and ill-organized public interest had to be favored over special, well-organized, and presumptively very powerful financial sector interests. This research tried to shed light on the policy process in financial regulation and the mechanisms that may lead to regulatory outcomes that favor a diffuse public interest over concentrated special interests. Given the limitations of capture theories in providing a satisfactory account of the full scope of the regulatory response to the crisis, this analysis presented a theoretical framework that centers on an element that existing explanations of regulatory reforms have largely neglected, namely: how have diffuse interests come to be strongly represented in the regulatory reform process spurred by the crisis, despite the greater resources mobilized by the financial sector?

My task in this chapter is to summarize how it was possible for putatively weak and diffuse interest groups to push for policy change, even under the difficult conditions posed by financial regulation, within the framework of which organized industry interests usually win the day. Tracing processes of policy change that reflect diffuse interests in four parallel case studies also allows me to draw some comparative lessons. I conclude that regulatory reforms promoting a diffuse public interest over a narrow financial sector interest occurred for the following main reasons, applicable to the positive and mixed cases examined here: post-crisis context, favorable political opportunities, mobilized diffuse interest groups, policy entrepreneurs, and active government allies.

During the post-crisis context, financial industry groups had only a limited ability to defend their interests (contextual conditions)

The case studies show how context matters in bringing about policy change in financial regulation that does not correspond to the interests of the incumbent industry. In order to function, the hypothesized causal mechanism needs to be situated within a specific context characterized by changed interest-group dynamics. After the damage the financial crisis had done to the economy, common mechanisms of regulatory capture were no longer in play. Instead, divisions among policymakers and the private sector occurred. Financial sector lobbyists in my cases felt "cut out," "isolated," "irrelevant," or, as "the ones to be punished." In the case of consumer protection regulations in the EU, representatives of financial sector groups reported that they found it difficult to lobby the European institutions. Some complained about diminishing communication levels and lamented that Commission officials and MEPs were giving financial sector lobbyists "a very tough time." The case of US consumer protection reforms evokes a similar picture. Industry representatives perceived lobbying in the post-crisis context as "frustrating" and "difficult." The fact that financial sector lobbyists were surprised about the content of the US administration's blueprint for reform testifies to their inability to influence policy-makers in those early stages of reform-making. Before the financial crisis, industry groups were used to exchanging information with decision-makers at early stages of the legislative process. In the post-crisis context, financial industry groups were clearly put at a strategic disadvantage and temporarily lost their political leverage.

The crisis drastically changed the lobbying environment in which financial industry groups had to operate in both the US and the EU. Afraid of public denunciations, the financial sector saw itself deprived of the usual lobbying repertoire. For example, in case of the EU financial transaction tax, industry groups refrained from openly speaking out against it in the early phase of the policy process. Findings of our case studies also confirm what Young (2013) showed empirically with regard to a range of regulatory reforms in response to the crisis, namely that financial sector groups started to adapt their lobbying strategies to the more hostile regulatory environment, refraining from attempts to veto regulatory change outright. For instance, in the case of the US consumer regulator, the ABA softened its lobbying position and offered to provide information and cooperate with policy-makers on proposed legislative reforms.

Opening-up political opportunity structures shaped the possibilities for success for diffuse interest groups to affect reform decisions

The financial crisis yielded opportunities and constraints for diffuse interest groups seeking to influence the reform process. As policy-makers pushed for financial reform in the direct aftermath of the crisis, diffuse interest groups found themselves positively affected in terms of access to the policy-making process, receptivity of political elites, and resource mobilization, all key factors for policy influence identified in the social movement literature. A qualitative shift in policy-making from technical discussion groups to parliamentary agendas opened up spaces for non-financial groups to have their voices heard in the legislative process. While earlier regulatory debates were usually dominated by financial sector groups, post-crisis reform negotiations were characterized by increased actor plurality. This plurality is indicative of the capacity of organized diffuse interest groups to adapt and find new spaces for influence that have emerged in the context of the financial crisis.

In both the United States and the EU, the degree of access to policy-makers, as well as overall political receptivity to pro-reform demands, increased notably in the aftermath of the crisis. In the EU case, access to national policy-makers who were sympathetic to the reform cause allowed advocates to press governments to champion a pro-reform stance at EU level in the Council of Ministers or the European Council. Simultaneously, diffuse interest groups had access to EU-level decision-making via the "Brussels route" by lobbying the European institutions. The responsible directorates-general at the European Commission became increasingly receptive to pro-reform demands. According to one Brussels-based consumer advocate, the political receptivity of DG Market to demands from consumer groups had changed "as day and night." Notably, MEPs were an attractive target for groups seeking reform. Asked about lobbying the European Parliament, interviewees for this research project reported that civil society groups had much easier access to the Parliament after the financial crisis than financial industry groups had. Similarly, in the US case, members of Congress increasingly responded to demands from consumer groups to restrict subprime lending and increase consumer protection after the crisis. Starting in early 2009, individual consumer representatives were repeatedly invited to testify in front of Congressional committees. In both cases, political receptivity was accompanied by the increased issue salience of the respective reform issues. The crisis had at least partly redistributed political leverage from financial to diffuse interest groups.

Non-financial interest groups mobilized and built pro-reform coalitions, effectively influencing reform decisions

In the positive cases examined here, diffuse interests enhanced their capacity for collective action by mobilizing as coalitions. Unprecedented and broad-based coalitions among a wide range of civil society actors emerged on both sides of the Atlantic to demand more substantial reforms of financial markets. The broad coalitions pushing for reform have been important in channeling public support for policy-makers' efforts to reform financial markets in light of massive bank bailouts at public expense. In the United States, the crisis served as a catalyst to bring together a wide array of organizations concerned with financial reform under the common umbrella of "Americans for Financial Reform." As their counterpart in the EU, a coalition named "Europeans For Financial Reform" set up a campaign for financial reforms. In both the United States and the EU, various groups came together in "Robin Hood Tax" coalitions to promote the introduction of a tax on financial transactions.

The outsider groups benefited greatly from favorable public opinion, which made policy-makers much more responsive to pro-reform demands. By explicitly adopting campaigning methods designed to demonstrate that their policy demands have broad popular support, pro-reform groups played an important role in transmitting public opinion to decision-makers. In the case of the US consumer bureau, advocates testified in front of Congress and its committees throughout the legislative debate. Groups also set up a database of collected testimonies of abusive lending practices, so-called "horror lending stories," which served as an important source of information for Congress. According to interviewees in Congress, this evident widespread public support in favor of stricter regulation also helped policy-makers to push for reform and overcome financial sector opposition. In the case of the EU transaction tax, groups also served as important transmitters of public opinion by organizing online petitions that were send directly as a citizen response to the Commission or by giving testimony in front of national parliamentary chambers.

It is noteworthy that diffuse interests were particularly successful when the opposition of financial sector groups split. Indeed, industry lobbying after the crisis was often marked by a lack of coordination. Instead of pulling together to jointly oppose the creation of the new consumer agency, industry groups in the United States moved apart. The Independent Community Bankers Association negotiated a political deal, which granted a semi-carve-out for small banks with assets under \$10 billion from the CFPB's oversight authority. In return, the Community Bankers did not oppose the bill during its passage in Congress. Deprived of a powerful ally who also had a more favorable public image, the ABA was left with little-to-no political leverage to oppose the legislative proposal. In the case of EU consumer protection, cohesion among industry groups was also weaker than has been commonly assumed and heterogeneous coalitions among stakeholders emerged, comprising both financial and non-financial stakeholders. Consumer protection measures were strengthened, for instance, when strange-bedfellow coalitions emerged among consumer advocates and the financial services industry. In the case of the EU financial transaction tax, diffuse interest groups succeeded during the early agenda-setting phase of the reform process, while the industry's response was still somewhat uncoordinated, with major banking associations not taking a transaction tax proposal seriously and refraining from active lobbying. This situation changed when industry groups stepped up their lobbying efforts to organize a coordinated anti-taxation campaign.

To date, the literature on financial regulation has largely ignored the question of how interest groups outside finance—in particular, civil society groups— can affect policy change and oppose industry groups. One contribution of this research is therefore to show the capacities and practices of civil society groups to address regulatory change in financial markets. In a short article examining the relationship between civil society and financial markets after the financial crisis, Scholte finds that civil society groups "play a fairly marginal role in the politics of commercial finance, thereby largely surrendering the advocacy field to industry lobbies and establishment think tanks." He concludes that "civil society activism to steer financial markets in the common good remains mostly muted and ineffectual, and governance of finance generally eludes democratic accountability" (Scholte 2013, 130). Similarly, Clark (2011) asserts that the financial crisis has been tough on civil society groups, reducing levels of public funding for civil society activities and increasing divisions within the sector who generally failed to provide a convincing alternative to policy-makers. These trends in turn have reduced the political influence and effectiveness of civil society's advocacy.

The present study has provided empirical evidence that confirms a very different claim about the influence of the financial crisis on group activity, and in particular on the activities and practices of politically less advantaged groups, such as NGOs, consumer groups, and trade unions. In case studies on the reform of consumer credit markets in the United States and the EU and taxation in the EU, this analysis shows that less powerful pro-change groups that traditionally have struggled to see their preferences translated into policy were able to take advantage of the shock of the crisis as an opportunity to promote policy change. Notably, civil society groups, such as Finance Watch, benefited from new sources of public funding that became available at EU level to support existing NGOs, as well as the formation of new ones to provide counter-expertise to financial industry groups in the financial regulatory process.

Empirical evidence from my case studies further suggests that civil society's strategy of campaigning to correct financial market regulation in response to the crisis has proven surprisingly effective. Diffuse interest groups engaged in advocacy played a central role by deploying key expertise and shaping regulatory content. The AFR coalition in the United States, Finance Watch in the EU, as well as the transnational Robin Hood Tax campaigns excelled in this role, by participating in consultations and hearings, providing language for legislative drafts, advising on technical details, and connecting decision-makers with financial experts. While in the case of the financial transaction tax, the success of the pro-reform groups was largely restricted to the agenda-setting phase of the reform process, advocates provided expertise and were actively involved in drafting legislative language in the case of consumer protection reforms.

However, the study also highlights the limitations on civil society capacity to influence regulatory change. In the case of the EU financial transaction tax, the findings suggest that the impact of pro-reform campaigns was largely restricted to the agenda-setting phase of the reform process. By contrast, the crisis-shaken private financial sector was back on its feet not long after the financial meltdown, increasing lobbying efforts and slowly trimming back reform advances, watering down financial reforms during the detailed policy-negotiation phase. This corresponds to Culpepper's (2011) argument about the rise of "quiet politics" in financial regulation. As soon as the interest of the public and the media starts to fade away, highly organized business interests "bounce back" much more quickly and capture the policy process through their lobbying capacity and under much less public scrutiny. Nevertheless, in the present analysis we have provided evidence that civil society groups are increasingly involved in financial regulatory decision-making.

Active government allies took the initiative in defense of a diffuse public interest

The findings of the positive cases examined here confirm the importance of "understanding where the preponderance of government support lies [...] in understanding when lobbyists succeed and when they fail" (Mahoney 2007, 54). An unmistakable pattern emerges in my case studies: high-level legislative allies (including presidents and heads of state, committee chairmen in Congress, European Commissioners, and European Parliament rapporteurs) advocated for reform and worked in tandem with mobilized diffuse interest groups to bring about policy change. Under conditions of salience, office holders had strong incentives to act in the defense of diffuse interests, rather than special interests. In the case of the new US consumer regulator, which represented the most sweeping policy change in any of our cases, not only the US President but also the two chairmen responsible for pushing financial reform legislation through Congress actively sided with consumer advocates to promote the new agency. Therefore, findings confirm that much of the success of diffuse interests in Congress hinges on the support of the President or party leaders who have an incentive to respond to broad interests as political leaders with "collective responsibility" (Derthick and Quirk 1985, 142).

In the case of the EU, the Commission and the European Parliament allowed for consumer interests to bear upon the regulatory reform agenda. Internal Market Commissioner Barnier became an important advocate for diffuse consumer interests, pushing for the same policy goals as advocates, despite financial sector opposition. Similarly, MEPs were quite sympathetic to consumer groups and amended the main directives in accordance with the demands of advocacy groups. In particular the S&D and the Green Party proved to be receptive to the preferences of pro-reform groups. The case study findings also suggest that the role of the rapporteurs proved to be instrumental in achieving consumer-friendly outcomes because they have to steer the legislative proposals through the ECON Committee and the plenary vote. The consumer voice can also be translated into policy when it coincides with member states' concerns for leveling the playing field as in the case of the support of the UK and Dutch governments for a Community-wide ban on inducements.

In the case of the EU financial transaction tax, the legislative proposal made it to the policy agenda due to key member state governments, as well as MEPs pushing for reform along with the preferences of a newly mobilized civil society coalition. However, with public salience fading during the technical negotiations among member states at the policy formulation stage, the principal condition for legislative allies to support legislation even against the preferences of special interests had been removed and financial sector lobbies successfully watered down the initial draft Directive. Ultimately, the joint opposition from financial sector groups and business groups towards a financial transaction tax contributed towards the dilution of the proposal at EU level.

In summary, the greater involvement of elected politicians in the design of financial regulatory reform under conditions of public salience helped non-industry stakeholders in particular. During the financial reform debates, policy-makers were generally accessible and willing to articulate a consumer viewpoint, as highlighted during several interviews conducted for this project. With voters beginning to pay attention to financial reform, electoral considerations became important to policy-makers. This suggests that, as long as the public remains engaged with policy debates, (politically) weak consumer interests can prevail over powerful business interests, even in a highly technical policy field such as financial regulation.

Policy entrepreneurship helped diffuse interest groups to organize and gain leverage

Faced with collective action problems, diffuse interest groups needed a helping hand in getting organized. In the case of the new US consumer regulator, Harvard law professor and consumer advocate Elizabeth Warren became an influential policy entrepreneur who promoted the proposal of a new consumer regulator in tandem with the newly mobilized reform coalition AFR. Warren's academic work served as important source of innovation, putting forward the idea of a new agency to protect consumers. She also successfully built supportive coalitions for her idea, thereby exploiting opportunities opened up by the credit crisis and the excessive industry influence over regulation that it brought to the fore. She was instrumental in rallying initial support for a single regulator among consumer, labor, and other interest groups. Throughout the reform process she served as key expert for the pro-reform side. The kind of policy entrepreneurship displayed by Warren in the US consumer protection case did not find any parallels in the other case studies examined here. One reason why policy entrepreneurs do not emerge in the European context can be found in the EU-level organization of civil-society access to the policy process. EU-based diffuse interest groups mobilize with the help of the European institutions and benefit greatly from resources provided by the Commission and the European Parliament. In the absence of public funding, US groups need to find alternatives to public funding schemes to mobilize effectively. Experts who are well-connected and politically savvy can provide groups with a jump start by playing an important leadership role to help groups mobilize around a common reform theme.

To sum up the analysis in the broadest terms, the explanation for success in my cases has three principal elements: the difficulty experienced by financial sector interests—although mobilized in opposition—to affect policy decisions due to a deep legitimacy crisis; the mobilization of diffuse interest groups as broad pro-reform coalitions channeling public support and deploying expertise; and the need of politicians for positions that were responsive to current public concerns in times of financial crisis and high salience. The analysis of the US case studies also suggests that diffuse interests are best represented in public policy if policy entrepreneurs and government allies work together in their defense. Policy entrepreneurs appear to be particularly important for the effective mobilization of diffuse interest groups in the United States, where interest groups do not benefit from public support schemes as in the EU. Indeed, the empirical analysis of the EU cases found that policy entrepreneurship is not necessary to explain the representation of diffuse interests in financial regulatory policies. EU-based diffuse interest groups did fare relatively well, even in the absence of a policy entrepreneur. This leads us to two slightly different theoretical models for political processes representing diffuse interests in the United States and the EU, whereby the role of policy entrepreneurs becomes redundant in the latter model. Routes to success for diffuse interest groups differ across the Atlantic, due to differences in the institutional structures of the two political systems.

In both the United States and the EU the key to success for diffuse interest groups is government allies sympathetic to their cause who actively pursue diffuse interests throughout the legislative process. The stronger the government allies they can recruit to defend their cause, the more likely diffuse interests are to succeed in the policy process. Adversely, advocates lose if they are not able to forge coalitions with well-positioned policy entrepreneurs, nor with potent government allies who would push their cause through the legislative process. The success of diffuse interest groups also depends on which political leader they can recruit as an ally. Diffuse interest groups succeed only if they find government allies who are central players in the policy process, such as the US President, Committee chairmen in the US Congress, the rapporteur in the European Parliament, or heads of states and government in the European Council. For diffuse interest groups to succeed in recruiting such powerful allies, issue salience appears to be more important in the United States than in the EU.

The findings of our case studies are also consistent with the results of Mahoney (2007, 54) who finds that the "EU system negotiates compromises which allow more advocates to attain their goals," while "absolute winners dominate clear losers" in the United States. Due to the characteristics of the US political system, shaped by direct elections and private campaign finance, these outcomes are usually biased in favor of more resourceful business interests. Accordingly, both US case studies presented here displayed clear winner-take-all outcomes, while both EU case studies resulted in compromise solutions, with most stakeholders involved winning a little. Indeed, diffuse interest groups in the United States attained either all or nothing, while in the EU, groups usually achieved some of their goals. These differences in lobbying success can be explained partly by the differences in likelihood of policy change. Whereas policy change is very likely in the EU system, where almost all Commission proposals lead to a policy outcome, policy change is much less likely in the United States, where initiatives can be killed at several stages of the legislative process. While US interest groups can lobby to kill a proposal (either winning or losing), EU interest groups have to work to modify it, making it more likely that some of their preferences are reflected in the final outcome (Mahoney 2007, 39).

Claims of "exploitation of the electoral process by moneyed interests" (Mahoney 2007, 54) seem somewhat exaggerated in both cases. Although the United States has usually been portrayed as a more electorally accountable system than the multilevel system of the EU, where policy-makers appear largely protected from the electoral threat, both systems displayed a capacity to defend diffuse interests in the policy process, even against business opposition. Nevertheless, ways in which diffuse interests get to be represented in the respective political systems vary. While diffuse interest groups are formally empowered through top-down public funding schemes in the EU, US groups mobilize from the bottom-up. The formal empowerment of groups representing diffuse interests in the EU through funding regimes for NGOs has no equivalent in the United States and might explain the variation in mobilization of public interest groups. Not only by funding but also by founding a new

NGO with Finance Watch, the European institutions aimed explicitly for a more balanced interest representation in financial regulatory matters. Although favorable public opinion is an advantage for diffuse interest groups in both cases, the political system of the EU seems more susceptible to diffuse interest representation in general.

Consumer finance protection

Consumer protection reforms across the Atlantic follow the expected pattern. Compared with the landslide victory in the United States, where consumer advocates successfully pushed for a new federal consumer protection regulator, the advocacy success of EU-based civil society groups seems modest. The process-tracing analysis of four different legislative initiatives at EU level suggests that private sector lobbying did not result in blockage of reform or weakening of regulatory standards at the agenda-setting or policy-formulation stage. Overall, the EU-level consumer protection reforms that followed the crisis remained rather incremental. All four legislative initiatives resulted in compromise solutions, with all stakeholders seeing some of their preferences reflected in policy. In the EU case, all elements of the hypothesized causal mechanism can be considered necessary to produce a regulatory outcome, reflecting diffuse interests groups' advocacy goals, except for policy entrepreneurship. In comparison with the US case, where Elizabeth Warren played a central role in the reform process as a policy entrepreneur, diffuse interest groups in the EU fared quite well without the helping hand of a policy entrepreneur. This difference might be explained by the fact that diffuse interest groups, notably Finance Watch, received a jump start in their mobilization efforts from the European institutions, which provided organizational, as well as financial aid. Hence, the empirical record of the case studies suggests that EU-based diffuse interest groups are at a slight advantage vis-à-vis their US counterparts, because EU groups can see their preferences reflected in public policy, even without the active support of policy entrepreneurs.

What is maybe more surprising is that in the case of the creation of the new US consumer regulator, consumer advocates won the day against financial sector opposition. Industry advocates trying to kill the proposal of a new regulator did not achieve their goals. One of the most interesting findings of the case studies examined here is therefore that winner-take-all outcomes are not always pro-industry. This finding is especially relevant in light of the dominance of capture theory in the literature on financial regulation. The new US consumer regulator was arguably the most contentious issue in the US reform act. The Wall Street Reform and Consumer Protection Act of July 2010 created an independent regulatory agency, housed at the Federal Reserve, with the sole responsibility of protecting consumers of financial products. In charging a single agency with consumer protection responsibilities, the reform succeeded in replacing a patchwork of different agencies, thereby consolidating and strengthening the regulation of consumer financial products. For consumer advocates, who saw all their main advocacy goals translated into policy, the creation of the CFPB was a major success.

To produce this winner-take-all outcome favorable to consumer interests, all four elements of the hypothesized causal mechanism played together.

A comparison of the policy processes in the United States and the EU reveals another interesting insight. Increased salience of financial reforms played an important role in both cases, providing a strong motivation for decision-makers to push for reform in line with the preferences of diffuse interest groups. In comparison with the US CFPB, which received enormous public attention, making it one of the key reform issues, individual consumer protection reform proposals in the EU received relatively little public attention. This suggests that US decision-makers are more prone to take diffuse interests into account if they are backed by widespread public opinion, whereas their counterparts in the EU seem to be more favorable in general to take diffuse interest groups on board. In other words, the salience of an issue is more important to the advocacy success of US-based diffuse interest groups than to their counterparts in the EU.

Financial transaction tax

The comparison of taxation reforms in the United States and the EU reveals the expected pattern of interest group lobbying success. The current legislative proposal for the EU financial transaction tax among 11 member states shows a clear tendency towards the usual compromise solution. Recent reform developments suggest a scaled-back version of the tax, reflecting the main objections of the financial industry to the initially broad-based tax. Contrary to the EU-level compromise, no policy change occurred in case of the proposed US transaction tax. US public interest groups advocating for a tax saw their lobbying efforts crushed under industry opposition and government rejection. In the aftermath of the crisis, proponents of the tax completely lost the political battle in Congress. These findings are in line with the lobbying literature which suggests that "zero-sum games"—with one side winning and one side losing—are common in US politics (Mahoney 2007). What explains these failures in advocacy for financial reform?

In our limiting case, the US financial transaction tax, issue salience was absent and the causal process that carried our positive cases was never set in motion. Although political opportunities opened up in terms of access and receptivity, the pro-tax campaign organized by a network of NGOs and trade unions was not successful in its mobilization efforts, which might have made a financial transaction tax salient and appealing to broader audiences or policy-makers. Different activist groups also failed to link their efforts successfully; potential policy entrepreneurs, including academic and private sector economists, made important contributions to support a tax, including reports detailing technical feasibility, economic utility, and social desirability, but none of the prominent voices could rally enough public and political support. Despite attempts, policy entrepreneurship defending diffuse interests largely failed at the national political stage; several legislative proposals were introduced to Congress, but stalled in political debate, because neither the President, nor chairmen of leading committees endorsed policy reform. Allies in Congress that pro-reform groups were able to recruit were too weak to bring broader political support on board.

In the case of the EU, a transaction tax seems likely to be implemented in a scaled-down version, which makes it a case of qualified success. Under post-crisis contextual conditions and with financial reform under public scrutiny, key member-state governments, including France and Germany, demonstrated a willingness to support an EU-level financial transaction tax, even in the face of firm financial sector resistance. During the early phase of the reform process, the hypothesized causal mechanism played out as expected: opened-up political opportunity structures provided incentives for the formation of a broad-based coalition among diffuse interest groups as a "Robin Hood Tax" campaign who found important allies in key politicians at national and European levels to promote a financial transaction tax in legislative debates.

During later stages of the reform process, with memories of the crisis fading, contextual conditions that had initially allowed the causal mechanism to work were largely removed. With public salience fading during the technical negotiations among member states at the policy-formulation stage, the principal condition for legislative allies to support legislation even against the preferences of special interests had been removed and financial sector lobbies, jointly with business groups, successfully watered down the initial draft Directive.

A comparison of the two cases confirms that the success of diffuse interest groups is highly contingent on issue salience and public opinion. As the salience of an issue to the public decreases, the likelihood of success for diffuse interest groups decreases in both the United States and the EU. Advocacy success of diffuse interest groups also hinges on the support of a powerful governmental ally who pushes for reform inside the legislative process. Ultimately, the advocacy success of diffuse interest groups is not determined by favorable political opportunity structures. To succeed, diffuse interest groups have to take advantage of increased issue salience favorable to their advocacy goals and recruit powerful government allies in defense of their interests. Otherwise, diffuse interest groups are likely to lose.

Business power

To better understand the limits of diffuse interests to influence public policy, it is useful to examine how business elites have tried to exercise power to resist change or reshape regulatory reform. For this discussion, it is helpful to recall the conceptual distinction between the instrumental and the structural power of business. Instrumental power is based on business groups' lobbying capacity and campaign contributions. The second dimension of power refers to the structural dependence of capitalist democracies on firms' investments, which provides the latter with political leverage even if financial sector groups do not actively engage in advocacy (Young and Pagliari 2015; Culpepper and Reinicke 2014; Utting 2012).

The financial industry's instrumental power is clearly brought out by the case of the EU financial transaction tax. Diffuse interest groups' advocacy success was largely restricted to the early phases of the reform process, which led to two Commission draft proposals. During this agenda-setting phase, financial sector lobbyists had largely refrained from lobbying the European institutions. The situation changed when industry groups started to take the proposed financial transaction tax seriously and to exercise instrumental power during the negotiation phase among Council working groups. In an effort to water down proposed legislation, EU-based financial industry groups not only started a massive outside lobbying campaign, presenting evidence against a transaction tax, they also formed strategic lobby alliances with central business groups, such as Bayer and Siemens. Financial sector groups also found important allies in the community of central bankers. The mobilization of groups not directly affected by the proposed regulatory reforms positively affected the financial industry's advocacy efforts. Due to this active opposition of financial sector and business groups, the numerous efforts of civil society groups to push for a broad-based tax with few exemptions eventually resulted in a diluted compromise.

This also provides empirical support to the "finance capital unity" hypothesis, which postulates that the broader business community is increasingly likely to mobilize in support of the financial sector when the latter faces new regulations (Young and Pagliari 2015). One reason why business groups only indirectly affected by financial reforms actively sided with the financial sector might be the centrality of finance capital in modern market societies. This centrality stems from the role of the financial sector in the provision of credit as "infrastructural" good to the rest of the business community. It might also stem from processes of financialization as underlying logic of capitalist systems that go beyond the provision of credit. In her often-cited study on the US economy, Krippner (2005, 174) defines financialization as "a pattern of accumulation in which profits accrue primarily through financial channels rather than through trade and commodity production." Financialization as primary regime of accumulation has promoted the financial industry to become the central player in contemporary capitalist systems in the United States and Europe alike (van der Zwan 2014, 104). Any attempt to re-regulate financial industry activities must therefore be understood as a direct challenge to the vested interests of finance capitalism. More important, re-regulations in the field of finance are likely to have repercussions not only for the financial industry, but for the wider business community, too. Business groups are therefore more likely to align with financial sector groups' advocacy efforts. Taken together, a combination of the instrumental and structural power of financial industry groups may explain why the lobbying demands of EU-based financial sector groups were eventually successful in diluting the proposed reform.

The structural power of finance may also serve to explain why a financial transaction tax did not become a politically viable idea in the United States and why US banking associations did not even start to actively lobby against reform proposals. Structural power shapes the preferences of decision-makers, who adhere to the same neoliberal worldview as financial services lobbyists. From this perspective, pro-reform advocacy was constrained by "cultural capture," whereby policy-makers indirectly promote the special interest in the belief that they act in the interest of the greater good (Baker 2010, 652; Carpenter and Moss 2014, 456). In particular, "structural power that works automatically through the anticipation of policymakers"

(Culpepper and Reinicke 2014) can be a strong motivator for politicians to follow business preferences. In the taxation case (unlike the consumer protection case) policy-makers' concerns about potentially harmful effects of the tax to the competitiveness of the financial industry and potential costs to investors and therefore also the broader economy could not be relieved. It was soon clear to US-based financial sector lobbyists that the likelihood of legislative success of a transaction tax was relatively low and that there was no need for explicit counter-lobbying.

The structural power of capital presents an important impediment to civil society advocacy, as Scholte (2013, 143) writes: "The entrenched structure of finance capital generates many strong forces that resist actual and potential civil society campaigns for significant change in financial markets." For the UK pro-tax campaign which had gained some momentum after the financial crisis in the late twentieth century, Utting (2012, 33), for example, concludes that it was "stifled" by the structural power of finance. Robin Hood Tax campaigns in response to the 2008 financial crisis seem to have met a similar fate.

Return to pluralism

Finance is a technical and highly complex issue area in which diffuse interests generally appear relatively ineffective against concentrated industry interests. Financial regulation is thus a difficult case with which to demonstrate the role of diffuse interest groups in public policy-making. In doing so, this research joins a number of studies that show that business power can be curbed. The findings of my positive case studies are consistent with existing studies that found evidence for limits on business power. In his empirical study on business group influence in the United States, Smith (2000), for example, finds corporate power to be constrained under conditions of high political salience and when public opinion is opposed to business preferences. This in turn amplifies incentives for politicians to listen to the mobilized public. Similarly, Baumgartner et al. (2009) find that the impact of material resources in achieving policy outcomes is not straightforward. Rather, wealthy interests sometimes win and sometimes lose. Most notably, business routinely loses when issue salience is high (Culpepper 2011, 187). The present study provides further evidence on how business power can be curbed, in line with other studies, which have focused on public salience (Culpepper 2011; Pagliari 2013), institutions (Hacker and Pierson 2002), and ideas (Bell and Hindmoor 2014). The argument here has focused on relations between interest groups and government officials to explain how increased mobilization of diffuse interests can affect the ability of organized concentrated interests to influence policy. The argument thereby goes beyond the dichotomy between instrumental and structural power. The pro-reform groups clearly relied much more on non-material resources than their counterparts did. One of the key findings of the positive cases presented here is that weak actors can combine several resources to bring to bear on the political process, including the capacity to capitalize on a crisis, to forge coalitions among themselves and with like-minded allies in the government and to provide the necessary technical expertise.

What are the broader theoretical lessons that we can draw from the findings of the case studies presented here? First, they provide some support for the pluralist theory. Detailed empirical analyses undertaken in this research project suggest that industry capture in the field of finance is in fact far more contingent than the logic of collective action leads us to expect. The case studies show that coalitions of non-financial advocacy groups traditionally considered politically weak—such as consumer groups, NGOs, and trade unions—have been much more influential in leaving their imprint on financial reforms than literature predicts. Drawing on literature on social movement research and regulatory politics, the analysis ultimately suggests that researchers seeking to understand the outcome of interest group conflicts must look beyond the variable of material resources. Coalition-building among weak interest groups and with important elite allies on the outside and the inside of government pushing for the same policy solution considerably enhances that group's ability to shape regulatory policy, allowing groups to affect policy decisions independently of their individual material resourcefulness. These findings correspond to Trumbull's (2012) argument that diffuse interests are generally represented in public policy and can serve as an important counterweight to concentrated industry interests.

Ultimately, the study suggests that IPE scholars would benefit from a more nuanced understanding of "politics as organized combat," as drawn by Hacker and Pierson. Our case studies still evoke a picture of "organized combat," but one in which interest group plurality is increased, allowing various actors to shape regulatory reforms. One of the main findings of the analysis at hand is that democratic politics still function, even in the area of financial regulation, in which the structural power of finance capital is said to dominate political decisions. Indeed, despite the ample material resources at its disposal, business has repeatedly found itself on the losing side. In many ways, the argument presented here echoes Helleiner and Pagliari's (2011) quest to devote "[m]ore detailed attention [...] to the entire question of private 'capture' of financial regulatory policymaking."

Recognizing the plurality of interest groups involved in financial reform debates, some observers have discerned signs of Polanyian counter-movements "that use the agency of the state [...] to counter the intensification of market-forces" (Clapp and Helleiner 2012). We should, however, not confuse specific victories of diffuse interest groups with the big picture. Overall, financial reforms have remained rather modest, falling short of a fundamental restructuring of the financial market architecture. Policy-makers ignored the more radical demands of civil society groups pushing for more substantive reforms, such as a higher tax rate for the financial transaction tax. Rather than emphasizing the success of a Polanyi-style "double movement," an alternative interpretation may therefore regard post-crisis financial reforms as rather incremental reforms "implemented at the margins of finance capital" (Scholte 2013, 138) to temporarily appease public discontent.

Nevertheless, the most general conclusion of this book is that concentrated interests do not always dictate public policy. The structural power of financial industry groups has certain limits. As seen in the cases of advocacy success of diffuse interests in bringing about consumer protection reforms, as well as in the agenda-setting success in case of the EU financial transaction tax debate, the financial crisis acted as an important catalyst for group mobilization and policy change. Business interests may sometimes lose, even when it comes to financial regulation. Non-financial interests, and notably citizen groups, can win significant victories. To dismiss the findings of the case studies presented here as marginal phenomena underestimates the power of the democratic mechanisms built into our societies to hold elected politicians accountable.

How to mitigate capture in regulatory decision-making

How can the findings presented here assist our understanding of regulatory capture in financial regulatory decision-making? First, the analysis suggests that we need a much more nuanced picture of regulatory capture than the one portrayed by the literature on financial reform-making so far. My findings therefore correspond to the conclusions recently presented by Carpenter and Moss, who found that "regulatory capture is not an all-or-nothing affair," but rather "a matter of degree" (Carpenter and Moss 2014, 452). The most important finding of this dissertation might be that capture of the policy-making process through financial interests can be kept at bay. Certain defense mechanisms to prevent capture, including elections to hold policy-makers accountable and interest groups channeling the preferences of the electorate, are built into the institutional setup of our democratic systems. This analysis revealed one capture-prevention mechanism that merits further attention. In the positive cases examined here, public salience, newly mobilized diffuse interest groups, policy entrepreneurs outside government, and allies inside government combined to shape regulatory reforms in ways that transcend the interests and influence of the financial industry. There are several proposals for prevention that we can derive from these insights.

Actor plurality and mobilization of diffuse interests

Diffuse interest groups—mobilized as grassroots movements from the bottom-up or top-down through formal empowerment—can act as a "countervailing force" to concentrated industry interests. Enhanced actor plurality, with more end-users of financial services, NGOs, and consumer organizations participating in the policy process, reduces the dominance of the financial sector voice during legislative debates. We could observe this pattern in the case of the CFPB, as well as the EU-level reform debates in which advocates mobilized as vocal pro-reform coalitions. Hence, actor plurality has important consequences for the design of regulatory policies: it reduces the risk of outright industry capture and makes a more compromised legislative outcome, reflecting various stakeholder preferences, more likely. The creation of participatory mechanisms for diffuse interest groups is one potential policy solution to systematically increase actor plurality in decision-making processes (Pagliari 2012, 15). The creation of Finance Watch in

2011 is one example of policy-makers directly sponsoring an NGO as a counterweight to the industry. Another example is the creation of the Financial Services Users Groups (FSUG) at the European Commission in 2010 as a standing panel to represent consumer voices. Our case studies suggest that both mechanisms worked well to include a consumer and user perspective in post-crisis reform debates. However, while the Commission is planning to continue to fund Finance Watch for 2017–2020, funding for the FSUG had been curbed by the end of 2016, which will make it difficult for the FSUG to continue its work in the future.

In general, the chances of diffuse interest groups' achieving their lobbying goals increased when they started to cooperate in broad pro-reform coalitions pushing for the same policy goal. The analysis suggests that policy-makers take the whole spectrum of interest group mobilization into consideration when making decisions. Hence, the more groups mobilize to promote reform, the greater the likelihood of success. In both cases, diffuse US and EU interest groups greatly benefited from working together in coalitions.

Transparency and public scrutiny

The empirical record of the case studies presented here suggests that public attention and increased media coverage are important factors in reducing capture on regulatory decision-making. The literature on lobbying would lead us to expect that public opinion matters a great deal more in the United States than in the EU, which has no integrated media and 24 official languages. The findings of our case studies suggest that public opinion in favor of reform was an important driver for both EU consumer protection reforms and the decision to introduce a financial transaction tax among 11 EU member states. Press reports about undue industry influence leading up to the financial crisis in 2008 presumably alerted a broader public and increased issue attention to financial reform-making. Politicians in turn have an incentive to promote reforms, when the public is watching. There are, however, objective limits to public scrutiny, as Baker (2010, 657) points out: "The problem here is that public anger and political interest in regulation are also temporary and inherently pro-cyclical." Although there is no guarantee that broader access will assure greater public interest, increased transparency—such as the publication of information about regulatory decisions on regulators' websites—could allow a broader public to gain access. Enhanced transparency of decision-making processes could be one policy solution to effectively prevent capture and enhance accountability in the long term.

Expertise

The findings from the present case studies break with predominant accounts of technical expertise as a monopoly of the financial industry. Although the provision of expertise is relevant for US and EU interest groups alike, it is particularly important for EU groups in their efforts to influence the European institutions. In the EU cases, diffuse interest groups became central for deploying expertise to the

European institutions. Consumer groups interviewed for this project reported that a permanent link of cooperation and exchange was established with the European Commission following the crisis. MEPs were also depended on the expertise provided by non-financial interest groups, such as Finance Watch. Interviews with European Parliament staffers testify to the close cooperation among MEPs of the Green Party and the S&D with experts from Finance Watch throughout the reform process, including so-called "group briefings," which took place at the European Parliament, at which Finance Watch staff met with MEPs, their assistants, and political advisors to explain the technical details of regulations. Moreover, the European Parliament regularly invited experts from Finance Watch to testify on financial reform issues. Pro-reform advocates were also important partners in providing both the European Parliament and the European Commission with the necessary technical expertise to counter arguments claiming that there would be economically harmful effects from the proposed financial transaction tax.

Similarly to the role of EU groups, in the US cases, all interviewees representing diffuse interest groups highlighted the importance of deploying expertise to policy-makers throughout the legislative process. Rather than pressing politicians, interviewees reported that advocacy groups served as an important source of expertise in the drafting phase of the legislation. In case of the US CFPB, Congress staffers testified to the role of consumer advocates as knowledgeable people who could draft legislative language when needed. Close cooperation also took place among pro-reform advocates and individual policy-makers on numerous bills introducing an US financial transaction tax since 2009. Diffuse interest groups, such as community groups specialized in housing, were also able to deploy technical expertise to policy-makers throughout the reform debate and contributed to drafting legislation in both the United States and the EU.

Coalitions among legislators and pro-reform groups

My positive cases lend support to Griffith-Jones, Silvers, and Thiemann (2010, 6), who stated that key explanatory factors for financial regulatory change are political leadership combined with lobbying efforts of diffuse interest groups, including trade unions, consumer, and civil rights advocates that could capitalize on the public outrage in response to the crisis. Empirical evidence presented here suggests that regulatory change was triggered by the lobbying efforts of pro-reform coalitions, including non-financial groups and policy-makers. The success of diffuse interests in the policy process depends largely on the extent to which policy-makers' preferences align with or diverge from those of mobilized diffuse interest groups. Putatively weak diffuse interests become powerful only if policymakers are receptive to their demands. Findings also confirm that in particular under conditions of high salience, politicians are inclined to push for public interest reforms, even against financial sector opposition. The lobbying success of diffuse interest groups increased with greater issue salience, when groups saw their position backed up by public opinion. One important finding is therefore that the influence of diffuse interests depends on the receptiveness of policy-makers, which in turn depends on the public attention an issue attracts. In sum, the financial sector is less likely to capture the policy process when pro-reform coalitions occur among diffuse interest groups on the outside of government and policy-makers inside government, who work closely together to push for the same policy solution. Most importantly, these findings suggest that governments have discretion over which interests they include and which interests they ignore.

Limitations and future research

Reforms of financial service regulation in the EU and the United States are far from complete and some of the regulations dealt with here (particularly in the EU case studies) are only being implemented at the time of writing. A weakness of the present study is that the empirical evidence presented here is somewhat incomplete. The case studies focus most on the agenda-setting and policy-formulation stage of financial reform-making, while largely neglecting the implementation stage of the policy cycle. In the realm of finance, the more opaque and technical implementation phase of regulation is, however, the stage at which financial sector interests are hypothesized to be most apt to capture the policy process (Pagliari 2012, 7). Indeed, financial services groups stepped up their lobbying efforts targeted at the implementation of new regulations. Since its creation in 2011, the number of financial lobbyists targeting the CFPB has increased considerably, from 140 lobbyists working for 37 organizations in early 2011 to more than 400 lobbyists working for 94 groups by the end of 2014 (*Financial Times* 2015). Due to the topicality of the case studies examined here, the present research has, however, left it to subsequent research to unpack the full implementation process of the financial reforms enacted in response to the crisis in order to provide a full picture of post-crisis reform dynamics.

Generally, process-tracing studies suffer from limited generalizability. The aim here was to trace a single, generalizable causal mechanism and to test whether the mechanism was present across a bounded context of cases. Therefore, the main limitation of this study is that it focuses on narrow, temporarily specific case studies, with all four cases examined here situated in the post-crisis context. In other words, the crisis was indispensable for the functioning of the mechanism. Hence, conclusions drawn from the case at hand do not allow for addressing larger questions of political and institutional change in "normal times." Rather the theory developed here is limited in its application to—albeit crucially important— cases in times of crisis. Regulatory capture has often been described as a cyclical phenomenon, "alternating between crisis and boom" (Pagliari 2012, 14). This implies that Olson's theory might continue to characterize regulatory decision-making as soon as finance starts booming again. Far from a long-term shift in the balance of power, developments in financial regulatory reforms after the crisis seem, however, to be more of a temporary setback for industry groups, following the usual boom and bust cycle. Additional case studies are needed to examine how diffuse interest groups fare during the implementation process of reforms.

Indeed, as Baker (2010, 663) remarks, "the pro-cyclicality of regulatory capture, and the failure to address it explicitly, may yet mean that the same processes re-emerge more strongly than ever, with the same dysfunctional outcomes, once the next boom emerges." Further research might explore this in more detail and expand the study of diffuse interest groups to other policy contexts.

The role of non-financial groups, notably civil society actors, in financial regulation merits further exploration. The case studies at hand find that a growing number of civil society groups have developed capacities to engage with questions of financial regulation. This study also shows that consumer associations and trade unions, together with many other NGOs, succeeded in making their mark on the recent financial reforms and got themselves noticed as active players in financial regulatory debates. As recent developments outlined in this analysis show, in response to the financial crisis, civil society groups have started to get organized in order to promote a fairer global financial architecture that no longer puts a diffuse public interest at a disadvantage. In some cases this struggle has been fruitful. Additional case studies would shed further light on the question of whether civil society can be a real vanguard for subsequent reforms of the financial architecture in the public interest.

References

Baker, A. (2010) 'Restraining Regulatory Capture? Anglo-America, Crisis Politics and Trajectories of Change in Global Financial Governance', *International Affairs* 86 (3): 647–63.

Baumgartner, F. R. et al. (2009) *Lobbying and Policy Change: Who Wins, Who Loses, and Why*, Chicago, London: University of Chicago Press.

Bell, S. and Hindmoor, A. (2014) 'The Structural Power of Business and the Power of Ideas: The Strange Case of the Australian Mining Tax', *New Political Economy* 19 (3): 470–86.

Carpenter, D. P. and Moss, D. A. (eds) (2014) *Preventing Regulatory Capture: Special Interest Influence and How to Limit It*, New York: Cambridge University Press.

Clapp, J. and Helleiner, E. (2012) 'Troubled Futures? The Global Food Crisis and the Politics of Agricultural Derivatives Regulation', *Review of International Political Economy* 19 (2): 181–207.

Clark, J. D. (2011) 'Civil Society in the Age of Crisis', *Journal of Civil Society* 7 (3): 241–63.

Culpepper, P. D. (2011) *Quiet Politics and Business Power: Corporate Control in Europe and Japan*, Cambridge: Cambridge University Press.

Culpepper, P. D. and Reinicke, R. (2014) 'Structural Power and Bank Bailouts in the United Kingdom and the United States', *Politics & Society* 42 (4): 427–54.

Derthick, M. and Quirk, P. J. (1985) *The Politics of Deregulation*, Washington, DC: Brookings Institution Press.

Financial Times (2015) 'US Banks Target Elizabeth Warren's 'Rogue' Watchdog', 30 March, available at www.ft.com/content/db42740e-d378-11e4-a9d3-00144feab7de (accessed September 2016).

Griffith-Jones, S., Silvers, D. and Thiemann, M. (2010) 'Turning the Financial Sector from a Bad Master to a Good Servant: The Role of Regulation and Taxation', unpublished working paper, available at www.stephanygj.net/papers/Fin-Regulation-SGJ.pdf (accessed September 2016).

Hacker, J. S. and Pierson, P. (2002) 'Business Power and Social Policy: Employers and the Formation of the American Welfare State', *Politics & Society* 30 (2): 277–325.

Helleiner, E. and Pagliari, S. (2011) 'The End of an Era in International Financial Regulation? A Postcrisis Research Agenda', *International Organization* 65 (1): 169–200.

Krippner, G. R. (2011) *Capitalizing on Crisis the Political Origins of the Rise of Finance*, Cambridge, MA: Harvard University Press.

Mahoney, C. (2007) 'Lobbying Success in the United States and the European Union', *Journal of Public Policy* 27 (1): 35–56.

Pagliari, S. (2012) 'How Can We Mitigate Capture in Financial Regulation?', in S. Pagliari (ed.), *Making Good Financial Regulation: Towards a Policy Response to Regulatory Capture*, Guildford, Surrey: Grosvenor House Publishing Ltd, pp. 1–50.

Pagliari, S. (2013) 'Public Salience and International Financial Regulation. Explaining the International Regulation of OTC Derivatives, Rating Agencies, and Hedge Funds', Ph.D. dissertation, University of Waterloo, available at www.stefanopagliari.net/pagliari_-_phd_thesis_-.pdf (accessed September 2016).

Pagliari, S. and Young, K. L. (2013) 'Leveraged Interests: Financial Industry Power and the Role of Private Sector Coalitions', *Review of International Political Economy*, 21 (3): 575–610.

Scholte, J. A. (2013) 'Civil Society and Financial Markets: What Is Not Happening and Why', *Journal of Civil Society* 9 (2): 129–47.

Smith, M. A. (2000) *American Business and Political Power*, Chicago and London: University of Chicago Press.

Trumbull, G. (2012) *Strength in Numbers: The Political Power of Weak Interests*, Cambridge, MA: Harvard University Press.

Van der Zwan, N. (2014) 'Making Sense of Financialization', *Socio-Economic Review* 12 (1): 99–129.

Utting, P. (2012) 'Elite Business Power and Activist Response', in P. Utting et al. (eds), *Global Justice Activism and Policy Reform in Europe. Understanding When Change Happens*, New York: Routledge, pp. 17–40.

Young, K. L. (2013) 'Financial Industry Groups' Adaptation to the Post-Crisis Regulatory Environment: Changing Approaches to the Policy Cycle', *Regulation & Governance* 7 (4): 460–80.

Young, K. L. and Pagliari, S. (2015) 'Capital United? Business Unity in Regulatory Politics and the Special Place of Finance', *Regulation and Governance*. doi:10.1111/rego.12098.

Annexes

List of conducted interviews

The semi-structured interviews were conducted between July 2011 and March 2014. Interviews lasted between thirty minutes and two hours and were held in English, French, or German. All material is dealt with anonymously so that citations cannot be linked to the authors or their institutions, because the majority of interview partners were otherwise not willing to provide information about the financial reform negotiations that were still ongoing at the time. Translations for French and German are my own. To allow situating individual quotations in time, the date of the interviews appears in the text, not in the list below. For the sake of research transparency, anonymized transcripts of the conducted interviews are stored in a database at the Max Planck Institute for the Study of Societies in Cologne and will be made available upon request.

Number of conducted interviews: 116.

European Union–List of interviewees

Berestecki, Maciej, Policy Officer, European Commission, DG Internal Market and Services, Retail Financial Services and Consumer Policy, Brussels.

Blaschek, Beate, Head of Department, Department of Financial Services and consumer education, Section III consumer policies, Austrian Federal Ministry of Labour, Social Affairs and Consumer Protection, Vienna.

Boer, Martin, Secretary General, European Financial Services Roundtable, Brussels.

Botsch, Andreas, Special Adviser, ETUC/ETUI - European Trade Union Institute, Brussels.

Chapman, Michael, Senior Policy Expert, Financial Education and Consumer Protection Unit, Financial Affairs Division, OECD, Paris.

Chouffot, Simon, Media & Policy Expert, Robin Hood Tax Campaign, London.

Corbi, Antonio, Head of the European Tax Committee, International Swaps and Derivatives Association, London.

Crasta, Elena, Senior Policy Officer, TUC Brussels office, ITUH, Brussels.

de Rossignol, Pierre-Thibault Aveline, Regulatory Policy Advisor, European Fund and Asset Management Association, Brussels.

Degirmencioglu, Ani, Project Officer for Financial Reform, SOLIDAR, Brussels.

Degortes, Emanuele Policy Officer American Chamber of Commerce to the EU, Brussels.

Diemer, Rolf Head of Unit European Commission, DG TAXUD, Brussels.

Dobranszky-Bartus, Katalin, Senior Economic Advisor, European Mortgage Federation, Brussels.

Donlon, Claire, Policy Advisor, ALDE Group, Committee on Economic and Monetary Affairs, Brussels.

Fily, Ann, Head of the Economic and Legal Department, The European Consumers Organisation, Brussels.

Fossati, Luca, Political Advisor, S&D Group, Committee on Economic and Monetary Affairs, Brussels.

Gauzès, Jean Paul, Member of the European Parliament, European Parliament, telephone interview.

Gondard, Cécilia, Coordinator, Europeans For Financial Reform, Global Progressive Forum, S&D Group in the European Parliament, Brussels.

Goyens, Monique, Secretary General, The European Consumers' Organisation, Brussels.

Greenhill, Jonathan, Policy Manager, Business and Industry Advisory Committee to the OECD, Paris.

Greeves, Rebecca, Strategy Manager, TheCityUK, London.

Grignard, Marcel, National Secretary, French Democratic Confederation of Labour (Confédération française démocratique du travail, CFDT), Paris.

Grout, John, Policy and Technical Director Association of Corporate Treasurers, London.

Habbard, Pierre, Senior Policy Advisor, International Trade Union Confederation, Trade Union Advisory Committee to the OECD, Paris.

Heegemann, Volker, Head of Legal Department European Association of Co-operative Banks, Brussels.

Henn, Markus, Policy Advisor for Financial Markets, World Economy, Ecology & Development, Berlin.

Hillman, David, Director, Stamp Out Poverty, Robin Hood Tax Steering Group, London.

Ingham, Vincent, Senior Policy Advisor, European Fund and Asset Management Association, Brussels.

Johnson, Jennifer, Head of Legal Affairs, European Mortgage Federation, Brussels.

Jorritsma, Jasper, Policy Officer, European Commission, seconded national expert, DG Internal Market and Services, Unit G3, Securities Markets, Brussels.

Kaiser, Roger, Senior Adviser, Tax & Financial Reporting, European Banking Federation, Brussels.

Kemp, David, Policy Advisor, The Greens, Economic and Monetary Affairs, European Parliament, Brussels.

Knott, Julian, Head of Secretariat, Transatlantic Consumer Dialogue, Brussels.

Kobylinska-Hilliard, Katarzyna, Deputy Head of Legal Department, European Association for Cooperative Banks, Brussel.

Lalucq, Aurore, Institut Veblen, Paris.

Larsen,Stine Laerke, Policy Advisor, S&D Group, Committee on Economic and Monetary Affairs, European Parliament, Brussels.

Le Rudulier, Catherine, Assistant Secretary General, Comité consultatif du secteur financier, Banque de France, Paris.

Malhotra, Rohan, Policy Manager, TheCityUK, London.

Maslennikov, Mikhail, Head of Secretariat, zerozero cinque campaign, skype interview.

Mathieu, Luc, Secretary General, French Democratic Confederation of Labour (Confédération française démocratique du travail, CFDT), banks and insurances, Paris.

Mazounie, Alix, Policy Advisor, Reseau Action Climat, Paris.

Meaulle, Matthieu, Economic Advisor, Foundation for European Progressive Studies, Brussels.

Metin, Inci, Policy officer, Federal Association of Public Banks in Germany, Brussels.

Monzane, Marcio, Head of UNI Finance, UNI Uni Global, telephone interview.

Morley-Smith, Jorge Head of Tax, Investment Management Association, London.

Mulder, Joost, Head of Public Affairs, Finance Watch, Brussels.

Naulot, Alexandre, Policy Advisor, Financial Transaction Taxes, Oxfam France, Paris.

O'Donovan, Martin, Deputy Policy and Technical Director, Association of Corporate Treasurers, London.

Pellé, Philippe, Deputy Head of Unit, European Commission, DG Internal Market and Services, Unit H3 - Retail issues, Consumer Policy and Payment Systems, Brussels.

Phillipponnat, Thierry, Secretary General, Finance Watch, Paris.

Plihon, Dominique, Professor, President of the scientific counsel ATTAC France, Paris.

Prache, Guillaume, Managing Director, EuroInvestors, Vice Chairman of the Financial Services Users Group , Brussels.

Robertson, Jennifer Deputy Head of Unit European Commission, DG Internal Market and Services, Financial Markets Infrastructure, Unit G2, Brussels.

Robinson, Anthony, Senior Policy Advisor, Financial Services Confederation of British Industry's, Competitive Markets Directorate, London.

Roux, Jean-Marie, Advisor for European and International Affairs Fédération des Finances, CGT Confédération, Paris.

Saldanha, Jean, Senior Policy Advisor, CIDSDE - international alliance of Catholic development agencies, Brussels.

Schmalzried, Martin, Policy Officer Association of Family Organisations in the European Union, Brussels.

Shakesby, Timothy, Policy Analyst, European Commission, Internal Market and Services, Asset Management Unit U4, Financial Markets Directorate, Brussels.

Simpson, Robin, Senior Policy Advisor, Consumers International, Brussels.

Singh-Muchelle, Arjun, Head of EU Affairs, British Bankers' Association, London.

Sjölund, Hanna, Policy Officer, UNI Europa, Brussels.

Solli, Petra, Policy Advisor, ALDE Group, Committee on Economic and Monetary Affairs, European Parliament, Brussels.

Stepnitzka, Andreas, Advisor, Financial Markets, European Association of Co-operative Banks, Brussels.

Stetter, Ernst, General Secretary, Foundation for European Progressive Studies, Brussels.

Strickner, Alexandra, member of the board of directors, ATTAC Austria, Vienna.

Terray, Jacques, Vice-President, Transparency International France, Paris.

Tudor, Owen, Head of European Union and International Relations, Trade Union Congress, London.

van Berkel, Marieke, Head of Department, Retail Banking, Payments, Financial Markets, EACB, Brussels.

Vassalos, Yiorgos, Researcher, Corporate Europe Observatory, Brussels.

Vincent, Bernard, National Secretary, French Confederation of Management, General Confederation of Executives (Confédération Française de l'Encadrement CFE-CGC), Paris.

Weigmann, Ole, Policy Officer for capital markets and taxes, Federal Association of Public Banks in Germany, Brussels.

Wengler, Christoph, Head of Unit, Federal Association of Public Banks in Germany, Brussels.

Wulf, Thomas, Secretary General, European Structured Investment Products Association, Brussels.

United States—List of interviewees

Abernathy, Wayne, Executive Vice President, Financial Institutions Policy and Regulatory Affairs, American Bankers Association, Washington, D.C.

Abrecht, Stephen, Steering Committee Member, Americans for Financial Reform, Washington, D.C.

Banks, Pamela, Senior Policy Counsel, Consumers Union, Washington, D.C.

Barefoot, Jo Ann, Senior Advisor, Treliant Risk Advisors, CFPB's Consumer Advisory Board, Washington, D.C.

Barr, Michael, Professor of Law, University of Michigan, former U.S. Department of the Treasury's Assistant Secretary for Financial Institutions, telephone interview.

Beales J. Howard, Professor of Economics, George Washington University, former director of the FTC's bureau of consumer protection, Washington, D.C.

Booth, Heather, Former Executive Director, Americans for Financial Reforms, Washington, D.C.

Calabria, Mark, Director of Financial Regulation Studies, Cato Institute, Washington, D.C.

Chon, Julie, Global Head, Perry Capital, Public Investment Strategy, former senior policy advisor to Senator Dodd, U.S. Senate Committee on Banking, Housing and Urban Affairs from 2007–2011, Washington, D.C.

Donner, Lisa, Executive Director, Americans for Financial Reform, Washington, D.C.

Elliott, Douglas, Fellow in Economic Studies, The Brookings Institute, Washington, D.C.

Engstroem, Rob, Sr. Vice President, National Political Director, U.S. Chamber of Commerce, Washington, D.C.

Flynn, Jennifer, Managing Director, Health GAP, Washington, D.C.

Geduldig, Courtney, Vice President of Global Regulatory Affairs, Standard & Poor's Ratings Services, former senator Corker Congress staffer, Washington, D.C.

Green, Andrew, Counsel and Staff Director, Economic Policy Subcommittee, Senator Merkley Office, Washington, D.C.

Hauptman, Micah, Financial Policy Counsel, Public Citizen's Congress Watch division, Washington, D.C.

Kalman, Gary, Director of Federal Policy, Center for Responsible Lending, Washington, D.C.

Keen, Michael, Professor of Economics, Deputy Director of the Fiscal Affairs Department, International Monetary Fund, Washington, D.C.

Kemp, Elizabeth, Legislative and Policy Analyst, National Community Reinvestment Coalition, Washington, D.C.

Mavrellis, Democritos, Financial Policy Analyst, U.S. Department of the Treasury, Office of the International Banking and Securities Markets, Washington, D.C.

Mayer, Robert Nathan, Professor for Family and Consumer Studies, University of Utah, Washington, D.C.

Mierzwinski, Ed, Consumer Program Director USPIRG, Americans for Financial Reform Executive Committee member, Washington, D.C.

Miller, Andrew, Senior Vice President and Director of Regulatory Policy, The PNC Financial Services Group, former senior counsel of the Financial Services Committee of the U.S. House of Representatives, Washington, D.C.

Miller, Jonathan, Deputy Director for Policy and Research Division of Depositor and Consumer Protection, Federal Deposit Insurance Corporation, former U.S. Senate Committee on Banking, Housing, and Urban Affairs, Washington, D.C.

Mombrial, Nicolas, Head of the Washington DC office, Oxfam, Washington, D.C.

Naylor, Bart, Financial Policy Advocate, Public Citizen, Washington, D.C.

Pearce, Mark, Director, Federal Deposit Insurance Corporation, Division of Depositor and Consumer Protection, Washington, D.C.

Plunkett, Travis, Deputy Director, Family Economic & Financial Security Portfolio, The Pew Charitable Trusts, Washington, D.C.

Redman, Janet , Co-Director, Sustainable Energy & Economy Network, Institute for Policy Studies, Washington, D.C.

Rheingold, Ira, Executive Director and General Counsel, National Association of Consumer Advocates, Washington, D.C.

Rivlin, Gary, Fellow, The Nation Institute, New York.

Rosenkoetter, Darlene J., Associate General Counsel, Global Regulatory Affairs

Standard & Poor's Ratings Services, former Senator Corker Congress staffer, Washington, D.C.

Saunders, Lauren, Managing Attorney, National Consumer Law Center, Washington, D.C.

Silvers, Damon, Director of Policy and Special Counsel, American Federation of Labor and Congress of Industrial Organizations, Washington, D.C.

Talbott, Scott, Senior Vice President of Public Policy, The Financial Services Roundtable, Washington, D.C.

Turbeville, Wallace, Professor of Law, University of Maryland, Fellow at Demos, former Goldman Sachs Vice President, Baltimore.

Weinstock, Susan K., Director, Safe Checking Project, The Pew Charitable Trusts, Washington, D.C.

White, Evan, Honors Attorney, Consumer Financial Protection Bureau, Washington, D.C.

Wilson, Mitria, Director of Legislative & Policy Advocacy, National Community Reinvestment Coalition, Washington, D.C.

Yingling Edward L., Partner Covington and Burling LLP, former president and CEO of the American Bankers Association, Washington, D.C.

Zavarello, Bill, senior staff member, House Financial Services Committee, former senior staff on the House Financial Services Committee Chairman Barney Frank's office, Washington, D.C.

Zigas, Barry, Director of Housing Policy, Consumer Federation of America, Washington, D.C.

Zinn, Ken, Political Director, National Nurses United, Washington, D.C.

Index

Note: page numbers in **bold** refer to illustrations.

Printed and bound by CPI Group (UK) Ltd, Croydon, CR0 4YY

02/12/2024

01798763-0007